THE GAMES DO COUNT

THE GAMES DO COUNT

America's Best and Brightest on the Power of Sports

BRIAN KILMEADE

10 ReganBooks
Celebrating Ten Bestselling Years
An Imprint of HarperCollins*Publishers*

HarperCollins books may be purchased for educational, business, or sales promotional use. For information please write: Special Markets Department, HarperCollins Publishers Inc., 10 East 53rd Street, New York, NY 10022.

FIRST EDITION

Designed by Richard Ljoenes

Printed on acid-free paper

Library of Congress Cataloging-in-Publication Data has been applied for.

ISBN 0-06-073673-9

04 05 06 07 08 PDC/RRD 20 19 18 17 16 15 14 13 12 11

To my wife, Dawn; my son,
Bryan; my girls, Kirstyn and Kaitlyn;
my brothers, Jim and Steve;
and my mom and dad—
with this team, how can I lose?

★ CONTENTS ★

FOREWORD

Jim Brown

In many ways, sports is like life itself; often, we dwell on things that are not that important. We rave about the Super Bowl, the World Series, and every other championship under the sun, leaving the rest of the season— the less significant failures and victories. The fact is, sports—the act of play itself—are valuable and not just as a pathway to leading to championship victories. They allow us to compete and sacrifice, to build character and, even if only a moment, to transcend the everyday. Brian Kilmeade's *The Games Do Count* has captured the real essence of the games we play: the beauty of the journey we undertake in sports, not just the outcome.

Each and every person featured in this book—great in their own right— has an important story to tell about the significance of sports in their lives. Not just of winning and competing, but of participating in the first place.

Sports basically saved my life. As a young kid growing up, sports was the only thing I really cared about, way before I understood the power and importance of education. If I had never gone on to play at the professional level, I can safely say that the lessons I learned on the playing field in junior high school and high school would have helped me through life in any other field. I walked away from those experiences knowing how to work hard, to concentrate. I knew how to get up after I lost and how to cope with the fact that I wasn't always going to win. These tough lessons helped me gain confidence. If I could accomplish things in a highly competitive world, I knew I could push myself further. This confidence allowed me not only to accept myself, but to know that I could hold my own against the best, to know that if I believed in myself, I could compete.

The people in this book are known for things other than sports. And in some ways that makes them more human. But the commonality is that we're all human beings and the experiences we have playing sports as kids are indelibly written on our minds, and although we grow up, we never grow past them. So even though they might be the CEO of a major corporation, or president of the United States, there is a commonality of experience that all of us can identify with.

One of the great things about *The Games Do Count* is that even though sports played a part in the lives of all the people Brian interviewed, as it did in my life, John Elway's life, and Michael Jordan's life, we learn that sports isn't life itself. In taking the shared experience, we see that it humbles you in a certain way. I think great, successful sports stars have a great appreciation of people who aren't stars, and in so many cases, love to play with them. They love to shoot baskets with them, teach them, even get their concepts on how they played and the things that they applied to their lives afterward. In many ways, my experiences as a champion are the very same experiences that the guy down the street had, and these experiences have taught both of us an important perspective on life, as well as giving us a perspective on how to help people and how we should live our lives.

Failure is a major part of sports, just as it is in life. You might have talent and skills others don't, but the most minor twists of fate can veer you off course. Sometimes, a little bit of luck saves you from failure. Other times, luck (someone else's) causes it. Sports teach you how to deal with failure and in this way it's the great equalizer. Whether you're a superstar or an average guy, sports will humble you.

Sports also teach us how to deal with pressure, whether it be the pressure of expectations on the field or simply the pressures that come to us in everyday life. The pressure on me was that I had to do something extraordinary in every game, or else I was nothing. I couldn't just have a good game. The expectation was that I needed to be great. We all experience the pressure to be our best. And many of us, whether we grow up to be an actor, a CEO, a mechanic or a football star, have our first brush with greatness while playing sports in our youth. In the end, the lessons we learn from our athletic experiences are remarkably similar.

God gave us a challenge when he gave us the ability to have emotions and to reason. Those challenging situations are always going to be there, but what we learn is that it's never too bad that we can't get up. And it's never so good that we're not going to fall down. But if you can learn to enjoy the journey and do your best along the way, you will live a good life.

In the end, participating in sports when you're young isn't about going pro. It's about taking part in a wonderful experience that offers so many life lessons. Sports gives us an opportunity to look at ourselves, to see what we're made of, to forge relationships with other people, some of which last a lifetime. Ultimately, of course, sports is about having fun, and any intrinsic value we put on it or on winning, is man-made. I like to quote former Dallas football great Duane Thomas, who, when told that the Super Bowl was the "ultimate game," replied, "If it's the ultimate game, why do you play it again next year?"

Few of us will ever make it to the Super Bowl or the World Series or Wimbledon, but by reading *The Games Do Count,* perhaps you will be able to relive your own version of those games and understand how playing them in your childhood helped shape the person you are today.

INTRODUCTION

We've all read the stories about sports legends like Michael Jordan, Tiger Woods, and John Elway. How they rose from humble beginnings and managed through hard work to turn their prodigious natural talents into fame, fortune, and incredible accomplishment. But there are other untold sports stories out there—stories about everyday athletes, talented, average, or otherwise, who turned their sports experiences into the lessons of a lifetime.

Such stories are almost universal; many, many people have learned such lessons. The people in this book are anything but average. In fact, every one of them has taken something very special with them from their early years playing sports—whether it be baseball, football, wrestling, boxing, soccer, golf, horseback riding, or basketball—and parlayed it into outstanding success in life.

Let's face it: As much as we admire what Dr. J, Joe Montana, or Hank Aaron have done, few of us are fortunate enough to share that kind of talent and performance. Most of us never came close to their level of success. And yet those early years standing in the outfield in the hot sun on the rocky sandlot ball field, or dribbling a basketball on the sizzling summer asphalt, or waving a broomstick at a rubber ball on an inner-city street, count for something when we get older—something other than mere pleasant memories.

Most of us, when we were young, dreamed of glory in professional sports. Though few of us actually made that leap, in those early years, we played with the passion of professionals, always hoping someday to join our heroes in the Hall of Fame. The fact that we went on to other things hardly means that we failed; in fact, for many it set up success down the line in the professions we chose.

My hope is that the reflections I've gathered here in *The Games Do Count* remind us all that the time we spent playing sports in childhood could not have been better spent. For me and many others I've spoken with through the years, sports have been nothing less than life's boot camp. We have won and lost (probably lost more than we've won, if you're anything like me), struck out at the worst possible times; dropped fly balls; been knocked on our butts, benched, and cut from the team. At the time, it probably seemed as though your life was over, that you could never hold your head high again. Little did you know how important those failures could be in preparing you for the game of life. Nor did you know how much the early experience in sports would prepare you to survive the tribulations and challenges in life.

Even if we would never have admitted it, most of us must have known even then that we would never really get a shot at Major League baseball, the NHL, the WNBA, the PGA, or any other professional sports league. So why did we practice so hard, sacrifice so much, give up our summers and spring breaks to train?

The benefits of hard work and hard play were evident in every one of the conversations I had for *The Games Do Count.* For example, we know Jack Welch as the ultimate winner, the take-no-prisoners CEO of General Electric. But did you know he still stings from being benched on his high school baseball team? Did you know how much credit Burt Reynolds gives to football in forming his character and keeping him out of reach of the long arm of the law? Or why boxer Tony Danza needed to pick himself off the canvas and score a knockout in the ring to grab the part of Tony Banta in *Taxi?* How much credit does President Ford give to his days in football for his success in full-contact politics? How did Jon Bon Jovi's genes short-circuit his dreams of playing for the Giants, and why did that have such an important impact on his life? Why did soccer, not stand-up comedy, play such a big role in Jon Stewart's staggering success in the kill-or-be-killed world of late-night talk?

I first realized how much we pedestrian athletes think about our athletic careers while hosting my less-than-coveted Saturday 12:00 to 4:00 P.M. shift on XTRA, an all-sports radio station in Los Angeles, in 1992. Sports in Southern California, I realized then, doesn't ignite the same passion displayed in most Eastern cities. On the West Coast, most people are outside playing, not watching sports on TV or listening to the radio. So one day, after spending one too many afternoons with just a few callers on the line, I played a hunch. Instead of talking yet again about Mr. or Mrs. Superstar Sports Legend, I decided to offer listeners a chance to talk about *their own* sports experiences: the memories they couldn't shake, the trophies they were proudest to win. Suddenly the lines lit up—and a flood of anonymous voices spouted out their personal stories, many of them with humor and insight, all of them with passion. Men in their fifties were calling and reliving the regrets from their lacrosse exploits during their junior year in high school. Soon this theme became a regular segment of the show, and I loved my newfound role as a host-therapist. Slowly, I realized that I wasn't the only one whose early sports dreams had been dashed—but I also realized how important a role such memories had played in so many people's adult lives.

The last piece of evidence that compelled me to pursue this book came to me after the events of 9/11, when we began learning the stories of the passengers of Flight 93. As we all know by now, that plane was supposed to crash into the White House or Capitol building on that sunny September morning. When the passengers on board learned of the hijackers' planned suicide mission, they took action. Led by Tom Burnett, Todd Beamer, Jeremy Glick, and Mark Bingham, they stormed the cockpit and scuttled the terrorists' mission. How, I wondered, could those average Americans have mustered the courage to formulate such a plan—and then execute it, even as they stared death in the face?

As I learned from those who knew them best, each of those four men was shaped in part by his early experience in sports—experience that must certainly have guided these heroes' hands under those horrifying conditions.

The stories in *The Games Do Count* illustrate not only how much our own athletic exploits meant to us in childhood, but how much they shape who we are today. By following the early sports exploits of seventy of this country's most well-known and admired people, and hearing how their athletic pasts paved the way for their stunning careers, I learned something about myself. Perhaps you will, too.

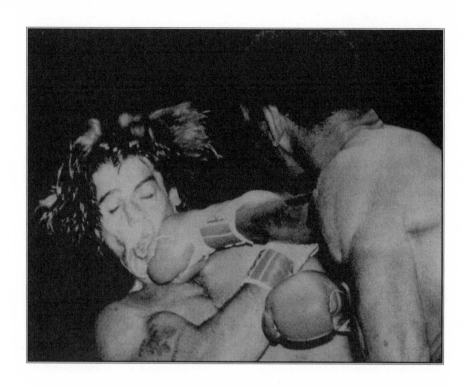

★ TONY DANZA ★

Actor

Boxing

I guess you could say that early on my main sport was street fighting, which just was like another game, especially if you were good at it. It was just something I did, not something I am terrifically proud of. When we were kids we used to go to a place and say, "Ah, there's no girls here, nobody to beat up, let's get out of here." You know, so it was kind of stupid, but that's the way it was.

When you're a kid in Brooklyn and you're little, like I was—only about 89 pounds and 4′ 11″ in tenth grade—you have to stand up for yourself. Plus, I had a big mouth, so guys used to love to throw me over the table, just because they could. Nobody got killed, nobody got hurt too badly. It was a time when kids fought with their hands and not with guns, and so a lot of times you ended up being best friends with the guy you ended up fighting with. It had to do with some kind of respect borne out of the fight.

"I THOUGHT I'D GOTTEN DRAFTED!"

When I got older, I owned a little piece of a bar in Long Island, and a bunch of my friends all hung out there. One day they got the bright idea to enter me into the Golden Gloves. They just filled out an entry blank in the *Daily News* and a short time later I got a notice to appear for my physical. For a second, I thought I'd gotten drafted!

I went to the bar that night, where all my friends were all laughing about it, and I said, "Okay, I'll do it." So I entered the Gloves in the sub-novice class at 175 pounds, light-heavyweight, which was a lot bigger than I was at the time. I should have been fighting at 160.

"I KNEW THERE WAS SOMETHING WRONG BECAUSE YOU'RE NOT THAT GOOD A LOSER."

I used to train like this: I'd sit at the bar and I'd go, "Aw, I got time for one more," and then I'd go fight.

I had a great first year. I knocked out the first six guys I fought. They were writing me up in the paper as the "Battling Bartender." "I serve mittens instead of Manhattans"—stuff like that. I could punch a little bit, so I did okay. But then, I ran into a kid who really knew what he was doing and he beat the hell out of me at the Downtown Athletic Club. I got knocked down and I remember, as I was going down, hearing my mother scream in this kind of vortex. It was the last fight my mother ever went to. The next thing I know, I wake up in the shower. I open up the shower curtain and I see the coach, Sarge, who was this old sergeant from the Police Athletic League. I said, "Hey, Sarge, what happened?"

"Well," he said, "we're going home a little early tonight." Then he said, "You went down, but you weren't knocked out. It was interesting, because you got up and you congratulated the other fighter, you thanked the referee, you congratulated the other corner. I knew there was something wrong, because I know you're not that good a loser!"

I was in Never-Never Land. I didn't know who I was. But even though I got beat up, I was hooked. I really loved it. It was that moment when you're young when you think, "I found what I can do! What I'm really good at." That's what it felt like to me.

I went back the next year in the open class, and this time I trained. I got down to 160. I figured, if I can knock out light-heavyweights, I'll kill middle-weights. I fought the champ in the first round. He hit me with three thousand jabs. I had him down twice, but I lost the fight. Then I turned pro. Five bucks and you got your boxer's license. I went to Gleason's gym, on 28th Street in Manhattan. It was the Mecca of boxing in New York at the time. There was an older guy sitting at a counter as you walked in the door, his name was Sammy Morgan, and he had this big, bulbous nose—obviously he had been a fighter—and he said, "What do you want?"

I said, "I want to be a fighter."

He said, "What?"

I'm looking around—there was all this noise—and just as I said again, "*I want to be a fighter,*" the bell rang, and it was quiet!

He said, "Chicky!"—that was Chicky Ferrar, the great trainer—"This guy wants to be a fighter!"

Chicky says, "He wants to be a fighter? Come on over! Has he got equipment?"

I got dressed and Chicky said, "Show me what you got." I got in the ring, and he put a little Vaseline on me and stuck my mouthpiece in. I turned around, and there was the number sixth-ranked middle-weight in the world, Eddie Gregory, sitting across, standing across the ring—later, he changed his name to Eddie Mustafa Mohammed and became World Champ. He beat the hell out of me. I lost my temper, which was one of my problems when I first started to fight. So I tried to hit him back and then he really beat me up. But I came back the next day, because I was hooked.

"IT'S LIKE A DRUG."

Boxing changed my life. It's like a drug; you can't believe how great it is! Let me tell you something, you hit somebody on the chin, the guy goes down, the crowd roars. . . . Wow! You really feel something! But it also does something else for you. First of all, there's this tremendous cama-raderie, because we're all in this together, and we all know what it takes to be in there. Then there's the bond with my trainers. You develop this father-son thing that's incredible. These guys really have a stabilizing effect on you, because they've been around. But boxing also gives you a tremendous amount of self-assurance, because you realize that if you can do this, you can probably do just about everything, and that carries on into the rest of your life.

My father, who passed away twenty years ago, was a tough guy, but he didn't want me to be a fighter. I finally talked him into coming to see me fight after I'd knocked out five guys in a row. I said, "Dad, I'm killing guys, come see me fight." I was fighting in White Plains at the City Center, and I walked into a right hand. I was trying to get out early. I thought I could knock the guy out, and the guy hit me right on the chin. I didn't go down, but my eyes rolled around in my head like a slot machine. When I came to, my father was sitting ringside, and he was as white as that wall. But then, I got him to come back, and I won a few for him.

"YOU KNOW, YOU COULD DO THIS."

Boxing also resulted in my getting the job on *Taxi.* A guy came into Gleason's and saw me training there—I was the only white guy in the gym, so I stuck out—and asked me to read for a pilot that he was developing called *Augie,* which was a combination of *Chico and the Man* and *Rocky,* about an old guy who had a gym and a young fighter named Augie. The old man, to keep the place, because he's down on his luck, rents half of it out to an aerobics instructor. So you have girls running around in outfits and you have fights. Pretty good idea, huh?

Anyway, he made me read for him, and he liked what I did. He said, "You know, you could do this."

I said, "All right."

But I thought it was a lark, so I went back to fighting. A couple of months would go by, and I wouldn't hear from him. Then he'd call me and say, "Look, I didn't forget you. I'm going to try to get you something." But I thought I was going to be champion of the world, so I wasn't interested that.

He called me up one day, and he asked, "You're fighting soon?"

It was a Wednesday and I said, "I'm fighting Friday night."

He says, "I got a couple of guys from NBC, they want to come see you."

"GET UP!"

I was nervous enough about the fight—I was fighting the state champion of Connecticut, Rocky Garcia—so I needed that like a hole in the head. I really wanted to look good—these guys were there and there were some other people there that were interested in managing me. The bell rang, and I came out. I was real good if you came to me, but I was pretty bad if I had to chase you. This guy came right to me . . . and I go "Ah, I'm gonna look good here," because I could really bang. He had this weird move, though. He looked like he was throwing a right hand, and then he threw a left hook. I couldn't figure it out. I get hit on the chin. Thirty seconds into the fight, boom, I'm down. The thing about a left hook is, a right hand knocks you down, but a left hook picks you up, throws you up in the air, you land on the back of your head with your feet up in the air. I was mad. I jump up, thinking, "I'll take care of this guy." Hits me the same punch. This time, I'm hurt.

Now, Rocky's full of adrenaline. He looked like he was breathing fire. He's yelling at me, "Get up! Come on and get up!"

And I was thinking, Should I?

I heard the referee saying, "Nine and a half . . ."

I got up and for the next two minutes I took a terrible beating. I'm following him around in the ring in a daze. Boom—he hits me on the chin—I start to go down. And suddenly, it's like in *Angels in the Outfield* where somebody puts a hand underneath you and picks you back up. I didn't go down. With fifteen seconds left in the round, we trade right hands, mine gets there first, I knock him down. I win the fight.

People were yelling, "You won! You won!" But I had no idea what they were talking about. The guy from Hollywood goes nuts! He got me a screen test here in New York. I get a call from someone who's doing a pilot in LA, would I like to fly out and audition?

So I fly out to LA and they said to me, "What have you done?"

I say, "I fought eight rounds at Prospect Hall."

I got the part and that started me on my show business career and eventually led to Jim Brooks casting me in *Taxi.*

Much later on, when I first started doing my song and dance act, I was so afraid of embarrassing myself, of failing. I even had an agent tell me, "What if it says on the front page of *Variety,* 'Danza can't sing!'" But boxing gives you a lot of self-assurance that if you can do that you can do anything. Even singing.

★JON STEWART★

Comedian and Television Host

Soccer

I began my sports career as a way out of the suburbs.

I grew up in a small town outside of Trenton, New Jersey, in the sixties and seventies, during the great suburban immigration. It was a soccer town, with a lot of immigrants, mostly Italian and Polish, so most of us gravitated toward soccer, while kids in most small towns gravitate toward football and baseball.

The best way to describe my ability was to say that after the game the other kids would say to me, "Way to try!" I'm not the largest fellow, and I was always a little young for my grade, which meant I was a little smaller than most of the other kids. I had to go through puberty in tenth, eleventh grade, and it was only then that I was able to compete on any kind of an equal level, without getting my head handed to me.

"IT WAS ALL ABOUT JUST GETTING GOOD AT SOMETHING."

I wasn't an All-Star, or anything like that, but it's always been part of my personality to be very dogged when I'm unsuccessful. So I spent a lot of time with a buddy of mine, Mike Faith, who lived up the block. Basically, we spent every night out in the street kicking a ball back and forth until eleven, twelve o'clock at night. Sometimes, we'd go up the block to the neighborhood church that had a huge, brick wall, and work on skills. I spent hours just kicking a ball against a wall, or kicking it to Mike, and running, doing anything that would help me get better.

I think back so fondly on just sitting out there in the street, under a streetlight, kicking a ball back and forth, just talking with my buddy, getting a feel for the ball, learning the necessary skills. But it wasn't until college, at William and Mary, that I really learned how to play the game.

I'm proud of my soccer career. I wasn't the greatest athlete in the world, but I tried like hell. I think I did about as well as I could have done. I don't think I left anything on the field when I walked away. I don't think anybody would say, "Well, that guy squandered the potential to be a World Cup athlete." Some of the best people I've ever met in my life I met on my college soccer team. I didn't know how to be friends with girls. I knew how to hang out with guys in a bus traveling to soccer games. So that was my idea of fun. The games were exciting, and there was a lot of passion, and for those ninety minutes it was wonderful.

"THERE'S ONLY SO FAR YOU CAN GO WITH A HAIRBRUSH AND A MIRROR."

Comedy and hosting a talk show is about the closest thing to sports that I have found. You don't know the outcome, and it really is up to you to do your best. If you lose, you lose, but you lose with dignity. You don't tank it— you stay true to how hard you want to play, or how you want to play the game.

When I played sports, it wasn't about, "I'm going to become a famous athlete." Instead, it was, "I want to be as good at this game as I can possibly be. I want to help my teammates be better. I want our team to do well." With comedy, it was the same thing. It wasn't, "I want to be a star of a sitcom, I want to do a talk show, I want to . . ." It was, "I want to be good at this, in a universal sense, not in a 'Jesus, he's only been doing it for a year, he's good for a year' sense." That's what it was like with soccer. You didn't want to be good for a small player, or good for a guy with no left foot. You wanted to be good, you wanted to take your best shot at the top guys and see how you came out.

Being funny is the same way as it was with soccer: You never think about the fans or the audience, because it's not about that. It's about the act of writing jokes. It's not about the spectators, although obviously, with comedy especially, if you don't have an audience, you're screwed. There's only so far you can go with a hairbrush and a mirror. Of course, you take into account their reaction to you, but that's not the thrill. The thrill is in the creation of the comedy, or the doing of it, just like it is with soccer. It's the playing of the game. That's where the real excitement is.

Also, as in soccer, when you're out there on stage you never think about how people might look at you. It's all about having a work ethic. I know what it takes to be good, and I have great respect and admiration for people who are good at what they do. And I know that that doesn't come easy. You don't wake up and just go, "I think I'm going to be a star today." You gotta pound it out. Competence is underrated. If you can achieve competence by hard work, then, Amen, you'll do fine.

CROCE IS AT LEFT.

★PAT CROCE★

Television Host and Former Part
Owner of the Philadelphia 76ers

Football, Martial Arts

I was first exposed to sports as a fourth grader playing knee-high baseball. I wasn't a very good player, but I enjoyed being a part of the team. From sixth grade all the way up into college, I played football. I loved the hitting, the camaraderie, the working out, the discipline, the locker room, and especially the celebration after the wins. To me sports was a way to celebrate, to show that when you practice and prepare and prioritize and prepare some more and then practice some more, your dreams can come true; you can get better at anything.

Sports didn't actually have to mold me, because my father was a very strict Italian task master. I guess you'd have to say that he was almost like my head coach in life. My father was really tough, and my brothers and I were almost like his team. If you didn't do it right, he wouldn't give out grass drills or pushups to do, he'd smack ya! But I think tough love made us do things right.

My old man was crazy! At the games, he would be in the stands, yelling, "Put Pat in!" He was a vociferous, emotional, passionate Italian guy, and everyone in the stands was laughing because he was so nuts. But he was the biggest fan of mine, even though I wasn't playing at the top level. He'd even come to some practices. So I think throughout my life—and I've never said this before—I strived to be better and ultimately to be the best at anything I'm touching because of him. Now, he's looking at me from heaven, and I believe he's still watching everything I'm doing. Fortunately, the other side of my family, the Irish part of me, always gave me positive thoughts: Pat, you can do this, you can do this. And everything in life, whether it's going to physical therapy school, or trying out for a team, or taking over the Sixers, or whatever it might have been, was always a case of, You can do this. So, I never had any real self-doubts. And I never thought of myself as a failure. Ever. Everything I did was a learning experience. If I failed, I just thought that I wasn't good enough yet. I still think that! I'm not good enough . . . yet! But with practice, with more will, with more skill, I'll be successful.

"I DIDN'T HAVE THE SKILL, BUT BY DAMN, I HAD THE WILL!"

I wrestled and played football in high school, but I never really started, probably because I was always outsized. As a senior in high school, I was probably about 5'8"—I'm 6'—and 150 pounds. I matured a little later in life, physically and mentally. My goal was to play for the Philadelphia Eagles, but I realized I wasn't big enough, nor fast enough, nor strong enough. I'm a hometown boy here in Philadelphia, and that, I thought, that would be the epitome. How great it would have been to be able to play for the Eagles! But when I realized that I was going to get killed out there, that's when my whole mind-set, my goals, my focus and my dreams changed to a different path in life that led me to become the physical therapist for professional teams. But I think that same pursuit of starting on the football team in high school transferred over to my work ethic in the classroom and in the work environment.

Not starting bothered me tremendously. In my mind, I believed I should have started, regardless of my physical immaturity or my being incapable of running the 440 or bench pressing 300 lbs. I believed I could hit. I believed I could read the offense better than other players. I believed I was smarter. But it didn't matter what I believed. The fact was, I didn't start. But I didn't say, "Okay, I give up." I just took it as impetus to do better, to train harder. And that's why probably to this day, I'm known as one of the fittest guys, because I still train hard. I think that was ingrained in me in my high school years, at a time when I said to myself, "I'm gonna start, by golly, I'm going to start no matter what it takes, even though maybe I don't have the talent of some of the other players." You know there's will and there's skill Maybe I didn't have the skill, but by damn, I had the will!

As a freshman in college—I was only seventeen and was six feet, weighing 170 pounds—I played at Westchester University. One day, the coach put me in because one of the linebackers got hurt. It was a close game, and I had the opportunity to make tackles that counted. When the game was on the line, I didn't let him down, I didn't let the team down, I didn't let the fans down, and most important I didn't let myself down, and that was very important to me.

"COACHES SEEMED TO LIKE ME. PROBABLY BECAUSE EITHER I WAS UNDERSIZED OR OVER-ZEALOUS."

What I went through as a young athlete helped me relate to the professional athletes I helped train. I've worked with some of the best—Charles Barkley, Allen Iverson, Mike Schmidt, Bobby Clark—and you get to the point where you can immediately recognize the guys who are given the skill but lack the will. You say to yourself, "Oh my goodness, if only I was blessed with these talents, I could play Michael Jordan . . ." I was fortunate enough to see some of the best athletes work miracles on the court, on the ice, on the field, and I could deal with them successfully because I always trained with them. For instance, when I was a conditioning coach and physical therapist for the Flyers and 76ers, I would never ask them to do something that I wouldn't or couldn't do. They'd be there at 7:00 in the morning every day or every other day, and I'd be waiting there with a key in the door, and, boom, we'd go at it. I call it the sweat factor—it's the common dominator among all people; when you sweat with someone you can relate with them. I never was in awe of them, no matter how great an athlete they were. I'm in awe when a writer writes a great book, or Bruce Springsteen sings a great song, or Mikhail Baryshnikov dances, but I was never in awe of the people themselves, rather what they accomplish. I like taking the big shots, whether it's CEOs in Fortune 500 companies or professional athletes, and breaking them down, ripping them off that pedestal, and letting them earn their keep.

ROBBINS IS NUMBER 16, SECOND ROW, THIRD FROM RIGHT.

★TONY ROBBINS★

Motivational Speaker and Author

Baseball, Football

I wanted to participate in sports in my life early on, but I had a lot of responsibilities at home and I wasn't that big or that strong. In fact, I was a bit overweight, and I was extremely pigeon-toed. As result, I walked a little bit like a girl, and I got harassed for that. They used to call me "cowboy," because I would wear cowboy boots all the time.

By the time I got to fifth grade, I had a new father, and he was a semi-pro baseball player. He was the coolest guy, and he really had a way about him. The singer Tom Jones was very big in those days, so everyone used to call my stepfather TJ. One day he said to me, "Why don't you play sports?"

I said, "Well, I want to, but I can't play because my mom won't let me." She was afraid I'd get hurt because I was so small, and she also said that we couldn't afford it.

But TJ said, "You're going to play baseball." So that's what I did.

"I ONCE I GOT HIT WITH THE BALL AND WAS BLEEDING ALL OVER THE PLACE, BUT I GOT UP AND SAID, 'HIT ME ANOTHER ONE.'"

I loved TJ so much, and now we were able to connect through sports, which was a way for me to create a relationship with him. I remember him going at me with ground balls, literally hours and hours and hours at a time. I can't tell you how many times the ball would come smack me in the face. I once I got hit with the ball and was bleeding all over the place, but I got up and said, "Hit me another one."

That was probably the most reinforcing experience in the world in helping me develop moxie, because when that happened TJ said, "That's my boy!" which made me feel great and more connected to him.

"I LEARNED THAT IF I GOT LOW, I COULD TAKE ANYBODY OUT."

What I found through sports was inner strength. I found it by pushing myself to the limits. I think the difference in the quality of anybody's life, whether it be an athlete or a businessperson, whether it be a Nelson Mandela or an Oprah Winfrey or a Maya Angelou, what sets them apart, is inner strength. It's emotional fitness and psychological strength. It's the ability to have enough mental toughness that you can get yourself to do the things you know you need to do to break through. Initially, I got that from practicing baseball with TJ.

As I got older, I got into football, but again, I was pathetic at it, in part because I came to it late—I was twelve or thirteen years old. Nevertheless, it toughened me up. Here I was a kid who was small, but I learned that if I got low, I could take anybody out. I became a little linebacker, the smallest linebacker they'd ever seen, but I would annihilate people. And being able to do that gave me the belief in myself that once I set my mind to something, nothing was going to stop me.

"I DIDN'T MAKE THE LAST CUT."

When I was a kid, I wanted to be a professional baseball player. I was a pitcher and a shortstop. The coach of the junior high school team was also the science teacher, and he was one of those really straight-laced guys. I had long hair, and he made it very clear that no player was going to play for him looking that way. So I went and cut my hair, thinking, Now I know I'm bald, but I don't care, man, I love this game. I'll give up everything for this game.

But I didn't make the last cut, and I was just devastated. So it made me reevaluate my whole life. It made me look at things more closely and I said to myself, Man, if I don't make the junior high school baseball team, how am I going to make the varsity team in high school? How am I going to get a scholarship to college? How am I going to make it to the minor leagues? How am I going to make it to the major leagues? And in that week of soul-searching, I decided what I'd become. I asked myself, What's the core of what I want? I love people, I love sports, I love lighting people up, I love the energy of the game, so I'm going to become a sportscaster, that's what I'm going to do.

"HOW AM I GOING TO GET AN
INTERVIEW WITH HIM?"

One day I was reading the *Los Angeles Times,* and I saw that Howard Cosell was going to do a book signing at Robinson's Department Store in LA. So I grabbed the tape recorder from school, called my mother, and said, "I have a private interview with Howard Cosell. I need you to drive me to Los Angeles." A total lie, but she checked me out of the school and drove me to LA.

I get to Robinson's, and Cosell was surrounded by dozens of people who are trying to get him to sign his book. I see this woman walk up to him, and she wants an autograph on a napkin she's holding, but she hasn't bought a book, so he says, "No ma'am, I don't give autographs, you have to buy the book." So here I was, this little kid, and I'm thinking, How am I going to get an interview with him if he won't even sign an autograph?

Finally, Cosell's publicist says, "I'm really sorry, but Mr. Cosell has to go."

I went into total panic. It was pandemonium. Photographers were snapping pictures, flashbulbs were going off. People were asking, "What about the Super Bowl, what about Muhammad Ali . . ." I fought my way through the crowd till I got up to him. I had these business cards I'd made up that said "Anthony J. Robbins, Future Sportscaster. Presently limited to brief taped interviews." My hand was shaking as I handed him my card.

He said, "Oh," and he flipped it over to try to give me an autograph.

I said, "No, no, no, sir. I'm here to interview you."

He looked at me, and said, "What, son?" He was a master, and so he used the moment, which turned out to be my advantage. He made everybody else wait. "No, I want to talk to this young man." He said, "You want to become a sportscaster, young man?"

I said, "Yeah."

He said, "All right, I'll give you a brief interview here. You get two or three questions."

I said, "Oh, great."

So we're standing there and I'm holding my microphone, my hand shaking like crazy, and I'm asking these questions, and he's really getting into it, going "To-neeey." The publicist keeps pulling at him to go, but I got him engaged. Finally, he said, "Well, I've got to go."

I said, "Can I ask one final question?"

He said, "Yeah."

Now there used to be a radio sports commentator in LA who used to rip Cosell every day, and his name was Jim Healy. So I said to Cosell, "Do you ever wish the morning after *Monday Night Football* that Jim Healy would wake up with laryngitis?"

The whole crowd started laughing, and then there was a silence. Cosell said, "I'm sorry son, but I've never heard of Jim Healy." He got up and stormed out.

The next day, the *L.A. Times* ran an article about how he didn't sign autographs, but how this young kid tamed him. So the local newspaper in my city tracked me down and called me up and said, "We heard you're the person in this article, would you like to write a story on it?"

I said, "Are you kidding me? I'm in journalism classes." So I wrote a twenty-two-page article that became six paragraphs. I got up at 5:00 A.M., got on my bicycle, and rode down there and got every one of those copies of the newspaper. And there was my picture with Cosell and me and my little interview. They loved me and it so much that they gave me a weekly column.

RIVERA IS IN THE BACK ROW, SECOND FROM RIGHT.

★GERALDO RIVERA★

Television Journalist

Wrestling, Football

I am not excellent at anything. Certainly not sports. I was average at almost everything, but I was able to maximize my average abilities. I guess you could say that I was way above average in terms of motivation. You know, I couldn't throw the ball as far as most of the guys, I couldn't hit as hard. I just wasn't as skilled. I was a competent athlete. But the difference between being a winner, or competitive, and being a loser, is attitude. There aren't that many Michael Jordans or Muhammad Alis. But you've just got to go out there and do your best. I think that the person who's most motivated most often wins in that kind of match up.

I was a marginal kid in high school, in the sense that a lot of my leadership skills were misapplied. I was a very street-oriented kid and I was co-founder of a group called the Corner Boys, which was kind of a gang. I was constantly at war between going the route of the football team or going the route of the streets. I really have to say that two of my coaches steered me toward the team, and really helped me in very important ways to get off the streets and to dedicate that energy, and whatever leadership skills I had, to something much more productive than the street life.

I was an asthmatic kid; I weighed only 75 pounds in seventh grade. When I was a freshman and weighed all of 115 pounds, I took up wrestling and football. I was so relieved to finally have mastered this crippling affliction, but I'd take three steps and I'd start wheezing. Sometimes I would do a wind sprint and I would be wheezing at the end of that. But gradually those wind sprints began to help expand my lung capacity and stamina. It was interesting to see my metamorphosis from a 98-pound weakling into a person who would ultimately be the sand kicker rather than the sand receiver.

What I found is, as Napoleon said, morale is the most important ally on the battlefield, more important even than the artillery. And it was really true.

One particular game comes to mind. We were playing Amityville, the perennial powerhouse in our neck of the woods. It was pretty early in the game and we were already down by two touchdowns, and we were dragging our asses on the field, thinking, "Oh my god, it's going to be a ninety-to-nothing game."

The coach saw this and came over, whacked me on the helmet and said, "What's wrong with you? Don't you see you're only down by fourteen points? That's two scores. This is only the second quarter! Now get these guys fired up!"

I remember thinking, Oh my god, we're only down two touchdowns. It isn't inevitable. We went on to give them the fight of their lives, barely losing the game.

After high school, I attended Maritime College, which was part of this whole evolution from street kid to being more career oriented. When I got there, I joined the rowing team. We rowed whale boats, eight-row crew and one coxswain, in the international seaman's race every year. We'd race against other maritime colleges in the country and overseas. And that, even more than the high school football team—getting up at five o'clock every morning to be in superb shape—helped me go from being the 98-pound weakling to someone who really was physically fit and formidable.

Knowing that seven guys could do great, but that one guy could sink it if he crabbed his oar, or if he didn't put out, if he didn't help, taught me the importance of working together as a team. The nucleus that developed between the nine of us was a very emotional thing for me. Even now, years later, I can still remember in great detail specific competitions—and with boxing, later on—specific matches, what the emotional feeling was at various points along the way.

I really love competitive sports, and I love team sports more than anything. The touch football game I played in for twenty-five years every Sunday in Central Park was a classic example of that. It was an eleven-on-eleven game, while most touch football games are six-on-six or seven-on-seven. I'd show up and play against these kids that every year got younger and younger, harder and harder. But it was such a wonderful event: the environment was wonderful, here we were all living in the city, but you get out every morning in Central Park. And then, as people started prospering, as they got older, people moved to the suburbs, but some of them would still drive two or three hours to be at that 9:00 A.M. choosing of teams. Because if you missed that, then you'd have to sit out until someone went out for an injury. We played all morning. You could cross body block and you could leave your feet to block, and in most touch games you can't do that. It was a really rough, tough game. I was a flanker, mostly, and a corner back on defense. Even today, I remember a certain catch or a certain "tackle" in a particular game. Some great people played in the game, like H. Rap Brown, who wasn't a great person, he was a political radical and later an alleged murderer; and there was Jerome Snyder, who worked with Milton Glazier who was the first designer of *New York* magazine. A lot of very successful people went through that game, and the fact that I played in it for a quarter of a century makes me very proud.

"CAN I STILL DO THIS?"

I also got something else out of playing sports that was very important. There's always the "thrill of victory, the agony of defeat," but it's also about matching your skills up against someone else, as well as answering the question, "Can I still do this?"

It's just the pure pleasure and the aesthetic of playing the game, like when you catch a pass with a full body extension, or when you leave your feet and make contact and tag out one of your opponents; or when your team does win when the other team was the favorite.

There were and are a lot of people who didn't credit my potential or the chance I had to compete. I know a lot of people along the way who said I'd be an overnight wonder. But I've been in this business now for almost thirty-five years and I'm still here. That's a very long night.

★CATHERINE CRIER★

Television News Reporter,
Anchor, and Author

Horseback Riding

I was always a jock. I started playing sports as soon as I could walk. I remember the year I asked for (and received) a basketball hoop and basketball for my birthday. The only reason to have a Barbie doll was to have something to put astride the plastic horses while pretending to ride!

I must have been nine when we got our first horse. I'd already learned to ride, but in 1964, my sisters and I were given a horse. That turned my life around completely, because within three years, we were enmeshed in the raising and showing of Arabian horses. I ran track, quarterbacked the flag football team, and played forward on the basketball team in my elementary and secondary school years, but the horses were my major athletic outlet.

Having horses is a lot of work. There is a 1,200- to 2,000-pound animal on the end of a line that you're training and grooming while hauling saddles, throwing hay bales, and dumping wheelbarrows full of sand. (I was the unofficial arm-wrestling champ in the seventh grade.) By the time I was in seventh grade, I would leave school, go straight to the barn, work horses until dark, and then go home. The weekend was spent riding. My experience was not that of a kid delivered to some private barn, placed on a school horse, and trotted around the ring under the watchful eye of an instructor.

Back in those days, you could skip a lot of school with a note from home. I "lost" a lot of relatives to excuse my absences as we hooked up the trailer and headed for the horse shows. I clearly remember my first big competition, the Houston Fat Stock Show, where I was the designated junior rider for a famous Arabian horse farm. I was about twelve years old and terribly nervous. I completely lost my voice. The trainer kept giving me sips of beer so I would relax. It must have worked, because I won the English Junior Championship, the Western Junior Championship, and the High Point Award for the show. That experience was the first in a wonderful show career in the Arabian horse world.

While I wasn't asked to my senior prom, I made up for it by winning several national horsemanship championships instead. At fourteen, I was National Champion Saddle Seat (English) Equitation Rider, and the following year, I was Reserve National Champion Stock Seat (Western) Equitation Rider. The horses were my great outlet; especially since I was a bit of a loner and a bit shy. I skipped my junior year in high school, and at sixteen I headed off to the University of Texas.

"YOU PLAY AS HARD AS YOU CAN AND THEN GO HAVE A BEER WITH YOUR COMPETITORS."

I pursued sports in a way that most men do—that is, you play as hard as you can and then go have a beer with your competitors. It's more than competing against someone else. It is really about competing against yourself and doing the best you can. Growing up in an environment of healthy competition encouraged me do things that many girls probably didn't feel comfortable doing, in athletics, academics, or simply life, when I chose to leave home at sixteen. Sports really contributed to that mind-set. I have always believed that the world is a big place, and if you mess up, then move on and explore new things. I might pen my epitaph to read, "courage to risk, freedom to fail."

Competing with the horses, much the same as in track and golf, it's just you. If you mess up, no one else is responsible. You can practice, prepare, and put on the best show possible, but then you must let the chips fall where they may. That's all anyone can do. It is important to judge the results through that prism and recognize the elements of circumstance and fate that contribute to the outcome. This lesson is valuable in all areas of life.

I didn't have a coach throughout most of my showing career. Even when I was at the top of my game, I had very few equitation lessons. Instead, I discovered my own way of learning. I would stand on the rail and watch a teacher working with other riders, then mentally envision my body, my muscles, moving as they should. Years later, I formally learned about psychocybernetics—the practice of mentally rehearsing tasks that I wanted to do, then going forward with skills achieved in part from this thought exercise. I remember reading about a study of two basketball teams. For several weeks, one team sat in chairs and mentally contemplated their game while the other team worked out on the court every day. When they played each other, the abilities were virtually the same. This sort of mental exercise has always helped me to prepare and perform, whether on television, as a lecturer, or in athletic endeavors. The mind is an amazing organ!

I am wired pretty tight. Had sports not been a big part of my life, I could have gotten into a lot of trouble. The horses, in particular, provided more than competition and self-assurance. They demanded an emotional attachment that helped me to develop other traits like empathy, love, and responsibility. Sports gave me game, gave me confidence, and gave me an extraordinary outlet that continues to support every aspect of my life.

★JOHN TESH★

Television and Radio Host
and Musician

Soccer, Lacrosse

I was a skinny, hideous-looking kid. I was the height I am now, which is 6′ 6″, in junior high school, and I weighed 150 pounds. I had size four-teen feet, and my parents put braces on me to straighten my teeth, and in those days that was like wearing barbed wire in your mouth. They sent me to school every day with a bologna sandwich, because they wanted to save money. So I smelled like bologna, and I had barbed wire on my teeth. The whole thing in junior high school is for girls to be interested, and the girls were definitely not interested in me.

What am I going to do to be popular? I asked myself.

At the time, anybody in that school would have said, "There's nothing Tesh can do."

I said to myself, Well, I can't run, because I don't have the power in my legs, but I can jump, so why not try high jumping? So I did, and I started get-ting a little bit stronger, and in seventh grade, I ended up setting a school record at 6′ 3″. Before that, I had never been over 5′ 10″, but I slipped when I jumped and something just happened and I flew over the bar. I set this record, and they announced my name in the auditorium, and all of a sudden I was a hero for about a week, until somebody else broke it. That really gave me the in-testinal fortitude to do other things, and that's when I started playing soccer.

"THERE'S NOTHING TESH CAN DO."

I was not naturally talented at all, and my parents were not athletes. If you go back and trace my life you would see that the decisions I made look like those of a kid who's trying to get noticed, whether it's being a musician or being on television or being on the radio or putting on little shows for Halloween or being an athlete.

Instead of hanging out at the 7-Eleven, trying to score alcohol, I was running wind sprints. I was always the most tenacious, the one who wanted to be the first in line to run the wind sprints, the one who would attack the ball if the goalie dropped it and not say, "Well, the goalie's got it . . ."

"MY REAL PRIDE AND JOY WAS MY LETTER JACKET."

I was on the soccer team, but I didn't start all the time. I played what they used to call halfback and also fullback, so I was basically a defender. I was still hideously skinny, but I had gotten pretty fast, and I was always the most determined one out there. I was the kid who got "most improved," the kid who always got the hustle award, because I knew I didn't have the talent the some of the other kids had. Even at North Carolina State, where I didn't get a scholarship but made the team as a walk-on, I was always the guy who stayed after the regular practice and did the dribbling drills and the wind sprints. It's the same way for me with music. I'm always the guy who stays after to practice the scales, because I know I'm average talent in a lot of these areas. So it was a real ego booster just to be on the team.

My real pride and joy was my letter jacket. I think I was the only kid at Garden City Junior High and Garden City High School who wore his jacket every day. It was like a little night-night pillow or something that a kid has.

I have one particular memory of playing sports, but it's not an especially good one. We were playing a game and I was at fullback. It was tie score, and a ball was coming right toward me. I kicked it as hard as I could to clear it out, and it spun off my foot and went right into the goal. Our own goal. I didn't bend it like Beckham, I bent it backwards. So, we lost the game, 2–1. That became a metaphor for my whole life: make sure you lean forward and connect with the ball. And make sure it goes straight.

"I WASN'T SCARED OF ANYTHING."

When you look at my career, it looks like I picked stuff up right away. But I was the kid at home with a tape recorder reading a paragraph in the *New York Times;* then I would look up and try to ad lib it. I was always rehearsing. I used to do play-by-play of ping pong games to try to prepare myself for the Olympic Games. Whether as a musician or as an athlete, it's all about finding the right way to practice. I think there's a lot of kids who look at anybody on TV, on MTV especially, and they say, "Oh my gosh, I want to do that." Well, between "I want to do that" and doing it, there's a lot of work. There is one key ingredient, though, and that is lack of fear. If you look at my career, what was I doing at WCBS as an anchor and a reporter at twenty-three years old, it's because I wasn't scared of anything. And playing sports helps you get to that point.

I really believe that there's a sport out there for everybody. I think it's really important to have the experience of working on a team, being a team player.

★OLIVER NORTH★

Marine Colonel, Author,
and War Correspondent

Baseball, Boxing

I grew up in a fiercely competitive family. My dad was an athlete who rode crew for the University of Pennsylvania during the Depression. He desperately wanted his boys to know the experience of what it meant to compete—in other words, what it meant to be part of a team, and what it meant to work hard at an endeavor.

When I was a kid my dad coached the Little League team. So, it was a no-brainer—my brothers and I all wanted to go out there and play. I didn't have all the gifts and talents to be a great baseball player. I'm a southpaw, but I was so wild on the pitcher's mound that I ended up playing first base, where it turned out I had some talent. I could move pretty well. I could make a good double play. And I turned out to be a pretty good base runner. Running the bases isn't just about eye-hand coordination, it's about how you move your body that ninety feet that it takes to get from one base to the other before the ball gets there and makes you out.

"NOT WINNING IS A DISAPPOINTMENT."

At Annapolis, everybody competes. It was, like at all the military academies, a requirement to go out for a sport. People ask why, and it's because of what you learn about yourself, what you learn about others, and what you learn about being a part of a team. In the military, being a part of a team is absolutely essential. If you don't learn those things on the playing field, then you've lost something when you're getting ready to go into combat. I look at that as being a very, very important part of what I was as a young man, and it has served me well to this day.

I also learned that not winning is a disappointment. Not that Dad or any of the other coaches I've had in my life would say, "You're a lousy player." But

I learned that winning does make a difference. People who go out there and say, "It's just to play the game, it's not to win," are losers. I hate to put it that way, but in my book, you ought to go out there to play to win, but you ought to play fair, you have to play by the rules, and these are things you should learn as a kid.

"YOU GIVE THE FIGHT TO THE GUY WHO HAD THE GUTS TO GET BACK UP AND KEEP ON FIGHTING."

One of the things I learned at the Naval Academy as a boxer came from my coach, Emerson Smith, one of the great, grand old men of boxing who was one of the U.S. Olympic coaches and a legend at the Academy. He could take a young guy like me, who hadn't boxed before, other than a little bit of sparring back in the old days of the AAU and the Golden Gloves, and make sure that every time you got in the ring, you were paired off with somebody of about equal level. One of the things Emerson Smith taught you right from the get-go was that when you get knocked down you have to get back up, dust yourself off, protect yourself, and start swinging.

One of the remarkable things that happened to me as a consequence of being a Navy boxing champion was years later when I was called back to referee the Navy boxing championships along with Rocky Marciano, the World Heavyweight Champ. It was a bantam-weight 135-pound bout. Amateur boxing is three three-minute rounds—the longest nine minutes of your life, is the way I describe it. I was collecting the cards after each round and giving them to the ringside announcer, so he would have the whole fight laid out by the time the third round is finished. At the end of the first round, everybody has scored the round to the guy who knocked the other guy down. He was knocked down once in each round. As I'm looking at the cards, I noticed that the champ had given the round to the kid who got knocked down. Second round same thing, third round same thing. The fight went to the guy who knocked the other guy down, but it was as the result of a decision, not a knockout.

Later on, in the locker room, we were taking a shower, cleaning up, and getting dressed in our street clothes, and I said, "Champ, I got a question for you. Why did you give the fight to the guy who got knocked down every round, usually in the first minute of every round?"

He looked at me and he said, "Son, you've got to understand something. I was a slugger. I never had real finesse in the ring. What you've got to understand, son, is you don't give the fight to the guy who knocked him down, you give the fight to the guy who had the guts to get back up and keep on fighting." I wrote that lesson into my first book, because it was so profound. I was a young officer, I'd just come back from Vietnam, and I'd been invited back to the Naval Academy, and you know what, that's exactly the kind of people we like to be around. We like to be around the kind of guy who gets knocked down, gets back up, dusts himself off, puts his dukes back up, and goes back at the guy.

"SOME OF US ARE NATURAL TALENTS. I'M NOT."

The first year I boxed at the Naval Academy, I lost in the quarter-finals. I said to myself, You know, there are a lot of other better boxers, but I'm going to stick with this and I'm going to keep working at it until I get good enough, because I know I can be a champion. The second year, I lost in the semi-finals. The third year I won the championship.

Now, when I coach young people, I tell them, "You've got to keep trying to get better." The good Lord gives us all certain gifts and talents. Some of us are natural athletes. I'm not. I worked hard at it. I kept my endurance up, so by the time I got to the Marine Corps and I was a commissioned officer, I knew what it took to excel at something like a physical fitness test. Life is full of those kinds of challenges. Whether you're an athlete or not, you're all being challenged in your day-to-day jobs, and you can draw forth from yourself those kinds of lessons that you learned on the playing field and apply them to everyday living. Whether it's marriage or business or relationships with other people, you can put those kinds of things to work.

★GERALD FORD★

Former President of the United States

Football

W hen I was ten or eleven years old, I started playing sports in a local playground in Grand Rapids. I liked the competition, even as a beginner. Somehow, it stimulated me and excited my interests.

Football was my principal sport in high school. I was captain of the team and All-State. I remember the hours I spent learning to center the ball for speed and accuracy. The center was forced to view everything upside down. The opposing lineman had the jump on you and to carry out your blocking assignment you had to be very quick. You also had to perfect different types of snaps.

My playing football and getting my name in the papers led to my biological father finding me. He surprised me one day when I was working in a hamburger stand. My job was to slap hamburgers on the grill, handle the cash register, and wash dishes. One day, at noon, I was behind the counter in my regular spot near the register when I noticed a man standing by the candy display case. He'd been there fifteen or twenty minutes without saying a word and he was staring at me. "I'm Leslie King, your father," he said. "Can I take you to lunch?"

I was stunned and didn't know what to say. I stared at him a minute and then I finally said, "I'm working."

"Ask your boss if you can get off," he said.

My father took me outside to a new Lincoln. A woman was sitting inside. He introduced her as his wife. They'd taken the train to Detroit from Wyoming, where they lived, had purchased the car, and now they were driving home through Grand Rapids. He asked me about sports and wanted to know all about my playing football at South High. We didn't mention the divorce or anything else disagreeable. After lunch, he drove me to school and handed me $25. "Now, buy yourself something, something you want that you can't afford otherwise." That night was one of the most difficult of my life. I don't recall the words I used to tell my parents what had happened, but I do remember that the conversation was a loving and consoling one.

My parents didn't really have enough money to send me to college, but I got a scholarship to the University of Michigan and I earned some money working at part-time jobs. I played on the freshman team and won the Meyer Morton Trophy, which was a silver football, as the outstanding freshman player at spring practice. That first year, I spent a lot of time on the bench, because we had Chuck Bernard, who was an All-American. But during my sophomore and junior years, we were undefeated and national champions. We used the "punt, pass, and prayer" style of playing. The theory was that if you had a good punter, a good passer, and a strong defense, you would always win. If you won the coin toss, you always kicked off and gave the other team the ball. You counted on your defense to force them into mistakes. Inside your own 40-yard line, you always punted on second or third down. If you were near your own goal line, you punted on first down. If your punter did his job, you could pick up 10 or 15 yards on every exchange. Them, if your quarterback connected on his passes, you could score and score again.

Our team fell apart my senior year, because we lost most of our starters to graduation and our quarterback, Bill Renner, broke his leg before the first game of the season and was out the whole year. Our most heartbreaking defeat came against Illinois. It has a horrible, rainy day, and the ball was so slippery it was tough to handle. We must have punted 15 or 20 times. Despite the slippery ball, I had a perfect day, but we lost, 7–6.

"AS A FOOTBALL PLAYER, YOU HAVE CRITICS IN THE STANDS AND CRITICS IN THE PRESS."

There's no question that my experience and exposure to athletics had a major impact on my future. In fact, I think that sports, particularly football, gave me an opportunity to be out front, to be a leader, which helped me later on, when I got into politics.

I think my dealings with the press had as much of an impact on my later life and the success I had as actually playing in Michigan Stadium. As a football player, you have critics in the stands and critics in the press. Few of them have ever centered a ball, kicked a punt, or thrown a touchdown pass with 100,000 people looking on, yet they assume they know all the answers. Their comments helped me develop a thick hide, and in later years, whenever critics assailed me, I just let their jibes roll off my back.

★GEORGE ALLEN★

U.S. Senator from Virginia

Football

Our family lived and breathed football. When I was in first grade, in the 1950s, my father was an assistant coach under Sid Gilman of the Rams. But coaching is not a stable profession, and when Gilman and all the assistant coaches got fired, he was out of a job and he wound up working in a car wash. I remember going to the car wash and thinking, This is great fun.

After the Rams, my father went to work for the Chicago Bears, and he would bring me to training camp with him. That's when I was first around football players. Papa Bear Halas was the coach, and those days they had players like Doug Atkins, Bill George, Bill Wade, and Richie Pettibone. I remember Halas would have the players running around in a circle with all sorts of exhortations, which made no sense to a little kid, and he used language a little kid shouldn't hear.

"MY FATHER WANTED ME TO PLAY BASEBALL RATHER THAN FOOTBALL."

Actually, my father wanted me to play baseball rather than football. His reasoning was that in baseball you'd have a longer career because there are fewer injuries, and you get paid more. But I just found baseball no fun whatsoever.

As a kid, I played quarterback. In high school, football players had to wrestle. I was pretty good. It's a tough sport and I didn't like it, but it got me in great shape.

I started out at UCLA, but then I transferred to the University of Virginia, because I wanted to be an architect or a lawyer. I made the All-ACC Academic team, but I was only an average college quarterback.

"HAVE YOUR OWN STANDARDS AND GO."

Growing up, my father had lots of advice for me. He said, "you're not to smoke, drink, or curse." And he had incentives: if you turned twenty-one and you didn't smoke, drink, or cuss, you'd get $3,000 or a car. I still don't cuss. And I don't smoke. But I may have a beer every now and then. At any rate, he taught us to be leaders. "Always be a leader, don't be a follower." He would say that all the time. "Have your own standards and go by them. Be a leader. You have a great future, great potential, don't screw it up by doing stupid things or wrong things."

What I learned from my father is attention to detail. He'd make the players do a certain number of perfect plays, and until they ran these plays perfectly, he wouldn't let practice end. It was a matter of being prepared. He'd always say the difference between winning and losing is often insignificant. He'd watch every detail of a play to figure out tendencies, so that his team, his defense, would know the tendencies of another team. From that, I learned that preparation is so important.

I also learned to work hard and to play hurt. If you're hurt, you keep playing, if you're sick, you keep going. But the other thing on a football team is that you learn that everyone is important. It's the same in a governor's administration, the senator's office, or a campaign—every player on a play has to do well. They need to have the snap count and then execute. If anybody fouls up, the whole team suffers. Everybody's got a different job, but the guard is as important as the quarterback.

My father loved, loved politics. The first time I ran for office—the Virginia House of Delegates, in 1979—I lost. And my father came and encouraged me—stick to it, and so forth. I ran again in 1982, and I remember that my father was campaigning at the polls. He loved it; he was so competitive. So we're in my office in Charlottesville, listening to the results come in from different precincts, and it's really, really close. We're waiting for Gladstone and Montebello, and we're saying, "Ah, if these places vote the way they normally do . . . ," and I was ahead by sixty-some-odd votes. But we had to wait for these two precincts that are so small they have paper ballots. And we're waiting and waiting, and it's just agony, listening to the radio. And finally my father said, "Well, what did you do in these precincts? Did you campaign there?

And I said, "Yeah, I went down there, and I was there alone."

And he said, "Well, I hope you did some good there."

I ultimately ended up winning by twenty-five votes. And when that came we all cheered in my office there in Charlottesville, and my father says, "Gosh, this is better than beating Dallas!"

BUSH IS AT LEFT.

★GEORGE H.W. BUSH★

Former President of the United States

Baseball

I started playing baseball when I was a small kid, just playing catch with my dad, who was a good college ball player long before me. Then, starting in grade school, I began playing baseball regularly. It became a very early passion, and my dad used to take us to Yankee Stadium or the Polo Grounds to watch the big guys play. And that, of course, only increased my interest in the game.

Sports have always played a major part in my life, because I think they have a lot to do not only with staying fit, but equally, if not more important, they teach you about teamwork. Sports also have a lot to do with character, and sports also have a lot to do with learning valuable lessons in life, like playing by the rules.

In the old days, in high school, I rooted for the Red Sox and I could tell you the average of every player on the team. I was an early Ted Williams fan, long before I became a friend of his. Then, I'm afraid I sold out when my son, the current president, got involved with the Texas Rangers. There went my Red Sox loyalty.

"DON'T BE PERSUADED BY THIS ONE DAY; HE'S NOT THAT GOOD."

I played baseball at Andover and was captain of the team in the spring of 1942. I think the only time I really did any good at the plate was against North Carolina State: a single, double, and a triple. A scout was there—he talked to Ethan Allen who was our coach. He said, "This guy Bush looks like a hitter."

And Ethan said, "Don't be persuaded by this one day; he's not that good."

Ethan Allen was a very much of an inspiration to me. He was a funny guy, a quiet fella, but he taught me an awful lot. He came out of the pros and took our team in '47 and '48 to the finals of the College World Series. So I remain very loyal to the guy. Although I have to say he didn't vote for me.

Baseball is the great American passion and pastime, and it's got a finesse to it that a lot of non-baseball players don't understand. It's a team sport in which all the players are rooting for each other. I'm very proud and appreciative of the fact that I played by the rules and loved the competition.

"I THOUGHT I'D DIED AND GONE TO HEAVEN."

Growing up, I wanted to be Lou Gehrig. He was my hero, but it wasn't just that he was a great ball player. He was a wonderful team guy and I remember that tearful farewell address at Yankee stadium. Babe Ruth was another hero, because he was a power hitter. Later on, Babe donated his papers to Yale and I was the one to receive them, because I was captain of the Yale team. That was a thrill to be with ol' Babe. At the time, he was riddled with cancer of the throat, so he croaked when he spoke. It was so sad. Everybody in the stands knew he was on his last legs, and sure enough he was. But just being there—it wasn't so much what he said—it was just being next to him that was so inspiring. I thought I'd died and gone to heaven. I was lucky to be the guy that was out there to take his manuscript.

Ted Williams was another hero of mine, and later on he became a very strong supporter and friend. In fact, even in his last years, I'd call him, or he'd call me, and we'd stay in touch. I went to the Manchester Sports Show, Manchester, New Hampshire, prior to the New Hampshire primary vote, and fans just flocked to Ted Williams. It was as if I wasn't there, which just showed me the hero worship they had for Ted. I remember when he came to the White House, celebrating the fiftieth anniversary of the year he hit over .400, and along with him was Joe DiMaggio, who was also celebrating the fiftieth anniversary of his hitting streak. That was a real thrill for me, even though I was president of the United States of America, just to be with those two guys.

FORD IS AT LEFT.

★ HAROLD FORD JR. ★

U.S. Congressman from Tennessee

Basketball

I started playing basketball when I was six years old at the YMCA in Memphis. I think I shot the ball every time I touched it. My motto was, "If it's leather, shoot it." I loved the smell of the gym, the smell of the ball. I was always excited about buying new sneakers each season. I was blessed that my parents could afford to do that. There was something about basketball season that got me going, got me excited. Getting up early and practicing in the morning and practicing in the afternoon, it was a good thing.

My dad was not a particularly active athlete. He came from a huge family, there were fifteen of them, and they only had three rooms in the house. He started working when he was seven, eight years old, so he didn't have much time for sports. And none of my uncles were particularly athletically disposed either. A few of my cousins actually were outstanding athletes. I have a cousin, for instance, who played the offensive line at Stanford when John Elway was the quarterback. But by and large, mine wasn't a particularly athletic family. It was politics that was big in my house.

Everybody wants their dad in the stands to see them play, but my dad worked so much—he was always traveling—that it was mostly my mom who came to the games. But when he did come, my maxim of, "If you touch the leather, let it go," was even more in play than other times, in an attempt to impress my dad. I look forward one day to having kids and sitting in the stands, whether they're girls or boys, and rooting for them.

At my house it was made clear that if you didn't maintain a certain grade point average, you weren't playing. And the school I went to was a very competitive private school, so everybody understood what they had to do. But in the household there was also a minimum level of achievement that everyone expected and sports was a part of that.

"THE MOST COMPETITIVE GUY IN THE HOUSE ON THE BASKETBALL COURT."

By eight or nine, I knew I was not pro material. For one thing, no one in my family was that tall, and there was no one who was particularly gifted athletically. But I always started. I was point guard. I played that position throughout my time in junior high and high school and I was as competitive as anybody. My colleagues in Congress joke that I'm the most competitive guy in the House on the basketball court—which is probably true—but I'm certainly not the most talented. But you've got to bring your "A" game every day to beat me.

I'll never forget my freshman year at St. Alban's in Washington, which was a small all-boys school. We scrimmaged against what was probably the best junior high school in the city. Their first team just destroyed us. It must have been something like 50 to 8 in less than 4 or 5 minutes. We had to call a time out, and Coach tells us, "You're not executing. These guys are very talented, but you gotta execute." So we go back out, and we score. I mean, we were even with them for the next four minutes. They were ahead by forty points, but we scored fifteen points, they scored fifteen points. We came back to the sidelines, we were so excited, and he was excited, and he said "Look, I want to let you guys know, you're doing everything I'm asking, but you need to understand something, that's their third team they have in now."

We ended up having a great season playing the teams that were more our speed. But I'll never forget that moment and how we all kind of looked at each and said, "We're not going to let these guys come in here and treat us like that." It was our gym, and granted, we knew they were going to kill us, but we weren't going to get beaten like that. So that was, that was kind of a moment that reinforced this whole notion of there's no "I" in "team."

"NOTHING RATTLES ME."

At a young age I realized that, although I may not play professional sports, I could be involved in some way, maybe as a general manager for a basketball team. I'm good with people, and I think I'm able to figure out ways to inspire them. A lot of that has to do with your interactions and experiences growing up. Nothing rattles me a whole lot, although I'd have to say that in sports it did. I was a little high strung. Now, I can tone it down, but at times I still do get a little high strung. I like to be the boss on the court, so that was one of the reasons I played point guard and one of the reasons why, even today in the House games, that's the position I play.

★PAT WILLIAMS★

Sports Executive, Motivational Speaker,
and Father of Nineteen

Baseball

My dad took me to my first major league baseball game when I was seven years old, and I remember it like it was yesterday. June 15, 1947. We had tickets on the upper deck, third base side for a Philadelphia A's–Cleveland Indians Sunday double header. I was absolutely captured by the sights, the sounds, and the smell of baseball. I never have gotten over it to this day.

That day at the ballpark, at the age of seven, I set a goal for myself. I can remember waking up the next morning absolutely galvanized. I knew what I wanted to do with my life: I wanted to be a major league ballplayer.

The first glove my dad gave me was a catcher's mitt, so that's the position I played. I could say that this ends up as a wonderful story, and that I ended up in the Hall of Fame, but of course, I didn't. I did play through high school, though. I went to college, and I caught for the Wake Forest baseball team, where I had some marvelous experiences. And then the Phillies gave me the opportunity to play two years of professional baseball. I got to ride the buses and get an experience of a lifetime as a minor league catcher. And that really helped lay the foundation for everything that later took place in my life, in the front office of various sports teams.

The first seven years of my professional career were spent in the Phillies organization—so in many ways, I'm still viewed as a baseball guy, even though I've been in the NBA now for over thirty-six years. But I think the fact that I did put on the uniform, that for two years I was a professional athlete, gives me a sense of what it's like—the insecurities, the ups and downs, the trauma—and believe me, being a professional athlete is a traumatic life, any way you slice it. It looks glamorous, but boy, there's an awful lot of pressure and a lot of difficult moments. And having to live through some of them, well, I think it gave me a much better feel for it.

"KEEP YOUR EYES AND EARS OPEN
ON AND OFF THE FIELD."

When I signed my contract to play with Bob Carpenter, the owner of the Phillies, his last words to me when he sent me to Miami as a minor league catcher were, "Keep your eyes and ears open on and off the field." In other words, he was telling me, "We are looking at you as a future executive as well as maybe a catcher." I listened to that and so, even as a minor league catcher, I was sensing that my future lay behind a desk, rather than behind the plate. But all I ever wanted was a chance to try and make it as a ballplayer, so I gave it my best shot for two years. But the Phillies obviously gauged my talent on the field and threw a coat and tie in my direction very quickly. They opened some doors for me, and at the age of twenty-four, I found myself at beautiful Duncan Park in Spartanburg, South Carolina, as the general manager at their minor league club.

Through sports, I've discovered in life that if you've got drive and desire and ambition, one goal simply leads to the next. There's never that point when you've arrived, because in sports there's always another game, another series, another season. You really can't rest on your laurels or look back in sorrow or in triumph, over anything that happens, because things are changing so rapidly. At this point in my life—I'm sixty-three years old—I want to live fully till the end. I don't think at any point you can simply say, "Well, I've done enough. My life is over, and now I'm just going to watch the sunset." I don't think that's the way we're meant to live, and sports, I think, offers us that lesson.

I still love to play baseball, and living in Florida is a huge advantage, because that's where the fantasy camps are. It's here that doctors, dentists, and lawyers pay $5,000 to come down in the dead of winter and spend four days being a big league ballplayer. It culminates on the last day with an actual game in the spring training site, be it the Phillies, the Mets, or the Braves. None of these old big leaguers want to catch, but I still strap on the tools, squat back there, and catch a Mitch Williams or a Fergie Jenkins or a Bob Feller at eighty-four years old, and I get the greatest thrill, because that is my big league appearance. Finally, at the age sixty-three, I'm catching big league pitchers. Granted, they don't throw anywhere near what they used to, but over these years, I've caught six or seven Hall of Fame pitchers. And to me, that's a great thrill.

"THE LIFE LESSONS LEARNED BY THESE CHILDREN . . . WILL NEVER LEAVE THEM."

We have nineteen children, and they all played sports. Fourteen of them are adopted, and the minute they got off the airplane from South Korea, the Philippines, Romania, or Brazil, I got a glove in their hand or got them into the swimming pool, or put soccer shoes on them, and got them involved immediately. Through all those youth sports, and through all the Little League periods, and on into high school, I think it was one of the most important things I did for them. If nothing else, it let them experience the magic of teamwork, getting along with other people. The self-discipline that it takes, the hard work that's involved, the respect for coaches, all that is so important. I fully believe that the life lessons learned by these children—who had come off the streets from the Third World countries—will never leave them. That's why I encourage parents to expose their children to sports, even if they aren't great athletes.

I often ask other people, "What do you think about in moments of quiet? Where does your mind flash back to?" And if I had to answer that myself, there is no question that my mind will flash back to athletic experiences as a youngster. I close my eyes and I can still see the old park. And I can still the A's down there in their white uniforms with the blue piping; and I can still see the Phillies in the red pinstripes. I can still see Robin Roberts pitching to Jackie Robinson. All of that is a very, very fresh, vivid memory in my life, and in my down times, that's generally what I think about.

★GEORGE WILL★

Newspaper Columnist and
Political Commentator

Baseball

Whittney I was growing up in Champaign, Illinois, right after World War II, we'd go down to the vacant lot and play touch or tackle football, but mostly it was baseball.

Back then, childhood wasn't as structured as it is now, so we had a lot of unsupervised time to ourselves. Today, it seems to me, the modern child spends the lion's share of his free time in the backseat of a station wagon or in a minivan being carted from one organized activity to another. But when I was a kid, you'd go out in the morning, and your mother would say, "Come back at lunch," and you'd come back and have a peanut butter sandwich, and then you'd go out and come back at dinner time, and that was it. It was spontaneous organization on the part of children, which itself was a learning experience. You learned how to organize yourself and didn't have it done for you.

I played for the Mittendorf Funeral Home Panthers. Our color was black. I sometimes played second base, but I also recall playing right field. But I was a *seriously* bad baseball player. I was earnest, but I had no talent whatever. The irony is, one day, Tom Selleck, who played basketball at Southern Cal and was a great athlete, and Kareem Abdul-Jabbar, one of the greatest athletes of all time, and me, which was absurd, were inducted into the Little League Hall of Excellence. Obviously, it did not refer to excellence on the field; it was for people who had done something else in life. When it came my turn to speak, I said, "I accept this honor for right fielders everywhere," because that's what I basically was—the kid they put out in right field, because fewer balls would come to you.

I've been competing at things and not excelling all my life. Baseball—it's a cliché, but like a lot of clichés, it's true—is a game of failure. The best hitter in baseball in a given year fails more than 60 percent of the time. If you bat

.350, you've failed 65 percent of the time. Ted Williams batted .406 in 1941, which means he failed to get a hit roughly 60 percent of the time. In any given year, the best team in baseball walks off the field beaten about sixty times. It's a very difficult game and a game of failure. That doesn't mean that some people aren't a whole lot better than others. And everyone was a whole lot better than I was most of the time.

But that didn't stop me from playing. Why? Well, first of all, knowledge of sports is one of the things that enables a child to converse on a reasonably equal level with an adult. You can talk about who the Cubs ought to be playing, and how Stan Musial is doing, and will the Brooklyn Dodgers win in 1955, which, indeed, they did. So there's a sense that everyone's opinion is as good as everyone else's, and it's a way of communicating.

On the field itself, it's a place where children, particularly, are sealed off from the outside world, within a cocoon of rules. You're on a playing field that has dimensions. There are rules: three strikes you're out, three outs the other team gets to come up, twenty-seven outs, the game's over. There's a kind of clarity to it. And you begin to learn what it's like to *strive* on an equal footing. "Level playing field" is more than a metaphor. It means that you're on an equal footing with others, and yet you will probably yield to superior talent. It's the kind of lesson you learn subliminally. You don't theorize about it, the events just teach you.

"THAT'S ONE OF THE GOOD THINGS SPORT DOES, IT TAKES AWAY ILLUSIONS."

About the time I was done with Little League, at age thirteen, I went to the University of Illinois education department's Laboratory High School— Uni-High, or as we were known in athletics, "Puni-Uni"—where I played basketball. Basketball is a sport you can practice by yourself. You don't need anyone to pitch to you, you don't need anyone to catch for you; you just go out in the snow and the driveway and shoot baskets. And I did an awful lot of that. But it didn't really help.

My senior year, our record was two and eighteen; we beat the same team twice. One thing I should say about "Puni-Uni" High is that we took a test to get in. We took seventh and eighth grade in one year, so all of us who went through were a year younger than the people we were playing against. That's as far as I can go in concocting an excuse for failure.

The next year, the school was consolidated, I think out of humiliation. A few years after I left Uni High, it had something like a 96-game losing streak. We were a bunch of faculty brats! Sort of, small people with glasses who read lots of books, did well on our SATs, and couldn't shoot the ball.

Nevertheless, I had a wonderful time. We played very small schools: Homer, St. Joseph, and Fisher, Illinois—these are little towns around Champaign-Urbana. But I was under no illusions. That's one of the good things sport does, it takes away illusions. It's all very well to think you're good, but you have to hit the ball, you have to shoot the ball, you have to do things. And sport gives you *instant* feedback, and objective measurements. It also gives children an immediate sense that everyone has talents, and not everyone has *all* talents.

I realized this the first time I played with a kid better than I was, which was the first time I played. You look at some guy swing and say, "Wow!" I have a son who's now twenty-eight years old, and he turned out to have been a terrific baseball player. There's no accounting for this. I don't know where the DNA got into his system that turned him into an athlete, but it wasn't from me.

"THE BIG PROBLEMS RESULT ONLY FROM NOT DOING THE SMALL THINGS RIGHT."

I've published twelve books. One of them has sold—I'm exaggerating a little bit—as many as the other eleven combined. That book was called *Men at Work: The Craft of Baseball.* It is, I believe, the best-selling baseball book ever. I had a wonderful experience writing it. I don't draw big political lessons from it—but the theme of that book is that the people and teams that succeed in baseball are the ones that do the little things right. If you do little things right—hit the cut off man, cover the base, cut the base on the inside when you're running it, hit to right behind the runner with a runner on second—when you do the little things right, you have no big problems. There is a lesson of life in that: the big problems result only from not doing the small things right.

When I was writing this book, I focused on a fielder, Cal Ripken; a hitter, Tony Gwynn; a manager, Tony LaRussa; and a pitcher, Orel Hershiser. When I finished, it suddenly dawned on me, after I'd been around for two years talking to *lots* of people in the dugouts, hotel lobbies, hotel coffee shops, and airplanes, that in two years of intense exposure to Major League ballplayers, I had never heard anyone brag. Never. Not once. That's because baseball is so hard, and so humbling, and there's always someone out there who can get you out, and someone out there you can't hit, and someone you can't get out.

Baseball is a humbling game. And it's great fun to be around a game you love and to understand that you can participate in it, contribute to it, be a part of it, without ever having been able to throw, let alone hit, a curve ball. But besides being a great game, it's also a complex social institution with roots deeper in American history than the airline industry. It predates the internal combustion engine. It's tied up in our history in interesting ways. It's a business, and business is interesting. It has problems in marketing and problems of transition to new generations as they come along. It's related to the political system in the fact that it needs ballparks, laws, and other things. So there are lots of things to do on it. But at the end of the day, it's just a very pretty game. And it's nice to be around. It's *weird*—I can't explain it more than that. It's strange that grown people, or allegedly grown people, such as George Will, get so lathered up about all this. I mean, last October, I traveled to Wrigley Field in Chicago to watch the Cubs lose the sixth and seventh games against the Florida Marlins. And I cared. And I didn't care that I couldn't say *why* I cared. I just cared.

And I still do, and I hope I always will.

★HENRY KISSINGER★

Former Secretary of State,
Professor, and Author

Soccer

I began playing soccer in Fuerth, the town where I was born in Germany, which is near Nuremberg. Fuerth has the same relationship to Nuremberg as Brooklyn has to New York; it's really the same town, but it has a different government due to a complicated history. Nuremberg used to be an independent city, part of Bavaria. That's significant for soccer, not for anything else, because it means those two towns were great rivals in the sport.

Fuerth, was to soccer as Green Bay was to football. It was a small town of 80,000 that in a ten-year period won three German championships. Going to the soccer game was the big event during the week, something we looked forward to.

"WE COULD ONLY PLAY AGAINST THE OTHER JEWISH TEAMS."

I started playing when I was about six. My grandfather had a farm near Fuerth, and they had a big courtyard and we played pick up games there. I played goalie for a brief period, then I broke my hand. After that, I played inside-right and then mid-field. I played until I was fifteen. I really wasn't very good, though I took the game very seriously.

Jews were segregated from 1933 on, when I was nine going on ten, but there was a Jewish team and I played on the junior team of that Jewish community. We could only play against the other Jewish teams. This wasn't just social segregation; this was the beginning of the extermination of the Jews. During that period, they tried to make life so unpleasant that people wanted to leave the country, which promoted immigration. That's why my family left Germany in 1938. So we were able to avoid the worst of it.

During that period in Germany, watching and participating in sports provided me with relief from the environment. I used to sneak out to watch the local soccer team play, even though, as a Jew, you ran the risk of getting beaten up if you were there and they recognized you.

"THE SYSTEM WAS TO DRIVE
THE OTHER TEAM NUTS."

When I was young, I was a bit of a strategist and something of a team organizer. As a teenager, we were scheduled to play another team that was really good and I devised a system that, as it turned out, is the way the Italians play soccer. I didn't know that then, of course. The system was to drive the other team nuts by not letting them score, by keeping so many people back as defenders. Good teams pass a lot, and if you keep thwarting them they get frustrated. It's the same as the Italian style of soccer, which is to stress defense, try to get a goal, and then pull everything back. It's very hard to score when ten players are lined up in front of the goal. And if you try to pick out the angle from which you can shoot at the goal, you're apt to hit somebody's leg every time you shoot. We had an inferior team, but instead of playing with five forwards we played eight people back and just kept two people forward. And if we were lucky, we could sneak a goal in.

Sports was an escape for me; it was also an occasion for comradeship. In sports there's very little room for phonies; you either perform or you don't perform. I wasn't just passionate about the Jewish club, I was passionate about my hometown club and the club of the next town, Nuremberg. Those were two huge rivals, like Yankees and the Red Sox. Nuremberg had five times the population of ours. So those were good games when they played.

After the war, I went there to see a game. Fuerth lost, and the referee got beaten up, which was standard practice. The German police couldn't rescue him, so the American military police came and rescued the referee, and one guy sitting down next to me got up and yelled, "So that's the democracy you guys are bringing us!"

★JACK WELCH★

Former CEO of General Electric

Baseball, Hockey, Golf

The first sports I remember playing, when I was seven or eight, were baseball in the playground and pick-up hockey on an ice pond in what was then called the Pit in Salem, Massachusetts. Salem was a scrappy and competitive place. I was competitive and my friends were, too. All of us were jocks, living to play one sport or another. We'd organize our own neighborhood baseball, basketball, football, and hockey games. We'd play from early in the morning until the town whistle blew at quarter to nine.

"IT WAS TOTALLY UNORGANIZED, BUT IT WAS GREAT FUN."

In baseball, it was the older kids who did that thing with the bat to choose sides: one hand over the other, one hand over the other. And then, when the last guy got picked, he'd go into right field. As the youngest, I was stuck in right field a number of times. And it was pretty much the same in hockey. We had great games; they were extremely competitive, and so it made a difference as to who got the first pick. We had bats that were held together with tape and nails. It was totally unorganized, but it was great fun.

My mother was a great influence on me, and the first taste I had of competition was the gin rummy games I played with her at the kitchen table. I remember racing across the street from the schoolyard for lunch when I was in the first grade, itching for the chance to play gin rummy with her. When she beat me, which was often, she'd put the winning cards on the table and shout, "Gin!" I'd get so mad, but I couldn't wait to come home again and get the chance to beat her.

She was a strict disciplinarian. One time, I cut altar boy practice to play hockey on the frozen pond at Mack Park near my home. During the game, I fell through the ice and got completely soaked. To try to cover up what happened, I stripped off my wet clothes and hung them on a tree over a fire we built. We shivered in the January cold, waiting for our clothes to dry. It was, I thought, a rather clever cover-up—until I walked through the front door. It took a second for my mother to smell the smoke on my clothes. So she sat me down, forced out a confession, and then delivered her own penance: whacking me with a damp shoe she'd just taken off my foot.

We didn't have Little League when I was growing up, but I played on school teams, and I played at the American Legion. The thing it taught me was that winning's a helluva lot more fun than losing. It also taught me that the team with the best players that worked together the best wins, and that competition is fun.

"MY FAST BALL NEVER GOT ANY FASTER."

As a player, my ability decreased exponentially as I got older. I was extremely good as a freshman in high school—I was a starting pitcher—but by the time I was a senior, I was on the bench. It was simply a case of my curve ball never got any better and my fast ball never got any faster. It was pretty much the same thing in hockey. I just wasn't fast enough. So my experience in competitive sports came to a pretty rude awakening as I grew older. But at the same time I was playing baseball, I was also on the golf team and I was getting pretty good at it. It was the same season as baseball, and it sort of took the sting away. Of course, golf isn't the same in terms of popularity in high school—at least it wasn't then—as being on the baseball team. I mean, the girls didn't come out and watch the golf matches.

I was a wild competitor. I was intense. I wanted to win. Particularly in hockey. I was what's called a "net rat." I wasn't that fast in hockey, but I was a very good stick handler, so I could score.

I was captain of all the teams, I think because I was a good guy. I was gregarious; I was good to my friends. In the end, being chosen as captain is almost the result of a popularity contest.

"THERE WAS NO PLAN."

Sports is a lot like business. You give a deal the best shot, you give it all you've got, and you want to win, but if you don't you turn the page and move on to the next thing. I am not the kind of person who goes back and analyzes everything that happened in the past. Next page, thank you. Even then, when I was playing sports, I was living in the day. I never had any dreams of what was going to happen or how it was going to happen, I was just trying to get from day to day. There was no plan.

I brought a lot of what I learned playing sports into the business world. Candor, for instance. I learned to listen to other people's views. I learned to build a team with the best players you can find. I learned not to pick on anybody when they're down. In sports you always know where you stand. And if there's one thing I know, it's who I am and where I came from, and that has affected every relationship I've ever had. Even when I've had problems with unions, for instance, they always knew where I stood. I've had vicious verbal fights with unions over certain points, but the thing is, we always knew where each other stood! One thing in life is, does everybody in your organization know where they stand? It may not sound like much, but it's a big deal.

★JAMES BROWN★

Television Sports Anchor
and Radio Host

Basketball, Baseball

The first organized sport I was involved with that showed me some promise of athletic talent was playing CYO [Christian Youth Organization] baseball in the eighth grade.

I was encouraged by my family but I'm sure, from my parent's perspective, it was just a way to make certain I was involved in a healthy and constructive activity. Back then, there wasn't nearly as much concern by parents as there is today in terms of wondering where your kids are. I was allowed, at that young age, to go four or five blocks away and play on a baseball field without there being any concern, because they knew I was with other adults, and that we were involved in a very wholesome activity.

I wasn't necessarily good at the outset. I think there was a lot of raw talent there, but what I did learn was the importance of listening intently to what the coaches were saying, being a contributing member of the team, and working hard to develop the latent skills and talent that was there. I got a chance to see the cause and affect that; if, in fact, you put in the time to hone your skills, working at it, does yield results on the back end. And certainly, that lesson in athletics carried over in the game of life as well.

"I BLEW THE LAY-UP."

Baseball was my first love, and that was my first foray into sports. We had some serious talent on our squad—we had a pitcher who had big league talent—and some other guys who went on to play college baseball. Our team went to the playoffs and, as a result, there were a lot more eyeballs watching us, including the legendary, Morgan Wooten, who coached at DeMatha Catholic High School, which was a school that back in 1966 beat New York's Power Memorial High School with Lew Alcindor. DeMatha snapped their 71-game winning streak. Morgan Wooten, who was both the football and basketball coach, was watching the baseball playoffs and he came up to me and said, "You know, you're a very talented youngster, would you consider me talking to your parents to see if you can come to DeMatha?"

I knew who he was and I thought, My gosh, this guy wants me to come there and play basketball. So I said, "Sure." But there was one problem. I did play basketball back at junior high school and I was horrible. How bad was I? Well, I remember making the team, mostly because the coach said that I was one of the most intense listeners around. He thought that was a good example to set for the other guys.

When he introduced the team to the student body at Assembly, we were to run the length of the court, make a lay-up, and then go stand over in with the rest of the guys. Of course, I blew the lay-up, and people started laughing. So that was my first foray into basketball. And talk about a seminal moment in terms of recognizing the importance of working on my game, because I didn't want to be in front of a crowd like that again and blowing something as simple as a lay-up.

"I WAS AFRAID OF CURVE BALLS."

Nevertheless, I was thinking, My gosh, I'd like to go to his camp, because basketball seemed to be more to my liking. Why? Because I was afraid of curve balls. We had that pitcher who had big league talent and I remember one time in practice he threw a curve ball at me. I fell in the batter's box, knowing that ball was going to hit me square in the head and, of course, at the last moment it broke over the plate. So I knew I didn't have the balls to stand there against a curve ball. That's why I wanted to go play basketball. And, indeed, I did go to Morgan Wooten's basketball camp, and I never picked up a baseball bat again after that.

My folks were very intent about us getting an education. They were both high school graduates and, like most parents, they wanted their kids to go further in life than they did. I was blessed to be the first one college-educated in the family. But it was at the continuous stressing of the importance of academic excellence as being the passport, if you will, that allowed me to get involved in extracurricular activities like basketball. My mother made that point loud and clear. I'll never forget how Morgan stressed the importance of working in the off-season. He told us, "Just think, over the course of the summer is when most guys who are serious about developing their game invest the time necessary to be excellent during the season. And if you're not out there, if you miss a day when you have the opportunity to go out there and hone your skills and you meet someone on the court who did put in that time over the course of the summer—all things being equal—who do you think is going come out on the top end?" I did not want that to happen to me. So, I spent four or five hours a day working on my game. I often teasingly tell people that I used to be white when I was a kid, but when I started practicing basketball in the dead of day with the sun blaring at 12 o'clock high, I got dark.

It paid off. People could not believe the radical change in me. I went from a gawky, skinny kid—I weighed about 175 pounds then—to the two-time high school All America and Player of the Year in the Washington, D.C., area. I was voted the Washington area's Best Player. In my junior and senior year, I was recruited by every major college in the country. So it was proof positive that if you put the time in, the preparation, that it will pay dividends on the back end.

When it came time to go to college, I firmly bought into what my folks stressed: Academic excellence is the key to success in the game of life. And although I may not have been a charter member of Mensa, I took note of Bill Bradley, one of my heroes, who was enjoying a tremendous amount of success in college. I thought, How neat is that, to be able to show the world that you can academic and athletic success. If I have a chance to go to an Ivy League school, I'd like to do that. And when I saw the letter on my coach's desk from Harvard, I thought, That is absolutely the ultimate.

I was able to get into Harvard, though it wasn't on a scholarship, because they didn't give out athletic scholarships. My folks thought I was crazy for not taking an athletic scholarship someplace else, but I bought into the notion that academic excellence was the best route to prepare for the game of life.

I gained a lot from my participation in sports, especially team sports. I got to know other people, their backgrounds, the different cultures, our religious backgrounds, which was tremendously helpful in understanding that the world is not homogenous. Sports also taught me the lesson that until the whistle has blown, the final whistle, no deficit is insurmountable. It can happen, *if* you are executing the right game plan, *if* you have investing the time in sharpening and honing the right skills to get the job done, and *if* you've got the right leadership in place and a belief in yourself and the ability to get it done. No lead is too big to overcome.

"HERE'S WHAT WE'RE GONNA DO."

Perhaps the best example of that was when I was a senior in high school and we played Long Island Lutheran High School, which at the time was a real powerhouse There was a guy named Billy Chamberlain who was a High School All-American and an outstanding forward/center, who later played at North Carolina for Dean Smith, and another guy name Gene Wilkinson, who was a teammate of mine at Harvard, who was an outstanding guard. We gave it everything we could, but unfortunately we had lost a lot of the big guys on the team, so I was the tallest guy on the floor, at only 6′ 4″, 6′ 5″. We were down by eight points with thirty seconds left. They had the ball. We came over to the bench whipped, completely spent, a look of defeat on our faces. Coach took about five seconds, he didn't say a thing, he looked each and every one of us in the eyes, and finally he said, "Fellas, let me tell you something. We have these guys right where we want them." And we're looking at him like, what in the world are you talking about? We're down by eight, with thirty seconds remaining, and they have the ball. He said, "Here's what we're gonna do. I've watched them all game; they're a little complacent right now, because they've manhandled us pretty well up to this point and they're lackadaisical. JB, you're going to be playing back at mid-court. Aubrey, you're going to press the in-bound pass, shading to the left. They're going to toss the ball to the left. Gene, you're going to go steal the ball. That will take exactly five seconds and after Aubrey scores the lay-up, we're down by six. Then they're going to panic; they're going to try to go up the court a little bit. JB, you're going to . . ." He went through the whole final thirty seconds and that's exactly what happened, and we wound up winning that game.

"I'M GOING TO GO IN A DIFFERENT DIRECTION."

When I got cut by the Atlanta Hawks as the last rookie on that team, Cotton Fitzsimmons said he wanted to talk to me. "Well," he said, "you went to a good school, you'll be able to do well in the game of life, but I'm going to go in a different direction," I was crushed. Crushed. *Crushed!* I mean, my dream was not going to be realized. I had the athletic rug, figuratively speaking, snatched from under my feet. I was thinking, This can't be. I was doing exceedingly well. I went home. I cried. I hid in the house for about two weeks. There was another player on the team, a big white kid from Missouri named John Brown. So my friends would see in the box score, J. Brown, and they thought it was me. They kept asking, "Man, how did you get home so quickly from a game on the West Coast last night?" It was really painful.

But, as opposed to pointing a finger or blaming, when I looked at myself in the mirror, the lessons I learned in the world of sports, and certainly from my coach, came back to bear. I remembered Coach Wooten said, "JB, you know if you don't work as hard to stay on top as you did to get there, it's going to ultimately tell." I felt that I didn't make it tough enough on Coach Fitzsimmons to cut me, because in college I was the big man on campus and certainly did not put in the same kind of time working on my game there as I did in high school, and that's the fruit that I bore later on when I got cut by the Hawks.

"I PROBABLY HAVE A FREE AGENT'S MENTALITY."

Now fast forward well into the game of life. I'm working as a professional now, and people rightfully accuse me of being a bit of a workaholic. But it goes back to that lesson learned—that painful lesson—that I wasn't prepared to capitalize on an opportunity because I had not invested the time necessary to capitalize on that opportunity when it came. I vowed never, ever to let an opportunity pass me by that I was ill prepared for, and that's why I try to do as wide range of things.

Even today, if you want to get the best out of me all you have to do is ask me, "Do you have what it takes to get it done?" That piques my competitive drive. There's a desire to want to excel. I probably have a free agent's mentality. I never, ever want to believe, nor do I believe, that I have it made. I remember talking to Mike Trainer, who was Sugar Ray Leonard's attorney, when I was trying to make a decision about whether to pursue a job in the broadcasting arena full-time or to stay in corporate America. Mike said, "You're so accustomed in being a high school superstar and doing well in college and you're asking for a safety net under whatever decision that you decide to make. It's almost like you have a scholarship mentality—you want to make sure that if you pursue this bit in the broadcast arena, and if that doesn't work, that you've got an absolute safety net to rely on to go back into corporate. Well, JB, it doesn't work that way. The only security that you have in life is in your ability to perform, no matter what. And even in those circumstances sometimes, if there's a change of management, you could be out. But if you can perform, and you've shown excellence, that will serve you well." I've never forgotten that. I'm always going to give it my absolute best, and employ the same kind of work ethic I did in trying to become a good basketball player, working three, four, five hours a day on my game and sharpening the skills, so that I'll be prepared for that opportunity.

WATTS IS IN FRONT AT RIGHT.

★J.C. WATTS★

Former Congressman from Oklahoma
and Ordained Minister

Football

In rural America, sports was our form of entertainment. During football season, after school, we'd go to the church grounds and choose up teams. During basketball season, we'd go to somebody's house and play basketball. In the spring, we'd go to the field and play softball. In the summer we played Little League. And, as kids, we all had dreams of someday making it to the big arena, but of course few of us made it.

"WE'RE GOING TO MOVE WATTS TO QUARTERBACK."

I didn't start playing football until I was in eighth grade. I had dreams of going to USC and being the next Ricky Bell or Anthony Davis. I played fullback and then, when we went to the "I" formation my freshman year, I played tailback. At the time, we had one quarterback who could throw but couldn't run, and we had another one who could run but couldn't throw. The coach knew I had some ability, so halfway into the season he said, "We're going to move Watts to quarterback." I practiced at quarterback for a day, and then we played the number one team in the conference two days later. We were down 22 to 0 before halftime. We came back and scored three touchdowns and ended up being down 22 to 20 at halftime. We lost 36 to 20, but I wound up playing quarterback the rest of my career, including at the University of Oklahoma.

There was a time in my neighborhood that the thing to do was just finish high school, get your car, and get a job that you'd hold for the rest of your life. Nobody in my neighborhood wore a coat and tie to work. My dad, for instance, didn't wear a coat and tie unless it was Sunday and he was going to church. But there was something inside of me that wanted more than just to finish high school, get a car and get a job. But I really didn't know what I needed to do to change that.

"I HAD NEVER SEEN ANYBODY ON TV THAT I KNEW PERSONALLY."

When I was in the seventh grade, there was an experience that totally re-ordered my world. It was 1971 and Oklahoma and Nebraska, numbers 1 and 2 in the country, were playing what was being called the Game of the Decade. I watched it on Thanksgiving Day, in the front room of my home in Oklahoma. I saw Lucias Selman, a guy I knew personally—he'd actually sat in my front room—and I had never seen anybody on TV that I knew personally. That birthed a dream that I really could do something besides finishing high school, getting a job, and getting a car.

My high school football coach said to me my sophomore year, after he'd moved me to quarterback, "Watts, if you keep your grades up, and you keep your name clean, you've got a chance to do what Leroy Selman's doing."

I was not a great student and I know I could have done a whole lot better academically, but I did as well as I did because I knew that in order for me to play on Friday nights I had to perform in the classroom during the rest of the week. And I had enough pride so that I would have been embarrassed if I would ever have been ineligible. So, sports became a motivator for me to do better academically, because you didn't want to show up on game night standing on the sidelines in your jersey and blue jeans. That was a sure sign to everybody that you were ineligible, that you had a failing grade.

"I DIDN'T KNOW IF I WANTED TO BE A RUNNING BACK."

I was drafted in the eighth round by the New York Jets. I remember getting the call. "JC, this is Coach Walt Michaels of the New York Jets. We've just selected you as our eighth round pick in the National Football League draft."

I went to their training camp in Hofstra and asked, "What are my chances of being quarterback?"

They said, slim to none. "We don't need help with quarterback, we need help with running back and someone to come in on third down, special teams and kick off returns, punt returns."

I didn't know if I wanted to be a running back, so I said, "I want to play quarterback." That didn't happen, so I went up to Canada where I played for a while, proved I could throw the ball, and then retired, because I thought it was time for me to move on and start develop something outside of football.

When I retired, I was only twenty-eight, twenty-nine years old. I became a youth director at a local church and in the early '90s, after I got into politics, I can honestly say that for about two or three years I hardly ever looked at a sports page.

"TEAM SPORTS TEACH YOU THE
CONCEPT OF 'BIG TEAM, LITTLE ME.' "

I tell young men and women all the time that if they take everything they learned on the football field, the basketball court, the baseball diamond, and apply those principles to the business arena, or to being a mom or a dad, or to being an elected official, they work, because they're universal. These lessons include an understanding of delayed gratification, which is the result of a lot of hard work that creates a mental toughness and the perseverance, sacrifice, and commitment it takes to excel. Team sports teach you the concept of, "big team, little me."

I don't care if you're on the first team or the third team, sports is a great educator for all the principles I just mentioned: hard work, sacrifice, and personal responsibility. Athletics teaches that personal responsibility means that if J.C. Watts throws an interception, he can't blame someone else for it.

"IN FOOTBALL, IT DOESN'T MATTER
WHO SCORED THE TOUCHDOWN."

I'm not so sure everyone understands the team concept in politics. In sports, if someone's wearing the same color jersey as me, it's my responsibility to help him, to block for him, for instance. You don't have players like the right guard saying, "I'm going to undermine this play, because it wasn't my play." In politics, however, it's often about empire building, trying to advance your own personal career, which is directly opposite of what you learn to do playing sports. In football, it doesn't matter who scored the touchdown, it matters whether the team wins.

I have seen enough of the world to know that you can go from goat to hero to goat in one play. I think you learn to keep it in perspective and keep a balance about it. I remember one game when I was playing in Canada. I had played just horribly. I came off the field and was in my locker feeling about as tall as grass, because I didn't perform well and we'd lost the game. The coach stopped by my locker and said, "Hey, keep this in perspective. The way to do that is to remember this: there's three billion people in China that don't give a damn about how you played." The important thing is, in athletics, as in life, to prepare yourself to compete. In business, you've got competitors out there and in athletics you've got other teams trying to beat your head in. It's the same thing in politics. You approach life the same way you'd approach the big game: You prepare yourself, you train, you condition, you make the sacrifices, the commitment, and you persevere.

★BILL O'REILLY★

Television and Radio Commentator,
Author, and Newspaper Columnist

Football, Baseball, Hockey

I started playing organized sports when I was seven years old, with the Central Nassau Little League team on Long Island. It was a social thing because when you're a little kid you get sick of rolling in the dirt, so you put on a little uniform and you go out there and play some ball. We were very competitive kids. In Levittown, where I grew up, there were so many kids, it was just a natural evolution to get into organized sports so you would compete against each other. It wasn't any of that touchy-feely stuff.

"IF THE FIGHT CAME TO ME, THEN I'D SETTLE IT."

I didn't play high school football, because my high school was a football machine that recruited players, so you couldn't really just walk on and play. I was a better player than a lot of the guys on the team, but it was a political thing so I didn't play as much as I should have. I played ice hockey in high school and the ice hockey and football seasons pretty much coincided. Actually, the hockey guys were tougher guys than the football guy and in Levittown, the biggest accolade you could have was to be a tough guy, and I would say that I was a pretty tough guy. But I wasn't a mean guy. I didn't go out and punch people, like a lot of people in the neighborhood did who went out and looked for fights. But I could absorb pain. For example, I was a goalie on the high school hockey team. My parents didn't have enough money to get me the goalie equipment you needed, so I had a catcher's mitt, a chest protector, a lacrosse mask, and pads that were like Gump Worsley used forty years ago. So I took a lot of shots with the puck, catching it on the elbow or someplace like that . . . and it hurt! I even lost a couple of teeth. But I didn't whimper. I went out and played. And I was a damn good goalie. There were fights in the games. I wouldn't look for the fight. But if the fight came to me, then I'd settle it, either by winning or losing it.

I didn't want my father to show up at the games because, like me, he was an emotional guy. I remember one of the baseball games my father came to—what a nightmare! I was about fourteen or fifteen years old, and I was pitching. The umpire had a son on the other team. The guy's name was Schultz. A little guy. No matter what I threw, the umpire called it a ball. Ball 1, ball 2, ball 3, ball 4. It got to the point where I didn't even bother to wind up. I just got on the mound, and I just threw it in—and he'd call it a ball. You can just imagine how angry I got at this guy. I was yelling at him, though I don't think I was cursing at him because back then you didn't curse at adults. Eventually, he threw me out of the game. When I got to the sidelines my father grabbed a hold of me, like it was my fault. That's the kind of father he was. I'd disrespected this guy, he saw it, and even though I was right, the bottom line was that I'd disrespected the guy. So I was in trouble. Afterward, I said to my father, "Look, just don't come to the games, all right? I'm a madman and we don't need two madmen in the game; you in the stands and me on the field. Just let me play." So, he didn't start coming back to the games until I was playing college football, because by then everything was ratcheted up and it didn't matter whether he was there or not.

I learned very early on that although my dream was to be a professional athlete, that wasn't going to happen. It was 1967 and I was eighteen years old. It was my senior year in high school. I was playing summer ball and I was getting scouted by the Mets and the Braves. I was pitching in a night game in Eisenhower Park out in Levittown. I really had everything working, even though we lost the game 2–1, because the left fielder dropped the ball. These guys came up to me after the game and wanted to know all the stats. One of them asked, "Did you play high school ball?"

I said, "No."

They were astounded. The Met scout said, "Look, we want you to come to Shea to show you some of the guys."

I said, "Great."

The rule in major league baseball is you can't go on a major league field and use the facilities unless you have a uniform. So I went in my little Connie Mack league uniform. I drove down to Shea Stadium, and there was the scout with his guys, and they took me out to the right field bullpen. They had a speed gun and some guy came out, he was the catcher, and I started warming up with him. I thought I was doing great. I'm throwing . . . bang, bang, bang, bang, bang. He goes, "Awww, let me see some breaking stuff." I didn't have a great breaking ball; I just threw it hard. All of a sudden, another guy comes out on the hill. I look over—I'm 6' 4"; this guy's about 6', maybe 5' 11" and I'm about 190, this guy may have looked to be about 175, 180. First pitch, whack! It hits the mitt, *whack*! There's another one. I'm looking at this guy, and I realize that my best stuff doesn't come close to his first warm-up pitch. I just stopped and watched. And boy, did that ball move. The ball was like, booom!, booom! And I look at the scout, and he says, "Yeah, it's a guy we think is going to be a big star. His name's Tom Seaver." I knew then that there was no way I was going to make it in the pros.

"SO I KNEW."

It was the same with football. I had enough proximity to the pros to know how good they were. And I was smart enough to know that I wasn't that good. I could punt the ball with the wind as far as any pro could. But against the wind, I couldn't. That was the difference. I played around with Curly Johnson who played for the Jets. I was booming them out there. He said to me, "Hey, you're really good, kid. But let's see how you are against the wind." I watched him and he'd cut that wind like crazy, because his ball was a tight spiral, while mine would flutter a little, and it'd go twenty yards less. That's the difference. So I knew.

Playing sports taught me a lot about life. Number one, it taught me that you have to be realistic in your expectations. You have to level with yourself. It makes you ask yourself, Look, how good am I? What can I do? Where can I go? Number two, it makes you very competitive, because if you play ball the way I did from age seven to twenty-two, you want to win. You're out there to be better than the others. But you take some shots in the process, and I took some unbelievable hits. As a result of ice hockey, I broke fingers. But a broken finger didn't matter to me. You go back out there and play. It was a matter of discipline, which I acquired at a very early age. So when I got into television news, which is a very competitive industry, I saw people wash out, because it was too tough. To me, sure, it was tough, but nobody was breaking my fingers!

★JON BON JOVI★

Musician and Actor

Basketball, Football

When I was growing up I remember watching ABA games with Rick Barry and Julius Irving of the Nets when they were out on Long Island. I had my red, white and blue ball, thinking I was going to be a basketball player. And if you played baseball, which I did, you "believed," just like Tug McGraw told you to. Of course, by the time I got to high school, I started to realize that those aspirations were fizzling. But fortunately, I found music.

I was a pudgy little kid. In football, I was a linebacker, and I was absolutely doing great until the day I went to weigh in and left my socks and jock on the ground and begged that scale to tip the right way. It tipped the wrong way, and I had to go up to the next weight class. And it was there that I got my butt kicked. It was all downhill from there. But fortunately for me, there was another way to get girls' attention.

"ROCK AND ROLL IS A TEAM SPORT."

I took some important things with me from sports. Part of it has to do with the physical discipline. We have a pretty athletic band. Tico's an avid golfer, and a very good one. Richie was always the best athlete in the band. Dave is a great soccer player. In my business, you've got Keith Richards on one end of the scale—he's an enigma, nobody quite knows how it is that he's still walking—and at the other end you've got Sting, and the guys from the Chili Peppers, and myself. You know, it takes a lot physically to stay on the road for a year, and to be able to perform on stage like that every night.

Another similarity is that rock and roll is a team sport. You're only as good as your weakest link. If you've got a drummer that's going left on you, the band's going to falter. So you have to become a good coach, or you have to become good quarterback, and you have to run the business the same way you would run a game.

Sports can also provide you with some great memories that you'll carry with you for the rest of your life. For instance, I remember the one and only homerun I ever hit in Little League baseball. I remember hitting it over the right field fence and sprinting around the bases, and the shortstop saying, "You've hit a home run, you know you can jog!" I don't know why I sprinted through it all, but I guess I'll never forget that moment.

COHEN IS AT LEFT.

★WILLIAM COHEN★

Former Secretary of Defense and
Former U.S. Senator from Maine

Baseball, Basketball

When I first started playing organized ball, I was pretty good. The first game I scored something like 27 points. I was an All-State basketball player in high school and All-State in college and was voted in as a member of the New England All Star Hall of Fame team. So, for someone who's just a shade under six feet, I did pretty well.

I was a pitcher in Little League. I threw the ball pretty hard but, unfortunately, I was also real wild. I guess you might say I was kind of a Nolan Ryan of my age. At twelve, I wasn't throwing any curve balls, because you're only 44 feet away, and it takes quite a strain on your elbow to bend the curves at that distance. But when I got to high school, I was throwing a curve ball and a slider, which was a pretty good mixture. At twelve, I was the first player to pitch a no-hitter in Little League baseball.

The memories of playing Little League baseball weren't always good. I remember pitching in a game in which I hit a couple of batters, and the fans in the stands were throwing beer cans at me. It was not a happy moment. That was one of the lesser highlights of my young career as a pitcher. In any event, I got redemption, because the next time I got up to the plate, I hit a homerun over the centerfield fence. I was clapping my hands as I was going around the bases, hoping that I just put it through the windshield of the guy that threw the can.

My dad worked eighteen hours a day, six days a week, and yet from the time I started playing basketball at twelve years old, he never missed a game. He would skip sleep and, with my mother, would follow me all over the state. Wherever I played, they were there.

My father was a pretty tough critic, though. In one of my more memorable moments, I scored 43 points in a church league game. He was watching and, when the game was over, I was pretty puffed up with pride to think that we only had eight-minute running quarters and yet I was able to put in 43 points. I walked over to him and said, "What'd you think?" And in total seriousness, he said, "If you hadn't missed those two foul shots, you would have had 45."

My father was a gentle man, but in terms of wanting me to excel, he was always looking for perfection, even in his own bakery. He never took a day off. But if he had a day off, he would travel to Boston to find out why their bread was better than his. He was always looking for the perfect roll, and he wanted me to always try to perfect whatever I was doing. I had a great relationship with him. It started out as a little boy, when he would take me on his bakery route and put me in his lap and put my legs through the spokes of the steering wheel, so that I'd be in control. That's how I grew up—in his arms.

"I WOULD SHOOT TO THE POINT WHERE I COULDN'T FUNCTION ANY LONGER."

My father always reached and made me reach. He encouraged me to practice, practice, and practice some more, which I did. I used to go out in the winter, to the basketball hoop on the base of the street where I lived and even though there was snow was on the ground, I would shoot. The ball would just drop, and I'd have to come and pick the ball back up, go back and shoot again. I would shoot to the point where I couldn't function any longer. Tears would be coming from my eyes and my was nose running and my hands frozen, and finally I would go home after spending probably an hour just shooting by myself.

I was usually chosen as captain of the basketball teams I played on, so would lead the team out onto the court when we broke out of the locker room. And I usually conferred with the referees on any kind of decision, so I played a leadership role throughout my athletic career. I had hoped to go on, believe it or not, to play professional basketball, but that was not in the cards.

The summer before my senior year in college, I had been teaching at a basketball camp run by Bill Sharman of the Boston Celtics and Richie Guerin of the New York Knicks, and I used to play against a guy named Jungle Jim Loscutoff, who played forward for the Celtics. He was the so called hatchet man of the Celtics at that time, but he became a friend of mine. At the time, the new league, the ABA, was starting up and they had a 3-point rule, which was not in effect in either college or the NBA at the time. I was

going to get a tryout with Sharman's team, but the team never really suc-
ceeded, and in my senior year I switched my thinking from basketball to the
idea of going to law school.

One of the highlights of my life came in 1987 when I was named to the
Silver Anniversary All Star team by the National Association of Basketball
Coaches. I like to joke about that because the people they had on the team
were John Havlicek, Dave DeBusschere, Terry Dischinger, Billy Packer, and
me. I had to accept the award that evening at the big dinner, and my comment
was "Thank God, the NCAA still believes in the affirmative action program."

SCHULTZ IS IN THE THIRD ROW, THIRD FROM LEFT.

★HOWARD SCHULTZ★

Founder of Starbucks and
Owner of the Seattle Supersonics

Football

I spent the better part of every day of my childhood in the school yard in Carnarsie, Brooklyn. I left my apartment in the morning when the sun was up and came home when the sun was down. My mother used to scream at me from the seventh floor saying, "Come on in! Come on in!" While I yelled back things like, "One more inning."

Growing up in that part of the world at that time wasn't only about sports, but about the diversity of the people. Sports was a great equalizer. It didn't have color. It didn't matter whether you were rich or poor, black or white. It really shaped me in many ways to be able to deal with a lot of different personalities and different cultures. Sports were the common thread.

In our neighborhood, we had a little bit of everything: Jewish, Catholic, Italian, Puerto Rican, and black. We were all thrown together at a young age, and the school yard had no color. It was all based on athletics and competition, and we were out there in the summer, our shirts were off, and we were drinking water from the water fountain, and we were competing.

I was a poor kid, from a blue-collar family. We lived in the projects—federally subsidized housing—and I think high school sports gave me a platform and a stage where perhaps insecurity about my family's financial situation was put in place because on the athletic field everyone was everyone was equal.

Playing sports also gave me the ability to recognize how important winning was, because in those days the schoolyard was packed with kids waiting to get into the game, and if you lost there was a long wait to play again. So, if we were playing basketball the competition really heated up because nobody wanted to sit. I think that shaped my competitive fire and my character in a number of ways.

"IT WAS ABOUT MAKING A
STATEMENT TO YOURSELF."

I was one of those kids who would dive on the asphalt floor and come up with a loose ball, and then I'd look at my shoulder or my elbow and I'd be bleeding. But that was the way it was. We're talking about a rough area of Brooklyn and in order to survive, you had to be competitive, you had to be tough. It was about winning, but it also was about making a statement to yourself in a way.

I was a very good schoolyard athlete in almost everything we played. I was the guy always organizing things, choosing the teams. I'm not sure where that came from, but obviously it's connected to the entrepreneurial attitude I had later in life.

High school sports was an eye opener for me. It was probably the first time in my young life where I realized what sports could be, and the opportunities it offered. So it was a heady time.

"IF IT HADN'T BEEN FOR SPORTS, I
WOULD NOT HAVE GONE TO COLLEGE."

I played football at Canarsie High School. We didn't even have a home field. Instead, we practiced on a dirt field in Seaview Park. It was not pretty. I was tougher and smarter than I was athletic, and I had a decent arm. I wasn't a real fast guy, but I was the kind of guy who could get in and out of tough jams within the pocket. But then I was a tough kid. I made mistakes all the time with trying to run over guys as opposed going around them. I was probably not as a good as I thought I was in high school. Even though I was the starting quarterback in high school, I was probably just a B player.

My senior year I was the quarterback, and I was lucky enough to get accepted to a very obscure school, Northern Michigan University, to play football. If it hadn't been for sports, I would not have gone to college, because my family just couldn't afford it. As it turned out, I was a washout, because I got injured. But in addition to that, the guy in front of me at quarterback when I was playing was a young guy named Steve Mariucci, who he ended up being a fantastic college and then professional football coach who now coaches the Detroit Lions.

It was tough at first, but eventually there was the recognition that I was not going to be good enough at that level. I went through disappointment and a fair amount of depression over it, but the truth of the matter is that sports, being on a team, understanding the responsibility of doing something collectively, and the power of that, the friendships I formed as a result of sports, the connections I made with people—those things are linked to how I approached my personal life, and ultimately, my business career.

★ROGER AILES★

Television Producer, Political Consultant,
Fox News Chairman, and Author

Basketball, Football

My dad was quarterback for the high school football team, and he ran marathons and sprints. I didn't really know that part of his life, but I did see a glimpse of it once when he was in his forties. He was racing my brother and me around the block. He was pacing us, letting us play around, and then we came around the last corner, he just opened up and killed us. At the time he was way out of shape, and we were in high school, so we should have been able to beat him, but we couldn't.

I had some injuries and illnesses as a kid that didn't allow me to play varsity ball, but I played every sport. I don't know whether I was attracted to sports because of my will to win, but it certainly reinforced my will to win. I would never quit. I could be nine runs down and still trying to win the game. Years later, when I was working at NBC, the *Tomorrow Show* played the *Today Show* in softball. Tom Brokaw was playing for the *Today Show,* and I was pitching for the *Tomorrow Show* staff. I couldn't run much anymore, but I could hit. I was able to turn triples into singles pretty easily. Late in the game, I got to first and knocked in a guy from third to tie the score. The third base coach waved me on. I came in, and the cut-off man threw it right to home plate. I saw the ball coming, and I realized they had me, so I just lowered my head and took the guy completely out. He dropped the ball, and I scored. They had to carry the guy off the field, and I thought, Geez, I feel really bad. But then I thought, Well, I don't feel that bad, I mean, I scored. And he's not dead, so we're okay here.

"GEE, THAT'S PRETTY COLD."

When I was a kid, my dad would always make me run, even though it was difficult for me because my legs were crippled up. I had been hit by a car, and I had a lot of bleeding in my joints, which froze them. He would make me run the half-mile track where they run the horses. There'd always be horse manure on the track and I remember falling down and my dad just said, "Don't fall down and you won't get any horse manure on you."

I thought, "Gee, that's pretty cold." I was mad at him. But the more I thought about it, he was right, if I didn't fall down I wouldn't get horse manure on me.

It was the same with fighting. My dad told me to do everything I could to get out of a fight, but if I had to fight, then I had to take the other guy out in the first ten seconds. Today, if you try to throw a punch at me, I can see it from my peripheral vision on either side, block it, and probably take you down. It doesn't sound like a great thing to do, but my dad said, "I don't want you to get hurt. So, get away, but if you have to throw the punch, or if you have to take somebody out, see it coming, block it, and counterpunch."

"IF I LOST, I WOULD USUALLY ASK FOR ANOTHER SHOT."

I learned early on that if you don't know how to lose, then you don't know how to win. I never was a bad sport about losing, but I was competitive to the end, and if I lost, I would usually ask for another shot. I had tremendous failures in my life. I went broke once when I put everything on a Broadway show. I've been divorced a couple of times. I've had plenty of failures, and I've made plenty of mistakes. So, I've certainly had failures in my life, but I've never let it stop me. I've never let it finish me. I've never said, "Okay, that's the end of it." I just pick myself up and keep going.

I think participating in sports shows the character and personality of people. It taught me a lot about reading people in real-life situations and in business situations. You can tell whether a guy's going to blink or not; you can tell whether they're going to quit the negotiation; you can tell whether they're going to back off; you can tell whether they are going to lose their cool. Consequently, because part my job now is working with talent every day and working with executives, I think I have a very good read on their emotional state. That comes from sports, which is driven by emotion.

Sports is critical in the development of people. There's pain involved—mental and physical—to be the best in anything. I try to be the best at running a network, being a television producer. Sometimes, just staying on your feet longer than everybody else allows you to win. A background in sports makes you healthier and tougher and better able to handle things that are going to be thrown at you. Whether you go on to be great is less important than what you can learn. One of the rules in life to success is knowing what you can do and knowing what you can do very well. Sports teaches you that.

"WAS NIXON ANY GOOD?"

I once talked to a guy who was one of Richard Nixon's coaches. I asked him, "Was Nixon any good?"

He said, "No, he was the worst player I ever had."

I said, "Well what's the story?"

He said, "He showed up first for practice every day. Guys would run over his position and stomp him into the ground, and he always got back up. I finally put him in a game, so he'd win a letter, because the guy never quit." You could see that in the man. You could also see it in Reagan by the way he walked and handled himself. It's true . . . people who win never quit.

LEARY WITH HIS FATHER.

★DENIS LEARY★

Actor, Producer, Writer, and Composer

Hockey

My father was an Irish immigrant and a huge fan of baseball and hurling, which is one of the national sports of Ireland. It's played with a stick and a ball on a field, but it was actually the basis for hockey. Transplanted Scotsmen and Irishmen started to play and they eventually discovered they needed to play on ice in the wintertime. So my father loved the sport of ice hockey once he came here. I remember very clearly not only hearing about Ted Williams, but about the second coming of Christ—the arrival of Bobby Orr. When they were signing him, when he was maybe fourteen years old, my father was already talking about Bobby Orr this, Bobby Orr that. So we were very hyperaware of when he was coming, because before he came, in the early sixties, the Bruins sucked. And they haven't been good since he left.

It was a real father and son thing. In those days, you slept outside the Boston Garden to get tickets for the playoffs and for the regular season, and if it was cold out, they'd let you inside the building. We did that kind of stuff.

Boston and Worcester—and all of Massachusetts, for that matter—were hotbeds for hockey. I started skating when I was three years old, at City Park, maybe four or five blocks away from where I grew up in Worcester. My older brother and I were very competitive, so I wanted to learn to skate as well as he could. The rink in my neighborhood was four blocks from the school, which was a block and a half from my house, so we used to go down there all the time. If we cleaned up all the garbage in the stands after a Friday or Saturday night high school game, the owner would let us skate from midnight to 2:00 in the morning for free. We played street hockey in the summertime, when we weren't playing baseball. They formed a citywide Street Hockey League by neighborhood, and we had a team in that league.

"NOBODY EVER BEAT US."

One year we played in the Citywide Street Hockey League, and went 16–0 in the regular season. To win the championship, you'd have to play another 8 games. We won the first series 4–0. We wanted to win the championship, but what we really wanted to do was go undefeated, because our coach was an ex-Marine and he kept saying to us, "If we could win four in the row in the second sweep, we'd have a perfect record and nobody will ever be able to do it again."

In game four, it was 3–3 tie, and it went to overtime, and we won. I will always remember that. Not only did we win the championship in the Citywide Street Hockey league, but we beat everybody. Nobody ever beat us. Some of the team members were fourteen at the time and you could only play until you were fourteen, so we lost a part of the team after that year, and it wasn't going to be the same team. The coach lived next door to the building I lived in, and we sat out on the stoop that night with the whole team. It was something that we did as a group of guys, and it would never happen again. And it never did happen in that league again. Nobody ever went undefeated. So that's something that will always stay with me.

"THEY'D BE AFRAID TO FIGHT ME, BECAUSE THEY'D HAVE TO GO THROUGH MY BROTHER AND THESE OTHER GUYS FIRST."

The great thing about a sport like hockey is that you cannot think of anything except what's going on in front of you, otherwise you'll get killed. There's no workout like it, because you completely forget about whatever your troubles might be. You've got to think about the action in front of you.

I was always one of the fastest guys in any sport I played. I had long legs and I was always lean. I've always felt I played a rock 'em, sock 'em style in hockey. I'm a tough guy, but I'm thin. I got away with a lot of stuff, because my brother was a huge guy, a lot of the guys I played with were really big guys, and I'd punch somebody in the face or say something, and they'd be afraid to fight me, because they'd have to go through my brother and these other guys first.

I was a wise-ass growing up. My brother and I would literally beat the crap out of each other every day. He was way bigger than I was and a much better street fighter. I never cried. I would just smile and say some wise-ass remark, and he would just grit his teeth, like "I can't believe that none of these beatings are working . . ."

I would hang out on the corner with him and his friends and my friends, and basically we'd be cutting each other down. It was the same thing in the locker room. One of the great things about hockey that has remained the same was, unlike the kinds of things you see in football and in basketball, where guys make a little play, and they're jumping around as if they just performed the greatest thing of all time, is that that would never fly, or else your teammates would beat the crap out of you. Hockey has a real work ethic built into it: that's your job, that's what you've got to do tonight, you'd better come into the locker room and be ready to be held accountable if you don't do it.

"THAT'S THE THING THAT SAVED MY LIFE."

I went to a very sports-oriented high school and. I was so much of a moron that in my freshman year I listened to the hockey coach who wanted us to play soccer so we could get our legs in shape. So, I played soccer and never cracked a book my entire first two months of high school. I thought because I was a good soccer player, and I was going to make the hockey team, that it was all going to be taken care of. That year, I came home with 4 Fs and a B−, and I was shocked that somebody hadn't fixed this. I flunked off the hockey team my freshman year and I did the same thing my sophomore year. I had a C− average, and that's when I became aware that I wasn't a very good student, and that I had probably screwed up my chances of getting any kind of hockey scholarship. That's what led me into doing a musical.

"I'M NOT DOING A MUSICAL, THERE'S NO WAY."

Usually, you skipped a class by saying you needed to go to the bathroom, and the nun would let you get out. Then you'd just walk around the halls for a long time. I was doing that when this nun grabbed me and told me I was going to be doing this musical. "I'm not doing a musical, there's no way," I said. Later, I was talking to my friends, and I said, "I can't do a musical, the guys will think I'm a fag." But I ended up doing it, just because the nun said that when they went into final three weeks of rehearsal I'd get out of school at noon. So, I'm like, "Oh, I'm doing the musical!" I did it, and there were a lot of great-looking chicks. Of course, my friends came to see it, and then they glommed onto the thing about the girls, and the next musical they had not only involved my brother, who was a football player and still in school at the time, by the way, and all of his friends, but all my friends from the hockey team trying out for the musical. Most of them got parts in the chorus, but it automatically became the coolest way to meet chicks.

"YOU NEEDED A WAY TO GET OUT."

Where I grew up, you needed a way to get out because it was a working class neighborhood, and your options were going to work for Coca-Cola, the Teamsters, or if your father was in the union or had a business, you could do that. My father was in the steel workers' union, so that was an option. My brother, once he graduated from high school, became a Teamster. Those things didn't interest me very much, so I had to figure out a way to get out. The only things I'd ever loved were sports and, from the couple of plays I did, acting. I liked it, and I liked the girls. The nun who put me into musicals in high school had a connection at Emerson College, a performing arts school in Boston, and she got me an audition. I ended up getting a scholarship, which kind of saved my life.

Growing up, I would say to my dad, "The coach said this and this and this. And he wants me to play second line."

And my dad would say, "Your coach is the boss, not me. I'm just a spectator in the stand. The team is the team." He was right. The team is a giant amoeba made up of all the different guys on the team. Everybody has to contribute and give up the individual for the group effort. That's a really important thing to learn, not only about ourselves, but about how you live in this country, and what this country's all about. We're all in it together, you know.

The greatest actors I've ever worked with, and some of them are Hall of Famers—the more about the teamwork they are. I did a movie with Robert DeNiro and Dustin Hoffman—that's a double header Hall of Fame shot—two of my favorite actors, by the way—and there was a lot of improv involved. All those guys cared about was not who got the best line, or who got the close-up, but about how the scene went, how do we make it better. I love those guys who lose a game, but in the locker room say, "Man, I had two assists and three goals."

"Yeah, but we lost, so what does it matter?" I'd rather have no goals and no assists and come out a winner.

"WE STOOD IN THAT LINE FOR THREE AND A HALF HOURS WITH ONE OF THESE MYLEC HOCKEY STICKS."

Whenever my brother Johnny or I had a game, my dad might not have been there for the whole thing, but I can clearly remember when you'd look up in the first period or the beginning of the second period, and he would be standing down in the corner, behind the glass, in his gas company uniform. After the game, he'd always have a couple of comments like, "I think you're doing this wrong, and you should stop yapping so much . . ."

Here's a story about my father. When they first came out with street hockey equipment, I think it was in '70, '71, Phil Esposito and Mylec came up with this product that was a line of shin guards and hockey balls and such. Phil Esposito was appearing in a store in downtown Worcester, and if you bought one of the pieces of this equipment, you could stand in line, and he would take a Polaroid with you, and he would sign it. We stood in that line for three and a half hours with one of these Mylec hockey sticks. The whole three hours, my dad's going, "Now when you get up there, make sure you have something you want to say to Phil." Five minutes would go by and he'd say, "And when we get up there, Espo's not going to have a lot of time, so whatever you're going to say to him, make sure it's really succinct."

I said, "Okay, okay. I'm thinking, thinking, thinking."

We get up there, Phil Esposito shakes my hand, shakes my dad's hand, my dad starts talking, I never get to say anything to Esposito. They take a picture of Espo and my dad, where only my head is like barely sticking out in the corner. He signs it, says goodbye to my dad, and we walk away.

I say, "Dad, you talked the whole time."

He says, "Phil took a liking to me, what do you want me to say?"

"I JUST CAN'T FATHOM WHAT I'D DO WITHOUT SPORTS."

I can't fathom what I'd do without sports. Just going outside and playing catch with your son, even without a game or having a family football game, which we do here every Thanksgiving, that's what it's really about. I like going to see the professional teams play, but to me it's more about watching my daughter high-five her cousin, because they just beat us. So that's where I really think the important part of it is.

Here's a piece of trivia for you. Name the two guys who skated with Bobby Orr, Gordy Howe, and Wayne Gretzky. The answer is Tim Robbins and Denis Leary. And the other thing is, I can also say I've been yelled at for not playing my position correctly by Gordy Howe, Bobby Orr, and Wayne Gretzky. So I'm very proud of that.

★MOLLY CULVER★

Actress

Basketball, Softball, Motorcycle Racing

I blew my knee out my sophomore year in high school on a motorcycle, which I was riding from the time I was eleven. It wasn't so unusual. My dad, who was a Navy jet pilot, and my brothers all rode motorcycles, so it was natural for me to do it, too. But after the accident, my sports career was pretty much done, although that didn't stop me from wanting to keep playing.

It never bothered me that I was a girl playing sports. I was always playing a little over my head because my sister or my older brother, Sam, would be the ones who organized the games. My brother would make my mother crazy by taping the strike zone on the garage. My sister went to college on a basketball scholarship, and my other brother played college basketball. They were such good players that it never occurred to me that to keep up with them you had to be good. It also didn't occur to me that just playing with them was really good training to be out in the world of sports. My brothers and sisters were competitive, but at the same time, we'd go home and we'd all love each other, so that was a lesson in sportsmanship. If you grow up in a family where nobody plays sports or you're an only child, I don't think you learn how to grasp the idea of team effort.

"I THINK LIKE A COMPETITOR."

They say the thrill in sports is winning, but I think the thrill is in the competition. There's nothing more satisfying, whether you win or lose, than competing against somebody who's really great. I compete against myself and I compete against other people, but ultimately when I come off the field or the motorcycle track, it's about doing the best that I can do.

When I'm competing for a job and I walk into a room where there are fifteen other really beautiful girls, I think like a competitor. If I see some girls who I know are super-talented, it makes me nervous. Naturally, I wonder if I'll get this job, but I also wonder if any of them can go 130 miles an hour with their knee on the ground on a motorcycle track. Or I wonder if they've ever played basketball and won the tip-off. I hype myself up in other ways like, I know I can do this, I know I can do this, and as a result the situation isn't so intimidating, because I've been in other situations where I've been against people who were really great, and I hung in there. I think that prior experience gives me a little edge on people.

"LET ME TELL YOU, THEY PLAYED TOUGH."

I played for the Christian Youth Organization in Daly City, in Northern California, where my sister coached basketball. I was two years younger than the rest of the inner-city girls, and let me tell you, they played tough. They didn't mess around. I fell down a lot, but it was still a lot of fun.

I had to play hard—I was a real scrapper—but I didn't play well. I knew that in order to stick around, I had to be aggressive. They used to call my sister "Butt and Gut Culver," because she'd just butt and gut and send 'em down, and probably my whole life's goal was to be my sister. She was so fantastic. She's about 5' 6", and she was fast and a really good player. I ended up being 5' 11", so I never played her positions, but I did want to be as good as she was and as focused. She can walk into a game, and there's nothing else going on for her, she's so focused. I walk into a game, and I'm much more easily distracted than she is.

"I WAS GEEKY, I WAS LANKY, I WAS NOT ATTRACTIVE."

I know it's weird to say now, but as a kid I was gawky, I was geeky, I was lanky, I was not attractive. It was tough, growing up, being taller than all the guys. But in sports being that height always helped. I felt like I could walk around knowing that I performed well in sports and that made me feel really good. I'm grateful I grew up in an era where women did compete, and it was respected, and that there wasn't that attitude that you weren't a girl if you played sports. It made such a difference in my life, because I really didn't fit in anywhere else and I always fit in in sports. It allowed me to find a group to belong to. It wasn't as if we hung out at the picnic tables together at lunch; it was just that we all came together and found each other on the court.

When I blew my knee out, my coaches were a little disappointed. After that, in my sophomore and junior years, things just kind of fell apart. Nothing was as inspiring to me. It was a tragedy. I had no ligaments. I had ACL surgery done the beginning of my junior year. They didn't have the technology they have now to reconstruct the knee and eight months later, you're good to go. Back then, I had a straight brace for six months. It was bad. I tried to play again, but when I did it popped out so many times. Every time I wanted to do a lay up I just would fall over, and it was so painful.

As an athlete you go through life a little more graceful. And having that background in athletics has helped me in what I do today. I can't tell you on a daily basis how it makes me feel to be able to do everything from catching the bar of soap before it hits the ground to throwing punches on *V.I.P.*

"YOU'RE ONLY AS STRONG AS YOUR WEAKEST LINK."

What's weird about Hollywood is that there are too many prima donnas who haven't learned to win as a team. They want to win individually and they want to stomp on whoever is in front of them to get to the top. It's so important when you're a part of an ensemble cast to know that as a team, you could be so strong. I've lived my life knowing that you're only as strong as your weakest link and that that person who is your weakest link isn't somebody you should cast out. Instead, it's someone you want to meet on Saturdays to shoot free throws with, to bond with, to help make stronger. When you walk into an audition, and you're in a scene with another actor, you'll often find that you're being upstaged by someone who just wants to be seen. They don't care how good the scene can be if you work together, they just want to look the best they can. That's the hardest wall I've come across here in Hollywood, and after being here five years, I know it's never going to change. I refuse to compromise my own morals and integrity in my life. But that's just the way it is out here.

"COACH MOLLY, WE DON'T WANT TO RUN NO MORE."

I can't play basketball anymore because of my knees, but I've played in three softball leagues in New York and I've coached some inner-city kids. At this level, when the kids are in first, second, and third grade, coaching isn't about winning these basketball games. They just want to be a part of something great, and it's not happening in their families at home—half these kids didn't even have shoes to play in. It's about getting them together and having a good time in something organized where they feel good at the end of the day. I'd have them doing running drills and they'd say, "Coach Molly, we don't want to run no more. Coach Molly, that's why they call them suicides, right, no thank you!"

"WHERE IS THE MODEL?"

I remember moving to Paris and going on my first "go-see" in my Brooks running shoes, a pair of jeans, and a Bruce Springsteen T-shirt. I really was sort of right off the farm. And this was Paris, where everybody was wearing black. I actually had booked this job and I sat there in my big down jacket waiting and I saw everybody kind of flipping out inside. They kept saying, "Where is the model, where is she?" I said, "Oh, I'm right here! Here I am." They thought I was the messenger. That was because I didn't understand how I should look. The girls and the groups of the people I was used to hanging out with dressed like they were ready to have a pick-up game. That's the way I am. I walk around in life ready to play a game, Any kind of game, from basketball to motorcycles—I am game.

I am a pick-up game waiting to happen.

RON REAGAN on His Father,

★RONALD REAGAN★

Former President of the United States,
Governor of California, and Actor

Football, Swimming

My dad wasn't the biggest guy in the world; I think he played at about 175 pounds, and he's a little under 6' 2", which was a little bigger for a player in those days than it would have been today. He played guard on his college football team, and he played against some pretty big people, including a guy named George Musso, who weighed about 300 pounds.

My dad was a little nearsighted, so he wouldn't have made a good end because couldn't see the ball coming. He also couldn't play baseball because he couldn't see the ball well enough to hit it. And he wasn't real fast, either. His brother, who we called "Moon," was the speedster in the family and he played end on the football team until he wrecked his knee. So my dad was usually the last one picked when they chose up teams.

According to the coaches, my dad was an impressive player. He'd show me techniques that he worked on to make up for his lack of size. He used to have this move where he'd sort of slap somebody upside of the head at the beginning of the play, which would drive their head down one way, so he could get around them.

For all his limitations, he was still a natural, talented athlete. But he also had to be gritty when the occasion called for it. He really wanted to play football and I'm sure he would've preferred to be quarterback, because when he used to come and play with my little friends and me in the front yard, he would insist on being the quarterback for both teams. But his skill set put him on the line.

"THE OPPOSING PLAYERS HAD A LOT OF GRASS STAINS ON THE BACKS OF THEIR UNIFORMS."

My father was a teamwork kind of guy. He always used to say, "There's no end to what you can get done, if you don't mind who gets the credit."

That was part of his personality. Not that he didn't have a healthy ego—you don't get to be president without one of those—but he was willing to do what he had to do, and he enjoyed being in the game.

He also had a very strong sense of fairness. I remember a story he told me that had to do with a guy who played tackle next to him who was an African American. My dad used to lifeguard every summer, and he'd come back really tan. They were doing some drill early in the fall training and he noticed the coach was standing behind them. They were lined up together with bare calves, their socks rolled down in the heat, and the coach was laughing, because my dad was darker than his African American teammate. There was a particular game, in which my father noticed that the opposing players were playing real dirty, piling on at the end of a play, gouging and punching, doing all those kinds of things to this teammate and obviously doing it because he was black. This made my father very angry. He could have responded in kind, I suppose—which means he could have started playing dirty, but he didn't. He just stepped it up a notch and from what I gather, the opposing players had a lot of grass stains on the backs of their uniforms by the end of the game.

"HE WAS TOLD THAT HE DIDN'T LOOK LIKE A FOOTBALL PLAYER."

Dad really wanted that job as the Gipper in the movie about Notre Dame's coach, Knute Rockne. He was more or less the same size as George Gipp. And, of course, he could kick the ball and run with the ball and throw the ball and do all of that kind of stuff. In fact, originally it had been his idea and he'd even started work on a screenplay that included Pat O'Brien as Rockne. But Warner Brothers beat him to the punch and didn't include my dad in the picture. The story goes that he went in and asked for an audition but was told that he didn't look like a football player. My dad came back with an old college football photo, and he got the part.

"HE WOULD POUND HIS OWN FENCE POSTS."

Not all actors are particularly athletic. They usually go out for drama club. My dad did that too, but he also played football. Physically, he was always younger than his age. Even when he was in his fifties and sixties, he was quite spry. After he was shot, he started lifting weights. Before that, most of his exercise came from riding horses and working on the various ranches he had owned since the 1940s. He would pound his own fence posts, saddle his own horses, build his own jumps, and build flagstone patios himself. It was quite physical work, and he enjoyed it very much. He's always enjoyed hard physical labor; he derived a lot of satisfaction from it. That may have had something to do with his athletic career.

My father's one of the physically bravest people I've ever met. There wasn't an ounce of trepidation in this guy. I can remember riding in this ancient jeep that we had forever and hauling big flagstones in a little trailer behind it, so he could make a little patio outside the ranch house in Santa Barbara. He was trying to go up this hill that was just too damn steep, and the rocks kept hauling us down backwards. On one side of us was a precipice going all the way down into the Simi Valley, and I thought, "My god, we're going to get hauled over this thing; we're going to die here." But he wasn't going to give up. By god, he just kept gutting that thing up that hill until we managed to haul those rocks up over the hill and down the other side. I was willing to go back the other way—let's take the low road! But not him.

"HE WOULD ESSENTIALLY KNOCK THEM SILLY BEFORE HE COULD RESCUE THEM."

My dad was a tough guy, and not just in football. Swimming was probably his best sport. He'd lifeguard on the Rock River, and there were seventy-seven notches on the log indicating the number of people he pulled out of the river. Some of them were kids who just went too far out, but some of them were these big, muscular farm guys, much bigger than my father, who at the end of the harvest season would come down from the farm and who couldn't swim worth a damn. They'd get into the river and start to drown and he'd have to swim out there and haul these people in. He told me he had to develop this technique where he would essentially knock them silly before he could rescue them. They'd be clawing at him and coming at him to drag him under, to try and hold themselves up, and he's have to hit them with a right cross to the jaw to sort of stun them to the point where he could get around behind them and pull them to safety.

He used to swim in the ocean and body surf until he was quite advanced in years. He was old-style, too. He wouldn't cut across the face of the waves and wear fins—he'd just go right over the falls. He'd catch a big wave and just ride over with the break.

I don't know where his fearlessness came from, but apparently he had it from a pretty early age. He was just a tough guy, but like most tough guys, also a very gentle person. He had very little patience for bullies, for people who would try to physically intimidate folks who were weaker than them. I remember coming home one time from some trip back to Washington, where he had discovered that a certain senator, who's actually still in the Senate, was given to physically intimidating his staff, and my dad was outraged by that. He took me aside and explained to me that when you've found a bully, you've found a coward. He said that a cardinal rule for any man is that you just don't pick on people who are smaller and weaker than you are, period. That's not manly.

"HE'D NEVER LET ME WIN."

Athletics were very important to my father. When he was working at home, say on the weekends, and I'd have some friends over, and we'd be getting a little football game together, I'd start coming in and bugging him to come out and play. He was the governor of our state and, understandably, he had work to do, so my mother would shoo me away. But you could tell he really wanted to play. His window opened up on the front yard of our Sacramento house and so he could see us out there, and I knew that would make it irresistible for him. Sure enough, in about half an hour or so, out he'd come and play with us. He loved little physical contests with me as we were growing up—swimming and arm wrestling, stuff like that. He'd never let me win. He told me at a very early age that he would not fake being beaten by me, because, he said, "Eventually you will be able to beat me, but how will you know it's real, if I'm always letting you win?" And, in fact, that's sort of what happened.

A lot of people who visited him in the White House would marvel at the fact that instead of being all-consumed by the affairs of state that he could switch to talking about acting or sports or lifeguarding or whatever it might be at the drop of a hat. He saw talking about that kind of stuff as a refreshing break.

He was always interested in Notre Dame, though we were officially UCLA fans, because the school is closer to where we lived. I remember sitting in the stands with him and watching the game in which O.J. Simpson broke that incredible sixty, seventy-yard run in the last couple of minutes and won the game for USC. I'm pretty sure he went down to the locker room afterward to congratulate the players.

"NO, SIR, I DROPPED THE BALL."

My sense of my father is that he understood that winning isn't the only thing; that how you play the game ultimately *is* the game. He would occasionally tell stories, and admittedly with my dad sometimes you'd wonder, Is this a real story, or is this just a story story? because if you're talking about decades old football games, you can't always know. I think he saw the football field, or any field of athletic endeavor, as a field of honor. That was the most important thing. Playing fair—playing hard—but playing fair. The tendency today is to say it's not cheating if you can get away with it—that was not him. Anyway, I remember he told this story, and again, I can't vouch for the reality of this, but it was—if I remember correctly—a college football game, and the underdog team had kept the game close into the waning minutes. As he told it, there was a last ditch, desperation pass into the end zone, which looked like it had been caught by the end on the underdog team. The crowd went wild. People were going nuts. It was a tremendous upset. According to my father, the player who apparently caught the ball, walked over to the referee, handed him the ball and said, "No, sir, I dropped the ball." And they disallowed the score. That was it. He lost his team the game. But in my father's telling, both coaches and at least a good number of the players knew who the real hero was that day—that this guy had done something way more important than catching a football. He'd upheld his own integrity, his team's integrity, and the integrity of the game by doing what he did.

There's a real lesson in that, I think.

★TOM RIDGE★

First Secretary of Homeland Security
and Former Governor of Pennsylvania

Baseball

I've got a photograph of me, I can't be more than four or five years old, wearing a little baseball outfit and holding a glove. That moment, when I first got that uniform, was huge, because at that moment you know that you're part of a team. And that's big time.

I played a lot of baseball and it was fun. It was probably my father who said, "Don't get flushed with victory, because you may see those guys next week, and they'll kick your butt." That's the beauty of sports—you always got a chance to come back.

My dad was very supportive of my playing sports. He was one of those guys who wanted the parents to get out of the way and just let the kids play the game. He worked two jobs, so many nights he would come to the field, drop me off, line the field, because he wanted to help, and then run off to his second job. Some nights he was able to come and actually watch the game.

I always loved to catch. Why? Because you're in charge. Nothing happens until you call for the pitch. You can even tell the pitcher what you want him to throw, and you can align the guys in the end field and the outfield, so it was a nice having that feeling at a young age.

I've always been very competitive from a very early age. It's not that I was a great athlete, it's just that I would be competitive one-on-one with my brother—and I still am—from a golf match to a YMCA pick-up game to baseball. After all, if it doesn't count, why keep score? I want to compete at the highest possible level, even in sand lot. It's important to get the most out of yourself and out of your teammates.

And I was damn good! If a singles-hitting first baseman or catcher ever had a shot at the pros, I'd have been it. But normally when you looked at those two positions, you want more than a good defensive singles-hitting player, so I had no shot.

"I DON'T THINK YOU'RE GOING TO BE PLAYING AND COMPETING WITH THIS TEAM."

I didn't play competitively in high school until the beginning of my senior year, when I decided to go out for the team. It was a cold spring day and I hadn't had a bat in my hand in a couple of years. I walked up to the plate and the pitcher threw a couple of zingers by me. I might have gotten a little wood on the ball, but mostly I just swung hard, hit a couple of foul balls, and missed most of the time. I may have been invited back for the second day, but I knew it was arrivederci. Nevertheless, I had a big smile on my face, because as this kid was throwing heat and I was missing it by a mile, I kind of concluded in my own mind, "Well, you know, you may like to compete, and you may like to play, but I don't think you're going to be competing and playing with this team." That's when the coach misinterpreted my own self-assessment to mean that I wasn't trying hard. Well, I was trying to make the team, I was just out of my league that day.

"CADDYING HAD A GREAT EFFECT ON ME."

I started caddying when I was ten or eleven years old. My dad would pick me up from my caddying job at the local country club, bring me a sandwich, I'd change into my baseball uniform on the way to the diamond, and I'd have a full day of sports.

Actually, caddying had a great effect on me. You learn a lot about human nature. Golf is a sport of integrity and character. You are responsible for knowing the rules and playing by the rules, and you're accountable to call the rules on yourself. I learned a lot about how people treat other people, and how people take to winning and losing. Once in a while you'd see somebody, if they were playing summer rules, move it in the fairway, or make an adjustment in the rough. But more often than not, it was how they'd handle a miss-shot that told a lot about them as people.

I remember one time when I had to pin the pin, which means pulling it out of the hole, because if the ball's on the green and the pin is still in, it's a two-stroke penalty. For whatever reason, it got stuck and the guy I was caddying for hit the pin, and got the penalty stroke and lost the hole. But he was a very decent guy and he handled it in a very nice way. He said, "I'm going to lose the hole on account of you not removing the pin. I know you didn't do it on purpose, but it's important you pay attention to these little things, if you're going to play golf. Because rules are rules."

"YOU COULDN'T GET A NICKEL
UNDER MY SNEAKERS."

I played a little basketball, but I wasn't very good. There was no arc on my jump shot, and on my best day you couldn't get a nickel under my sneakers. I play a little bit now with some of the guys from the Homeland Security Council, and it's the same thing. But I hustle and the advantage of being secretary is whether I deserve to get the shot or not, I do get the ball once in a while.

I think the competitive impulse is one of the reasons I'm in government. At the end of the day, particularly on the political side, you count 'em up and somebody's got more than the other. But that's good.

"YOU DON'T WIN 'EM ALL IN SPORTS,
AND YOU DON'T WIN 'EM ALL IN LIFE."

I think you're molded when you're young, and most of the clay hardens at an early age. In sports, you learn not to get too excited when you win or too disappointed when you lose, because there's always another day, another opportunity. You don't win 'em all in sports, and you don't win 'em all in life. You've got to learn to enjoy victory, but not to be intimidated or paralyzed by defeat. My favorite quote is from Teddy Roosevelt: "It is not the critic who counts, not the one who points out how the strong man stumbled or how the doer of deeds might have done better. The credit belongs to the man who is actually in the arena, whose face is marred with sweat and dust and blood."

★BURT REYNOLDS★

Actor

Football

I noticed very early that the guys I was hanging out with on one side of the street—the greasers—were on their own, while the guys on other side of the street—the ones who had the letter sweaters—had fifteen more girls over there with them than there were on our side of the street. That had a pretty big effect on me, and it was as good a reason as any to get involved with sports.

One day in eighth grade gym class, I outran everybody. A little guy came over, who had about ten letters on his sweater and said, "Hey, you're pretty fast. Think you can you out race Vernon Voss?" I said, "I don't know who that is, but yeah, I'll race him." So, the next morning, about 7:30, before school started, a bunch of us started walking down to the football field. All of a sudden, it was like I was Gandhi, because there were about a hundred people following behind us. We got down to the football field, and I looked over, and this kid was sitting there. I shook hands with him. His name was Vernon, but the little guy called him Flash. I thought, This is not good, his name is Flash. Meanwhile, they were calling me Mullet. I thought, If I don't win this race, I'll be Mullet for the rest of my life. So, I figured I had a lot more at stake than the other guy.

I won. And when I finished the 100 yards and turned around to come back, the little guy said, "That was a good race, buddy." And from then on my name was Buddy. By the way, that little guy was Dick Howser, who became manager of the Yankees and won the World Series.

"WELL, IT SOUNDS LIKE I COULD GET A GREAT EDUCATION HERE."

In football, you have to like to hit and get hit. I liked that, so it was a perfect sport for me. In football, you can take somebody who had a lot of desire and a certain amount of skill, like hand-eye coordination and speed, and they can make the team. That's not true in a sport like baseball or basketball, where you need special skills. In football, you can make it if you've got the "I'm-going-to-get-up-off-the-ground-and-kick-your-ass" attitude.

I never knew playing football was going to get me to college, but I figured it was probably going to get me dates. I was planning to go to go to Miami on a football scholarship. Howser, who we called "Peanut," was going to Florida State on a baseball scholarship and he said, "You oughta come up there and look around."

I thought, Aaaa, I don't want to go to Florida State, but I'll go up and take a look. They were bringing in major animals, guys that had already graduated from Mississippi Southern, and had two names, plus a lot of veterans from the Korean War.

The coach was a guy named Tom Nugent, who invented the "I" formation, the Typewriter Huddle, and the Lonesome End. He was an amazing guy and very, very quick-witted and sharp. "What are they giving you at Miami?" he asked me.

I said, "A lot."

He said, "You'll start here." And then he said, "Are you aware, Mr. Reynolds, that this is a girls' school, and there are twenty-two girls here for every guy."

I said, "Well, it sounds like I could get a great education here."

When I arrived that first day of practice before school started, there were 300 guys who all thought they had a four-year scholarship. Some of the guys were twenty-eight or twenty-nine, big, tough, bad guys—and it was going to be the last thirty-two guys standing. Lee Corso and I were the only two eighteen-year-olds that made the varsity. When we go back for reunions and Corso says, "You know, Burt, you look great," I say, "Yeah, compared to those guys, I do."

I was a fullback in junior high and high school. In those days, they ran out of T-formation, and they would switch me over to halfback on certain plays. When I went to Florida State, Nugent had the "I" formation, and if you were the deep back in the "I" you had two guys in front of you that were in the backfield with you but were essentially pulling guards. We did great in my freshman year, winning nine games, I think.

In those days, I weighed 192 pounds and was what they called a "big back." In terms of the pros, I had a cockiness about me that made me think I could play with those guys. But then, after I met some of them, I wasn't quite so sure. But then I was out partying one night and I was in a car wreck and I busted my spleen and re-injured my knee, and so the dream was over after that.

There are some similarities between actors and professional athletes because they both have had some success in their lives and then some failure and then some success again. It's one thing to be successful, which is hard to handle for a lot of people, but to crash and burn and then come back from it with some kind of dignity that's what football and sports in general teaches you. You're not going to win every game, and when you do lose you have to get up off the ground and go on. That's what the game is about. It gives you a focus, and it also gives you pride in who you are.

"I WANTED MY DAD'S APPROVAL MORE THAN ANYTHING."

My father was the chief of police. You can go one of two ways when you're the preacher's son or the cop's son. I went the other way. I hung out with outlaws and I was in trouble a lot, and football saved me. Without it, I would definitely have ended up in bad trouble, because I was heading that way.

I wanted my dad's approval more than anything, but it was hard to get my father to even say, "Good game." We didn't really make peace with each other until he was ninety—he lived to be ninety-four. Thank God, he lived long enough that we could say it to each other. He was enormously proud of me, but he just was from that generation where they didn't know how to put their arm around their kid and say, "You did a great job." I wanted that a lot. I think much of that had to do with being in the South and having an authority figure, because I remember Rip Torn once said to me, "In the South, no man is a man until his father tells him he is."

"HEY, IT'S JUST A MOVIE!"

The Longest Yard was not an easy movie for me to make, even though I had played college football. The other day I had lunch with Pervis Atkins, who was in the picture—he played for Frank Kush, and he was a tough guy—and he said to me, "We all said 'Let's kill this son of a bitch.'" They all wanted to kill me! Because to them I was just this Hollywood ad. So I had to prove myself, and when you have to prove yourself to guys like Ray Nitschke, you really have to prove yourself. Nitschke had this game he played called "Kill the movie actor." He'd try to take my head off every frickin' day.

I'd say, "Hey, it's just a movie," and he'd turn to me and say, "Not to me!" And it wasn't to him. To him, it was a matter of, "Don't put that helmet on unless you're ready to go to war."

We played from eight o'clock in the morning until five or six o'clock at night. I found out the very first day that they were not going to play patty-cake with me, and Robert Aldrich wasn't going to let them do that anyway. He was real smart. If it's staged, it always looks like crap, so he would have four cameras and he'd tell the offense to try to score.

For one scene, we were on the one-yard line and Aldrich had them throw me the ball and he said to the defense, "Don't let him score." And to the offense he said, "Okay, if you score, you can go home." It was four o'clock in the afternoon and we'd been playing since eight o'clock and I could not get that yard.

We went into the huddle, and Sonny Sixkiller and a couple of other guys said, "Damn it, Burt, please score. They're killing us."

Pervis said, "Step on my back."

I said, "What?"

"Step on my back, man. You know, you got that jump. You can jump." So I ran to the right, came back and I stepped right on his back and leaped high as I've ever been over the line. We finally had it! The reason the celebration in the movie looks so real is that it was. We didn't have to go out there and have Nitschke kill us—we were going to get to go home. It wasn't acting, it was reacting.

And that's as good an analogy between sports and acting as you can get.

KELLY IS IN THE BACK ROW AT THE CENTER.

★RAY KELLY★

New York City Police Commissioner

Football, Boxing

I grew up on the West Side of Manhattan and started playing ball in the street at the age of five or six. We'd use one of those pink Spaldeen balls for stoop ball or stickball.

Sports were a safety valve for me. With some of the things that went on in the environment I grew up in, I could easily have gone the wrong way. I think sports kept me out of trouble because, in my neighborhood, there were a lot of street fights. It was usually Irish versus Puerto Ricans. I remember one time my mother made us a boxing ring in the backyard and I fought another kid there. I also boxed a little in the CYO [Catholic Youth Organization].

The amazing thing about boxing is that it actually changes how your face looks from fight to fight. I broke my nose while boxing, probably because I had short arms and in boxing, without reach, you're going to have a pretty hard time. I did have a relatively powerful upper body, though. In order to win, I had to get inside, but once I was in there, I usually did okay.

Football was my next sport, and it wasn't too far from the little guy street fighting to the little guy in the ring fighting to getting into it on the football field. It was all tied into the ongoing process of proving myself. I have a fairly aggressive nature. I think it's a primal instinct and it definitely helps me in my career and in life. I think I learned it from competing on the street.

By the time I was seven or eight, I got involved in CYO sports as well as joining a Pop Warner football team. I was a running back and on defense I was a linebacker. I broke my thumb and wrist on three separate occasions.

I always liked the competition. In fact, I even liked the pain. My mother wanted me to stop playing. She was always asking me, "Why do you do it?" And the answer is that it's a testosterone thing that drives you to it.

Growing up, I was always small and yet I liked to hang with the big guys, which meant that I played with the big guys. I had to tackle these big guys and

I learned that if I was going to be able to do it, I had to get the jump on them, tackle them early.

You learn things about yourself playing sports, and one of the things I learned was that although at the time I didn't realize it, I had this Napoleon thing where I had to take on the big guy. I thought they were going to underestimate me—I was sure of that—and I would try and make them pay the price for it.

"I URGE EVERYONE ON THE FORCE TO STAY IN SHAPE."

I go to the gym and work out every day. I stretch and I do cardio exercises. There a tradition of fitness associated with this job that started with Teddy Roosevelt when he was Commissioner in the late 1890s. He was a sickly kid who became a really fit adult. He built up his chest when he boxed at Harvard. He had this cowboy kind of mentality. And that's something I can relate to.

As commissioner, I urge everyone on the force to keep in shape. We have them playing baseball, soccer, football, lacrosse, running. I like to have former athletes on the force, because they always display the discipline they learned from playing athletics.

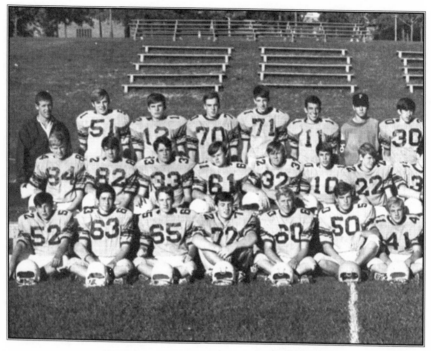

DREIER IS NUMBER 51, BACK ROW, SECOND FROM LEFT.

★DAVID DREIER★

U.S. Congressman from California

Baseball, Football

I was a terrible athlete, but I'll never forget one of the great moments I had and, as it happened, my father was there to see it. It was during a fifth grade baseball game, and everybody thought that David Kander was going to be up to bat, and they were cheering. But it turned out it was David Dreier who was coming up to bat. And everybody sighed. The upshot was that I hit a triple, which brought three people in.

That was a very memorable moment for me, especially since everybody else in my family was better at sports than I was. I remember being at a swim meet when I was seven or eight years old and, after a very long swim, I wound up last. But my family was very nice about it and encouraging. They celebrated the fact that I made it to the finish line.

I went to boarding school when I was twelve years old, and that's when I participated in virtually every sport. I played soccer, and I broke my best friend's leg during a scrimmage. At the time, we laughed, and then the next day he came into school with a huge cast on and I felt awful.

I was the student body president, class president, and all that stuff, but I was never a star athlete. It wasn't easy, but it was something that I accepted. I don't want to say I was jealous, but I really admired the people who were better than I, which was virtually everybody else.

There's a funny story concerning my so-called "athletic career." When I got this position in Congress as chairman of the Rules Committee, the *New York Times* and the *LA Times* wrote profiles. They interviewed my chief of staff, Brad Smith, who told them that I was quarterback on the football team. When I read the article, I said, "What the heck is this? I was center on the B football team."

Brad said, "You know, you've talked about football so much that I just assumed you were the starting quarterback!"

By the way, they printed a tongue-in-cheek correction.

I did play ice hockey and tennis, too. What was most memorable was not my teammates, although I certainly have fond memories of them, but my coaches.

"I JUST WISHED THAT I HAD HAD MORE TALENT."

The real defining moments centered around the discipline that came from these coaches who, in our eyes, could do no wrong. They were about the closest thing to the Almighty. They were the closest thing to God in my life because they disciplined us. I had to do extra laps and extra push-ups and all that sort of stuff. I just wished that I had had more talent, because I did practice. But I think that, although I didn't realize it at the time, practice paid off for me now because that discipline shaped me in many ways.

I was a runner and some of the things I learned from our track coach, Jack Eyerly, I still think about when I run today. I've come up with more ideas and solved more problems when I've been running than I do when I have other distractions.

"I OFTEN FELT LIKE I WAS DOING COMBAT DUTY."

My father was a great athlete and a Marine Corps drill instructor. I often felt like I was doing combat duty. Obviously, he had a great influence on me. I still do 200 push-ups and 500 crunches every day. It's all about discipline, which I think has allowed me to do other things like take the skeleton run at Lake Placid or go bungee jumping, which I did last year in New Zealand.

My father passed away a few years ago. He was sixty-eight and in perfect shape—he'd just won two tennis tournaments—but unfortunately he got sick. He was very competitive, and I know that I disappointed him many, many times. In fact, one of the last experiences I remember having with him was playing in a father/son tennis tournament. I missed a shot, and he reamed me out. Afterward, I let him have it. I said, "Listen, Dad, come on, give me a break. I tried for the shot, but life is too short to get upset about something like this."

"WE TALK ABOUT COMPETITION."

Politics is a sport. When you think about politics, you can easily use football analogies. For instance, you can say, "We want to move the ball down to the ten yard line, and we're going to make sure that when we get to the ten, we're going to score." We talk about that regularly when we're talking about moving the agenda for the American people.

Another strong connection between politics and sports is the competitiveness that exists in politics and in government, both domestic and global. For example, we regularly debate the issue of international trade, and we talk about competition. I like to say that when American workers compete, they win. Look at the experiences and references to sports that presidents make. I think our athletic endeavors really do have an impact on our governance of this country.

"DISCIPLINE IS CONTAGIOUS."

I've known Arnold Schwarzenegger for fifteen years. He's very disciplined. He still works out all the time. When I started hanging out with him, especially through the campaign, we were together almost daily, and if I didn't see him, I'd talk to him two or three times a day. Whenever we spoke, he'd always ask me about my physical regimen. "Okay, how many push-ups did you do this morning? How far did you run this morning? How many crunches?" He rides the life cycle for 45 minutes every morning, and then he pumps iron at night.

I find that by associating with people like that, their discipline has a tendency to rub off on me. Discipline is contagious.

★GRAY DAVIS★

Former Governor of California

Baseball, Basketball, Golf

As a young kid in the 1950s, I remember going to Ebbets Field as part of a Boy Scout troop, and I got to meet Gil Hodges. I still have a picture of that meeting, and ever since then sports have been a big part of my life.

Our coach, Nat Reynolds, who also taught history, was the person who motivated me the first year, when I was a high school freshman and couldn't make the baseball team. It happened one day when the team was out on the field with the coaches hitting ground balls to the infield and fly balls to the outfield while I was just sitting on the sidelines. Coach Reynolds came over to me and said, "You know, Gray Davis, I've been watching you, and you have talent. You have real abilities, so just learn to apply yourself. Your problem is you have no direction, no motivation, no desire."

"I WAS BLOWN AWAY THAT HE HAD PAID ATTENTION TO ME."

Looking back on those days, that was probably an accurate description. People who've met me since find that hard to believe, but I was kind of aimless and didn't know what I was going to do in life. Remember, this was back in the '50s, when people weren't quite as sure what they wanted to do with their lives as maybe they are now. What stunned me was not that I wasn't playing but that he'd actually noticed me and told me that if I had any problem with my homework or needed to get his counsel any time. He even gave me his home phone number. I was blown away that he (1) had paid attention to me, (2) believed in me, and (3) was willing to help me.

I said to myself, "Well, if he believes in me, I have to believe in myself." That conversation turned my life around, because I took his advice to heart, not only in athletics but also academically. And when I became a senior, Coach Reynolds made me the captain of the team.

"OH PLEASE, GOD, LET SOMEBODY CATCH IT."

I always hit for a pretty good average in high school. As a matter of fact, I won the league batting championship one year, but I rarely hit home runs. Although I do remember one particular game. There was no fence on our field, just a log out in left field, which was probably about 289 feet from home plate. Beyond that, people would park their cars when they came to watch the game. My mother was at this particular game and I hit a high fly to left field, and I heard Coach Reynolds say, "I think that's up with the jet stream, that may get out of here."

I was running to first base and I heard my mother say, "Oh please, God, somebody catch it, don't let it hit my car." So, in the best of all worlds, it landed over the log and bounced underneath the car. I had two home runs that year, and she got to see one of them.

I tried to play when I got to Stanford—baseball was always my first love—but even in those days, the players were 6′ 2″ and 220 pounds, and I was about 6′ 0″, 175. They were faster, stronger, bigger. So I ended up playing on the golf team.

My mother was a pretty fair golfer, and she had played in a number of amateur contests, back in the days when they played match play. Every time she got to the finals, she won. So I always would tell myself that, whenever I had a critical time at bat, or when I was preparing for debates, or running for governor back in 1998, that competition is in my genes. If Mom can do it, I can do it.

"YOU HAVE TO HAVE A LOT OF PERSEVERANCE."

I think my experience in sports has helped me through every election, because you have to learn how to win and how to lose and still come back the next day to play again. I've been in fourteen elections and I ended up losing two of them, but an election is an act of faith. All you can do is make your case as to what you have or what you will do and hope people respond. I always had confidence in the voters of this state that they would make good judgments, and even though I lost in the last election, you know, I still have a lot of confidence in people in the state. Generally, they're fair-minded and make good judgments.

PACE IS IN THE BACK ROW, EIGHTH FROM LEFT.

★PETER PACE★

General and Vice Chairman
of the Joint Chiefs of Staff

Baseball, Soccer

We lived across the street from a schoolyard where kids played basketball and baseball and stick ball, and so in my younger days, I probably spent a lot more time watching sports than I did playing them. My older brother played Little League, and I used to watch him go out of the house wearing his uniform. I thought that was kind of cool and that it was something I'd like to do someday.

When I finally did get a chance to play Little League, my natural skills were not at the top of the heap, which is why I'm not playing pro ball these days! But I enjoyed the game, and I learned a lot about myself as far as the desire to play. I did not like sitting on the bench, and I ended up finding out that a guy with average skills who tried real hard could still play the game.

"IT DID IRRITATE ME TO BE SITTING ON THE BENCH."

Even though I wasn't a starter, I never remember having any thoughts that Steve or Charlie or somebody else shouldn't be out there and I should. I was always able to accept the fact that there are guys in this world who were smarter than I am, who could run faster, who had better skills than I had. But it did irritate me to be sitting on the bench, and I think that spurred me on to work harder to get to the above-average level that would allow me to play.

I remember the game in which I hit the only homerun I ever hit in Little League, and it was as a pinch hitter. That taught me the value of doing the best you can, when you get the opportunity, and that everybody can contribute.

"YOU'RE NEVER GOING TO BE WORLD CLASS."

In seventh grade, I started playing soccer. I did all right, but I was still pretty much a substitute on the team. In tenth grade, we had a coach named

Bill Powley, and if he hadn't been a high school soccer coach, he probably would have been a good drill instructor. Through getting us to run further than we thought we could and train harder than we thought we could, he taught us to work together as a team. He taught us that the limits we thought we had in our heads were nowhere near the limits our bodies could reach if we gave them a chance.

One day he sat me down and said, "You know, Pete, you're never going to be world class, but you've got a lot more in you than you realize. I want you to go on the track team when you're not playing soccer, and I want you to strengthen your running ability."

So I did just that. I started running the mile on the high school track team as well. Our track coach, Coach Ryan, had us running quarters and jogging quarters and running quarters and jogging quarters continually through the entire practice until we had four, five, six miles under our belts. By the time I finished high school, I was running a 4.20 mile, which was pretty good in those days. That taught me that if you don't like the results, change it. Do something.

We were the League Champions my senior year in high school. I credit that to team play and to Coach Powley, who died five or six years ago of a heart attack. He taught us the value of teamwork, the ability of everybody to contribute. Personally, he taught me that an average player can perform at an above-average level.

"HEY, COACH, YOU NEED ME AND I NEED YOU."

An interesting sidelight is that when I applied to the Naval Academy, I flunked the physical. At that time you had to have 20–20 vision, and mine was 20–40. So I got the appointment, and I had the academics, and I had everything I needed, but I could not pass the eye exam. So I wrote Coach Warner at the Naval Academy and said, basically, "Hey, coach, you need me and I need you." He had me come down to the Academy, I did an interview, took another physical, and failed the eye exam again. He got in touch with Coach Powley and asked him to write a letter. To make a long story short, my soccer association, and the fact that I did well in soccer, allowed me to get a waiver to enter the Naval Academy. So right there is a very direct connection between sports and the unintended consequences of doing the best you can.

My dad always expected us to produce as scholars in high school. That's a word I wouldn't have used when I was a kid, but he and my mom were both most interested that we get good grades. As a matter of fact, the reason I didn't wrestle in high school was that my sophomore year in high school I came home with a C in English. All the other grades were B's and A's. But my father said I was off sports until I got all my grades back up to the B's and A's. So, although dedication was important to my dad, he clearly had his priorities for me set: one, academic; two, sports.

There is an analogy between being involved in athletics and being a member of the military. You can understand how being on a great team brings out the best in you. It gives you the opportunity to play at a level you didn't even know you had the capacity to play at. The Marine Corps did that for me because of the enormous number of really talented, dedicated folks in the military. I've worked hard, but I've also had the great good fortune to be put on some great teams inside the organization that have done some things that I've been proud of.

"HE HAD SACRIFICED SO MUCH MORE THAN I HAD."

I was inducted into the Little League Hall of Excellence. I'm glad they put it that way, because "Hall of Fame" would have meant I had some kind of outstanding skill, which I really didn't. Instead, the honor is bestowed on folks who have played the game and who, in the eyes of the Little League, have gone on to make a mark of some kind. I was truly honored to have that recognition. More important, the day that I was inducted they also inducted Wilbert Davis, a great young army staff sergeant, whose skill level as a Little League player was much greater than mine. He was a pitcher in the Little League World Series. My team never got out of Teaneck, New Jersey. His team made it to the World Series. He was killed in combat in Iraq. So for me, it was a very poignant moment in that, clearly, he had greater skills than I had and he had sacrificed so much more than I had. It was a humbling experience to be on the field receiving the award at the same time his family was accepting the award on his behalf.

★HENRY KRAVIS★

Co-Founder of Kohlberg,
Kravis, Roberts & Co.

Football, Golf, Wrestling

I'm very small, so I was always the smallest person on the football field, but I loved football. I remember my dad telling me, "If you don't eat your food, they're always going to say, 'Look at that little guy on the field.' And you don't want to be known as that."

I said, "Yeah, but do you know what they're going to say, Dad? They're going to say, 'Look at the little guy on the field, but look how he can run!'"

Flash forward to when I was in the ninth grade. I went to a school up in Massachusetts, and my parents came up for visiting day when we had a football game. I took a punt and I was running down the field. Someone was standing right next to my dad, saying "My god, look at that little guy run!" My father told me that story and it stuck in my mind so much, that I said to myself, You may not be big, but if you're fast and you're flexible and you out think the next guy, then you're always going to be able to play any sport.

In football, I always had coaches who said, "You're too small."

So I said to myself, Fine. That's the way he feels, then I'll just have to try harder, and I'll have to be better than the guy bigger than me. And that's what I did.

I've always been a very determined kind of person, so size didn't worry me when it came to playing football, which I loved. I'd go into practice, they'd line me up against some of the linemen to learn to block against them but it didn't matter that they were bigger than I was. I remember the first time I took some big guy down and I saw stars. I said to myself, That's the badge of doing what you have to do.

"IT'S ABOUT TRYING TO IMPROVE YOURSELF."

I really focused on two individual sports—wrestling (I was captain of the team when I was a senior in high school) and golf, which my father got me into—and one team sport, football. The good part about golf and wrestling is that they are individual sports. It's you against you. It's all about trying to improve yourself. When you're on a team, you can get a lot of help from other people and that can make you look awfully good.

Good conditioning is always an important part of the end result of a game or contest. It's the same thing in business. If you haven't thought out your game plan, if you haven't done your homework, if you haven't positioned yourself properly in order to buy a company, you're not going to end up being very successful in our world of financial sponsors and private equity.

I'm very proud of the fact when I ask a CEO, "How'd our team do?" he says, "You guys did better than anybody else that came through here looking at our company. You knew more about the industry; you asked better questions than anybody else, you were better prepared than anybody else." It's all about conditioning, about being ready for the game.

"YOU'RE GOING TO BE SURPRISED AT WHAT YOU CAN DO."

I'm very competitive, and I actually like when somebody tells me I can't do something. I've told my children for years, "Just take the word 'can't' out of your vocabulary. I don't want to hear I can't do this, or I can't do that. First of all, you don't know whether you can or you can't until you try it. And you're going to be surprised at what you can do when you set your expectations very high. If you set your expectations low, then you're going to end up low." I'm an optimist. I want to find a solution to a problem in business. I always get worried when people say, "God, what a great buy," when we're buying a company. I think you should congratulate me not when we buy the company, but when we sell the company. Because if we sell the company, that means we have something to sell, and we've probably done pretty well with it. Anybody can buy a company, just pay enough and you'll own the company. The key is what you do with the business once you own it.

"I WANT A GUY WHO IS PREPARED TO GET HIMSELF DIRTY."

I've learned a lot playing golf with people over the years. You can tell if they are prepared to cut corners, and if they are, that's not for us. If they mark their ball wrong on the green on a consistent basis, what's he going to do in the big leagues? Same thing if you're playing golf with a guy and you know his ball's out of bounds and suddenly the ball shows up somewhere else. I get turned off by people like that. I want to watch how people behave under pressure. The guy doesn't have to be a good athlete; but it is important that he's got some breadth, that he's not all business. That guy's a bore. I want a guy who can laugh at himself, who doesn't take himself too seriously, and is prepared to get out on the field and get himself dirty.

"I'M GOING TO HAVE TO THINK THREE MOVES AHEAD."

I'm from Oklahoma originally, and wrestling is big in that part of the world. I wrestled three weights: 110, 121, and 129. The hardest thing about it for me was losing the weight. In those days in high school wrestling, you could use a rubber suit, or go to the steam room, which in hindsight was probably pretty stupid. But I did, because I loved it and I was determined to come down in weight as much as I could without killing myself. I was fast and a big part of being a successful wrestler is having some speed, but you also have to have some strength and be thinking all the time. I like sports where you actually have to think. You've got to out-fox the guy; you've got to think ahead. It's not just one move, it's not just trying to escape from a hold. You have to say to yourself, "Okay, I'm going to have to think three moves ahead. If this move doesn't move work, then what am I going to put back to back on that?"

It's the same thing in business. You have to think ahead. You have to consider what the issues might be and where you might run into obstacles. In wrestling, you're not going to score points every time you try to do an escape or try to do a take-down. You have to be thinking, If that doesn't work, what's my second take-down going to be?

"HOW CAN I BE A LEADER WHEN I'M NOT IN SHAPE?"

Sports taught me how important it was to be in shape. I was captain of the team and it was an exhibition match. I had had an injury, so I wasn't in really that good of shape before I wrestled. I was ahead nine-one in points in the third period when suddenly I just ran out of steam and I got pinned. That lesson was incredibly valuable for me. I was embarrassed by it, asking myself, How can I be a leader when I'm not in shape?

I learned another lesson while playing golf in the National's small college division of the NCAA in Davenport, Iowa. I was in the first threesome teeing off, there was a fairly large crowd standing around watching us, and I was very nervous, so nervous that I just about whiffed the ball on the tee shot. Fortunately, the ball stopped just short of the little creek in front of us, which couldn't have been more than twenty yards ahead of me. The reason I missed the ball was that I'd gotten out of my routine when playing competitive golf. Usually, right before swinging, I'd go through a mental check of how I wanted my swing to be. In this case, I was thrown off by all the people in the crowd standing around watching on that first tee.

"THE DOOR'S ALWAYS OPEN."

My partner, George Roberts, and I run our company like a team. George and I run the firm, but the door's always open. We don't have a hierarchy, there's zero politics at our company. Our employees are too busy to focus on that, and a lot of that comes from my experience in sports. Nobody's going to remember that I won my golf match. They don't post that. What they post is how the team did. You can win your match, but if your team loses, you feel that loss. When we set up this company, that's exactly the way we did it; everybody is compensated on how well the team does, not how well the individual does.

★BOB KERREY★

President of the New School University
and Former Senator from Nebraska

Football

I grew up in Lincoln, Nebraska, in a house where everyone played games. There were seven of us and John, the oldest, was a genetic athlete. His body was big, he was fast, he was strong. My dad encouraged me to take part in sports, but he wasn't an athlete, and it was probably my brother I wanted to impress more than my dad.

"I'LL CONTRIBUTE TO THE UNIFORMS IF YOU'LL LET MY BOY PLAY."

In those days, we played what was called "midget ball," and I probably started playing when I was about ten years old. I remember just hoping not to be picked last. That's a fear that I had. I was never in a situation where I really hoped to be picked first, because I was small, slow, and weak. Later in life, I met the guy who was the coach of the team, and he told me that my father once went to him and said, "I'll contribute to the uniforms if you'll let my boy play." I can understand why. I don't think I was 80 pounds until I was fourteen or fifteen years old. And I had childhood asthma, which probably kept my size down. The onset of the symptoms usually began around Labor Day, and I'd start having difficulty breathing. Of course, that's when football begins, and it made it very difficult to put on weight, which is what we were all trying to do. I even did the Charles Atlas dynamic tension system to try to build up my body, not that it particularly worked. I was listed on the roster as being 156 or 160 pounds, but I really wasn't that heavy.

"I'VE GOT TO GO BACK AND FIX THIS."

I played on the sophomore team, and I played on the junior varsity team in my junior year, but I didn't start. I made the varsity roster my senior year, as center and linebacker. My expectation was that my senior year, since I'd watched all these other centers move on, I would be the starting center. I worked all summer long, making the long snaps for punts and such. I remember it was a particularly bad asthma season. And then, on Friday, the last day of practice, the big moment came when the roster was put up on the board for the opening game and my name wasn't there.

I was crying as I got on my bicycle and I headed home to tell my father that I wasn't going to be playing football anymore. But as I rode home, I started to think about it and realized that I didn't know whether it was going to be harder to face my father or my coach. I decided it was my father, so I said to myself, "I've got to go back and fix this." I turned around, went back and confronted the coach directly. He said, "Don't quit. Hang in there, and I'm sure you'll get a chance to play." As luck would have it, in the opening game, the kid who was playing center had a bad day, and I started every game afterward.

That was a very important moment for me, because it taught me a lot about myself. It's not that I thought I'd ever go any further athletically than I did. I never thought I was going to be walking into Memorial Stadium, other than maybe as someone selling hot dogs. It never occurred to me when I would go to the knothole section as a kid to watch the Nebraska football games that I would be playing for the team.

"THE CLOSEST I GOT TO TACKLING GAYLE SAYERS WAS A FEW MINUTES AGO, WHEN I SHOOK HIS HAND."

I did get to play against the great Gayle Sayers. It was the fall of 1960 and I was playing linebacker on my high school team. And I have to tell you, I barely touched the hem of his garment as he blew by me for two 70-yard touchdowns. We played a good game, and I think we stayed within a touchdown, but he was like a different species. He became a legend that year. He went to a track meet, won the hundred-yard dash, and set a long-jump record that stayed on the books for a long, long time. You knew you were watching something special.

We graduated the same year, and he went to the University of Kansas and I went to Nebraska. I met him a couple of years ago at a benefit. I shook his hand and when I delivered my remarks, I said, "The closest I got to tackling Gayle Sayers was a few minutes ago when I shook his hand."

"DO IT TILL IT'S DONE."

I've learned that there is a definite relationship between effort and accomplishment. I also learned that you're a lot better than the worse thing you ever did. I missed tackles on Gayle Sayers, and I got my face driven into the dirt by guys bigger than me. I went out for track and was lousy at it. They made me run the mile, because no one else would run it. Through it all, I learned to take some satisfaction in what I was doing regardless of what anybody else thought. I learned before I got into athletics from my father that whatever you're doing, you just do it the best you can, that's all you can do. And do it till it's done.

★HANNAH STORM★

Television Sportscaster

Soccer, Softball, Track and Field

My dad was a sports executive for almost the entire time I was growing up—he was commissioner of the ABA for a time—so I was always involved in sports.

My parents grew up in an era in which sports participation for girls certainly wasn't recognized as being as important as it is now. But my mom and dad were fantastic in that they always had me involved in one activity or another. But they didn't push me into it. They let me do things I thought were fun, and so I kept doing it. And that's really one of the essentials in keeping girls, in particular, involved in sports—that it be fun.

In high school in Atlanta, I was the school mascot—a wildcat. So, obviously, I was really into school pride and team spirit—that was a big deal to me. My parents were always there for games, whether I was the mascot or in a track meet. That really validated my participation in sports, and it really bled over into me participating in a lot performance type things.

"I SHOWED UP FOR THE MEET ANYWAY."

I wasn't an outstanding athlete, even though I lettered in track and field. But nevertheless, what I think I got out of it was self-esteem, and I was able to reach a comfort level with myself physically. Every week our track coach gave an award, a star for best performance of the week. It was something you could put up in the locker room, where we had the names of people and how they had scored in the meets. I remember once I was really, really sick, and I showed up on an extremely hot day in Atlanta for a track meet that didn't mean anything. It was just a nominal meet, but we needed a certain number of people there to have our team be able to qualify. I remember feeling like I wanted to throw up, but I showed up for the meet anyway. I did a terrible job. I probably jumped a foot off the ground. I went home and went to bed. I came back to school that Monday, and I had the star!

By doing that, my coach sent that *incredible* message to me: that just in showing up you could be recognized and rewarded. It's just like life, a lot of times you don't feel like doing something, you don't feel like playing the game—whatever the game is—you don't feel like going into work, you don't feel like cooking dinner again, or whatever it is, and you do it anyway. And the times when it's the most special are the times when it's the hardest for you to execute it. To me that one little story stands out, because it was a great life lesson.

I spent twenty years observing the team mentality. Rather than a physical observation, it was an observation of the psychological, and how teams would either rise to the occasion or else crumble under the pressure. I would say one of the big lessons I learned in observing teams is how to handle pressure. When teams put an enormous amount of pressure and expectation on themselves, they generally can't handle it. That's what undoes them much more than any physical limitation. I also saw how, even though people weren't necessarily best friends on a team, they could put that aside and work together. I think that's a really valuable lesson for the workplace. Even if the people you work with might come from a completely different place and a completely different background, if you work together, you can really accomplish great things. I also learned that individuals who are only worried about their individual glory can undermine a team. I think that in the workplace, one has to realize that you've got to pass the ball. You've got to work together with other people. You're not always going to be the one to shine, and that's okay. That's something that really translates exceptionally well, I think, into broadcasting.

"YOU HAVE TO RELAX A LITTLE BIT."

Another thing I've learned from participating in sports is that rather than forcing the issue, you have to relax a little bit. Stay focused, yet at the same time, stay relaxed. That's what all the good ball players do. If you look at a baseball player, they've got to sit on the bench a lot. But when they do come up to bat, they have to marshal all their energies. That's the way it is with us. We're sitting around, but when it's our turn to do the interview, we have to come to play.

I hosted four Olympics at NBC, and to me, that was the real pinnacle of achievement. I wanted to host the Olympics and parlay that into working on morning television, believe it or not. And that's exactly what happened!

The great thing about sports broadcasting is that every day brings a new challenge. Off the air and on the air, it's a huge learning curve. It's like golf: You never master the game. And I think that's what makes it so much fun.

BIDEN IS NUMBER 30.

★JOE BIDEN★

U.S. Senator from Delaware

Baseball, Football, Basketball

I have a picture of me and my dad with my first Little League team in Green Ridge, Pennsylvania. My dad was one of the coaches, and technically I was a little too young to be on the team. I can still remember that day, and how the parents all worked to get the field ready, and then it rained. I thought it was the end of the world.

I loved baseball so much I used to take my baseball glove to bed. I would rub the glove with linseed oil, put the ball in it, and then take my belt and tighten it around the ball and the glove as hard as I could to form a pocket in the glove. Then I'd take it to bed and lie on it and make sure it all got worked in. That's how important baseball was to me.

"THEY USED TO JOKE THAT I WAS LIKE SHOE LEATHER."

When I moved to Wilmington, Delaware, I played my first organized football as a halfback on the Holy Rosary eighth-grade team, and I was still playing baseball and basketball in the CYO leagues. My problem—and, as it turns out, also a godsend—was that I was always the smallest kid in the class; I grew about five inches between the end of my sophomore and junior years in high school.

I was always a good athlete in the sense that I had great hand-eye coordination. They used to joke that I was like shoe leather. You could keep beating me into the ground, but it wouldn't matter, you'd have to kill me to win. I think that's what happens when you're relatively good, you're competitive, and you're small. You just have to compete a little harder.

"WHAT SPORTS DID FOR ME WAS GIVE ME SOME SELF-CONFIDENCE."

I was always the leader, even though I was the little guy and I stuttered. I was the kid picked first or second in the pick-up games, no matter what the sport was. I guess looking back on it, the sport that was most natural to me was baseball, but the sport I cared the most about and devoted most of my time to was football.

I went to a Catholic high school in which for all four years every student had to be in a public speaking class. As a freshman and sophomore, we had to get up on Tuesday morning and do a twenty-minute presentation before the entire school. Up to the time I graduated, I was the only one exempted from that, because I stuttered so badly. What sports did for me was give me some self-confidence to make up for the embarrassment of stuttering.

Looking back, I realize that the only guys who could beat me were those who were more confident than I was. There were guys who were better than me; there were guys who were bigger than me; there were guys who were faster than me, but there wasn't anybody I played with who I ever thought that on balance was singularly superior to me in sports. So it really built my confidence that there wasn't much I couldn't do.

"MY DAD SAID, 'WHEN YOU GET KNOCKED DOWN, UNLESS YOU CAN'T WALK, GET UP. GET UP RIGHT AWAY.' "

My dad worked was a general manager for an automobile company for thirty-five years. He worked twelve hours a day. He would leave in the morning, drive us to school, come home for a quick dinner, and then go back to work and close the place up. Still, he would go out of his way to make most of my games. My dad was not a Little League baseball dad. He grew up in fairly affluent circumstances and was an equestrian. He rode in the Maryland Cup; he was a steeple chaser; he played polo. He wasn't great at it, but the sports he played were not the sports I was interested in.

When I was a halfback playing against St. Elizabeth's, I got knocked out on the field, and my father wouldn't let my mother go out there to see how I was. When I came to, they took me out of the game and my father asked, "You were knocked out, right?"

I said, "Yeah, Dad."

He said, "Well, just remember one thing son, when you get knocked down, unless you can't walk, get up. Get up right away."

That was the *only* thing I can ever remember my father talking to me about sports, because he never had the experience of playing team sports himself. But the one expression he had that pertained to sports, and everything else for that matter, was "Never complain and never explain. Never let 'em see you sweat." It was always about competing. It was not about "You have to win." My dad used to always say, "It's a helluva lot harder to be a graceful winner than a graceful loser, and I expect you to be a graceful winner." For him, it was more about *how* to play the game, rather whether I should play the game or not. My dad wouldn't compliment me, but what he would say was, "I was proud of you, you got up."

My senior year, my last game I scored four or five touchdowns. I had a great game. There was a guy who was an all-state quarterback playing for us, and we had another terrific halfback. We were all seniors and there was a little friendly rivalry in the backfield. We were probably on the twenty-five-yard line and one of the guys said, "All right, we each get a chance to run the ball one more time in our careers." The guy who gets the ball last has the best chance of scoring, right? So he turns to me and he says, "It's your ball. We're going to run a thirty-four counter."

I looked at him and said, "You're not getting the goddamn ball back!" And I ran about a seventy-yard touchdown.

Afterward, my dad got a big grin on his face, and it wasn't about the fact that I'd scored all those touchdowns. He said, "I'm proud of you, Joey. You didn't give it back."

"I DON'T WANT TO PLAY HALFBACK."

My junior year in high school, everyone assumed that I was a lead pipe cinch to be first team All-State. I'd been shifted to end from halfback because we didn't run a winged T but rather a straight T formation, and I had very soft hands. The quarterback would throw the ball to me and if it got close, I'd catch it. My senior year, we got a new coach, a real gung-ho guy. He turned out to be a great guy, but he and I didn't hit it off right away, in part because he decided that for the good of the team I ought to play halfback, because I was the best open field runner. It turned out he was right, but hell, I had my heart set on making first team All-State at end. So, I went to him after the first scrimmage and said, "I don't want to play halfback." Of course, that violated an absolute rule: "I'm the coach. I'll decide what's best for the team and you'll do exactly what that is and you won't question it." I ended up doing it, but that put us off on the wrong foot. To make a long story short, I believe we had an eight-game season, and I scored ten touchdowns, and I had an awful lot of yardage in the year. I think my combined yardage was somewhere around 1700 yards, with something like 700 yards of it on the ground.

I didn't get picked for the All-State team, which was probably the biggest disappointment I had in my life. But the guy who was chosen as coach of the team picked me as one of five players to play in the All-Star game, and he wanted to start me in the backfield. But out of stupid pride I said, "No, I have to work." That *is* my biggest regret. My foolish pride. To this day, the coach likes to tell the story to anyone who'll listen how because Biden didn't accept his offer to play in the All-Star game, and his team lost, because Mike Fay fumbled in the end zone.

The point of this story is that my father was really disappointed in me in that I let my pride get in the way of doing what he knew I loved to do and what I was asked to do. Not that my father cared whether I played or not. He thought that's not what a gentleman should do. And he was right. I disappointed him as well as myself.

"I MIGHT BE ABLE TO MAKE IT."

I was a little too small to make it in the pros, but remember, there were smaller players like Tommy McDonald for the Eagles and Frank Gifford for the Giants, so it wasn't completely out of the question. I had good speed and I had good moves, and so I actually thought, Well, you know, as a flanker-back, I might be able to make it.

But that didn't happen. In any case, playing football was inspirational for me in the sense that it made me think I could do things I never thought I could do. It taught me a lot about what was really important and what wasn't. It sounds corny, but I think of that famous expression by, I think it was Churchill, that "wars are won and lost on the playing fields of Eton." I think that's true in the sense that team sports make you realize, no matter how good you are, you cannot do it alone.

"SPORTS MAKES YOU REALIZE THAT IF YOU WORK AT SOMETHING, YOU CAN REALLY ACTUALLY GET BETTER."

I think so much of what I admire about sports is heart. It really offends me that we factor out the thing that makes sports special, the thing that allows people to be heroic. We used to do what we called "riversides," because we practiced overlooking a river and we would do sprints at the end of the day. The phrase you dreaded hearing from your coach was, "Riverside!" meaning "Back to running again!" But I think that kind of thing ought to be rewarded, because having "heart" allows you to live your life in a way that lets you stretch yourself. Sports makes you realize that if you work at something, you can really actually get better.

How many times in the middle of winter did I go outside, shovel the snow off the road, strap a flashlight to the top of the basket, and then shoot the ball? How many times do you think you stood there as a kid and shot at a basket? A million? How many times do you think you picked up a baseball? Maybe a million? How many times did you pick up a ball and throw it to a kid at the other end of your yard holding a glove? Maybe a million? Don't you think you learned how to intuitively throw the ball so you didn't have to aim it? And because you threw it a million times, you knew what force you had to throw it at to get where you wanted it to go.

I remember, on summer nights, I used to climb out my bedroom window and drop down six feet, take my basketball, and run down to the school-yard, about a mile and a half or two miles away, and, by the light of the full moon, shoot baskets for two hours, then sneak back, put the garbage can up against the house, and climb back into my bed. Think about it. Thousands of kids do that stuff! It doesn't take long to realize that if you stand there at the free-throw line, and you do it 500 times, 1000 times, 2000 times, you're going to get the job done. And that translates later into business situations.

"HUSBAND, FATHER, SON, ATHLETE."

In 1988, I was diagnosed with two cranial aneurysms. The joke among neurosurgeons is, "How do you know that someone has had an aneurysm?" The answer is, "They're on the autopsy table." I wanted to talk to my boys, who were then in high school and a freshman in college, before they took me down. I was trying to be light-hearted about it, and tell them what I expected of them, and I said, "Look guys, if I die . . ."

They said, "Dad, don't say that."

I said, "If I die, I don't want any of this senator stuff and chairman stuff on my tombstone. I just want four things on the tombstone: husband, father, son, athlete.

FLIGHT 93

AFTER THE 9/11 ATTACKS ON THE WORLD TRADE CENTER AND THE PENTAGON, I COULD NOT PICTURE A DAY WHEN I COULD READ SPORTS THE SAME WAY AGAIN. THE METS PLAYOFF RUN, YANKEE GREATNESS, TYSON ESCAPADES, WHO CARED?

LEAVE IT TO RICK REILLY OF <u>SPORTS ILLUSTRATED</u> TO BRING ME BACK TO EARTH. WHEN HE RESEARCHED THE BACKGROUND OF THE FOUR LEADERS OF THE HEROIC STRUGGLE TO TAKE BACK FLIGHT 93 FROM THE TERRORISTS AND SAVE THE CAPITOL BUILDING OR THE WHITE HOUSE FROM BECOMING A RAGING INFERNO, HE FOUND OUT THAT THEY ALL PLAYED, THRIVED, AND SHINED AS LEADERS IN SPORTS. I'M NOT SAYING THAT BY PLAYING RUGBY, BASEBALL, OR FOOTBALL OR BY WRESTLING, YOU COULD BECOME A HERO, BUT THEIR LOVED ONES CERTAINLY BELIEVE SPORTS PLAYED A MAJOR ROLE.

BINGHAM IS AT LEFT.

DAVE KUPIECKI on His Friend

★MARK BINGHAM★

Rugby

I met Mark in the fall of 1989 at Berkeley, while I was going through the fraternity rush system. I ended up joining because of him, and we became immediate friends.

There's a lot to say about Mark. He was someone who really made everyone feel like they were the center of attention. He was not a conceited person, he didn't blow people off. He always had time for everyone. He was completely fun-loving, in a kind of goofy way. He was just a big kid.

Actually, that's probably the first thing that would strike you about Mark: that he was big. I guess he was about 6′ 4″. But he was the kind of guy who would stick up for someone smaller. Sometimes, in college, after drinking a little too much, we might find ourselves in a confrontational situation, and when we were, he was always there for anybody who had gotten into trouble, or was going to get into a fight. He was always ready to step in there for anybody.

One thing Mark and I had in common is that both of us were about as far from silver spoon kids as could be. We were both going through school on borrowed money and we were definitely not the kind of kids who were living large. He had that sense of humility about him and even later in his life, when he was doing quite well financially, he had a real grounded sense of himself.

"HIS INTENSITY LEVEL WAS SO HIGH."

When I first met Mark, he was on the rugby team at Berkeley. He had played in high school and the coach at Berkeley really wanted him so they helped him get in through a junior college. I didn't know much about rugby.

It wasn't played in the Midwest where I grew up, and I'd never seen it played at the high school level. I started learning a little bit more about it, because Cal was a really good team, even though they hadn't won a championship yet.

I consider myself a pretty good athlete—I came to Berkeley and walked onto the soccer team. I was completely outclassed, but at least I was good enough to play on their freshman team and not get laughed off the field. I remember playing basketball with Mark on this court set up in the fraternity courtyard—and I stink at basketball, by the way—and I noted that he didn't move with the grace of a natural athlete.

I'd watched Mark play basketball, and he was pretty good but not particularly graceful, and we'd played some street hockey together, but he just kind of bumped and bruised his way through that. But when I watched him play rugby, I couldn't believe my eyes. I remember thinking, Here's this big guy, but he's a very graceful athlete. It was like he was made for the sport. He was on a field with the best players—guys who went on for the U.S. national team—and in my mind, he was the one who stood out. He might not have been the best player out there, scoring all the points, but he easily made a difference. His intensity level was so high. I'd never seen him like that; it was like watching a different person. I was awed by his fearlessness and his physicality. When you're not wearing any pads and you're diving in with your head and shoulder to tackle someone, the injuries are right there in front of you, and it was if he didn't even care about that. He never gave up. He wasn't someone I thought of as an endurance athlete—I didn't see him running up hills or waking up at 7:00 any morning to go jogging—but he didn't quit that whole game. Not for one second.

The most amazing thing about him was even though he had risen to that level of being one of the best players, he wasn't conceited about it. He didn't talk much about himself and the team. The only time he talked about his accomplishment was after they won that first title in '91. He was very proud of that.

"HE ALWAYS WANTED TO HANG OUT AFTERWARD."

Mark was an extrovert to the extreme. It was that outgoing personality that took him into PR. One of the things he really liked about rugby was the camaraderie afterwards. You know, you go out and bust each other's faces in for however long, but afterward, he loved the part of sports where everyone hangs out and goes drinking. Even when we played intramurals at the fraternity, he always wanted to hang out afterward and just shoot the breeze about the game and over-analyze it and goof on each other.

"MARK WAS UP IN THE FRONT."

I don't know everything that happened on Flight 93, but I do know that they got separated into two groups. The passengers in the main cabin were in the back, and Mark was up in the front, in the first class cabin. Both his mother and his aunt were United stewardesses, and they got him a companion pass, so he often got the upgrade to first class. When some of the other guys on the flight called their wives, they told them they were going to do something, but not Mark. He didn't say anything specific to his mom. And those of us who knew Mark know that's just the way he would have behaved, because she would have worried. He was very matter-of-fact, but that's because he was always very cool under pressure. He just said, "Hi, Mom, this is Mark Bingham."

"I CAN'T IMAGINE HE SHOWED ANY FEAR."

No one knows what actually happened up there, but I think they probably did overpower the hijackers in the cabin, and there's a lot of reason to believe that Mark was involved in it. I can't imagine he showed any fear, because I never saw him show fear in any circumstance. I've been to Hawaii with him and seen him jump off a giant cliff. He just walked right off it. I never saw the fear emotion in him.

I can imagine him springing into action—that zero-to-100 percent kind of explosion I saw from him so many times. It always used to amaze me how he'd go from calmly standing there to an explosion of action and tackle somebody. I just see him doing something like that in that situation.

"HE LIVED HIS WHOLE LIFE LARGER THAN LIFE."

Mark lived his whole life larger than life. I admired him, even envying him a little bit. He's a huge person in my life. Saying he was my best friend doesn't do that word justice. I think he had to go out like that. In a big way. That was Mark.

A lot of activities I remember about Mark revolved around athletics, whether it was tossing a ball around or going out to play basketball. It shaped him, for instance, to the extent that he didn't hold long-term grudges against people. This came, I think, from going hard on the field but then, afterward going over to your opponent and saying, "Oh, I'm sorry about that," or "Hey, I didn't mean to do that." It was the same thing in life. I knew him for ten-plus years, and there were definitely people during that time I've seen him have fallouts with, some stronger friends than others, but they always came back. They all had that sense that when it came down to it, they were friends. It was the same for him in the business world. His attitude was, "We might be two guys at two different PR firms trying to get the same client; I'm trying to win this business, and you're trying to win their business, so we're competitors; but let's go have a drink at the bar together or this great show and shoot the breeze." I'm not sure other people understood. They might say to themselves, Oh, you're the competition! I can't hang out with you. He just didn't see it that way.

LLOYD GLICK on His Son,

★JEREMY GLICK★

Judo, Lacrosse, Wrestling, Soccer

Jeremy was athletic from the time he was seven. In high school, he played lacrosse, soccer, wrestling—he was captain of the team—rugby, and of course judo.

Jeremy wanted to wrestle in college, but he wound up going to a school that didn't have a wrestling program. But he continued to do judo on his own. As a matter of fact, when he won the NCAA championship, he went to the NCAAs without a team and without a coach. And he won. It was a pretty amazing accomplishment.

Like all athletes, Jeremy learned to think under pressure, to deal with difficult situations, as well as to deal with winning and losing. We knew they were going to take action, that they were formulating a plan, because Jeremy had a half-hour conversation with his wife from the plane. He even joked. At one point, he described to Liz that they had box cutters as weapons, and he said, "Aaaa, but you know, we have our plastic knives from breakfast."

Jeremy did no less than what I would have expected of him, but I still get angry over the whole circumstance and the fact that it was unnecessary.

BEAMER IS SECOND FROM LEFT.

DOUG MACMILLAN on His Friend

★ TODD BEAMER ★

Baseball, Golf, Basketball

I met Todd on the softball field, playing for our church team. Almost immediately, we hit it off on the field and then we realized that we lived about six or seven houses apart. We became fast friends after that.

I tell everybody that I have no regrets in my life at all. But the truth is, I do have one regret, and that is that I didn't know Todd in college, because he's one of the best athletes I've ever seen. I would have liked to have seen him in his prime. When you're in your thirties and carrying an extra 20 pounds, it's a lot different from being in your twenties and being in shape.

No matter what sport we played—we also played in a basketball league together and played a lot of golf—it was very evident that Todd had tremendous athletic skills. He was a big guy, 6′, 6′ 1″, 190 pounds, and you could see how he developed as an athlete, how his different abilities transcended each sport. As a leader, he was always the one to be there to coach, to help others, to chime in with his opinion about a particular situation or play. He was very competitive. He had that kind of leadership ability where he could say, "This is what we're going to do, this is how we're going to do it, this is . . . we're going to win this thing, and let's just go do it."

A day or so after the plane went down, I was interviewed by a newspaper reporter, and he asked, "Why didn't Todd do something?"

This is what I said: "Look, this is the type of character Todd had. He would have been the type of guy to say, 'Not today, this isn't happening. This is what we're going to do, who's with me, let's get it done.'"

A couple of days later, after more of the story came out, that same reporter came over to do another interview and he asked, "How did you know that?"

I said, "Because that was Todd. That's the type of person he was." I wasn't shocked that Todd's story came out about what he did with the others on the plane. I knew that's the type of person he was and knew that's what he would be doing on that plane. Doing what was right and putting others ahead of himself.

"WE MODELED HEROIC CHOICES AFTER TODD."

I think there are a couple of different aspects as to what molded Todd's character, and I think athletics is one of those. First and foremost, of course, it was his family and his faith. But I think sports played a big role in it, too. Athletics taught him teamwork and camaraderie and discipline and motivation, and how to set goals.

We modeled heroic choices after Todd. First and foremost, he was somebody who loved other people unconditionally and was ready to take action, to make a difference and make a stand. We're trying to teach children to have that same type of character trait that Todd had. We try to teach them to understand that they're going to face adversity, but that they after to get over it. We try to teach them how to be strong, how to communicate and work well with others. These are many of the same principles that Todd learned himself on the athletic field, and that he taught in others via mentoring and teaching Sunday school and just playing with kids in the neighborhood. We're trying to impart those same type of character traits.

"HE WAS A GREAT LEADER."

There's nothing that's come to light since 9/11 that has made any different impact on my regard for Todd. The Todd I knew for that number of years is the Todd that everybody knows now. It doesn't surprise me that under that amount of stress and that amount of frustration they must have been going through on the plane, Todd never wavered from his true character. To me, that's just amazing!

I'm thrilled that that is the Todd that everybody got to see. Because he was a great leader, a great listener, a great motivator, and a great communicator. He was very quick to listen and slow to speak. He would process everything, and then very succinctly come out with what was needed, a plan to be put into place to accomplish things. He was very analytical and then from being very analytical, he would become very practical, saying "This is what you need to do."

"LEARN FROM IT, GROW FROM IT."

I'm glad I have those memories of Todd, and that I have the ability to reflect on it. I wouldn't trade that for the world. It's one thing to get on with life and not allow a tragedy even to hinder you, but there's also a lesson we can teach our kids from it. "Yes, you're going to face adversity, but it's not the end of the road, it's a stepping stone. Learn from it, grow from it. Don't forget what you went through and don't forget the memories and things you had, but use that to continue to develop as a person and to overcome."

As for me, I'm always reflecting on Todd, almost on a daily basis.

DEENA BURNETT on Her Husband,

★TOM BURNETT★

Football

Tom used to speak often about his involvement in team sports, and how it prepared him for obstacles throughout his adult life, and I have no doubt that the leadership that he learned by playing quarterback in high school and college assisted him in decisions he made on Flight 93.

He was very proud to be a team leader, to be the guy who called the plays and made the decisions on the field. He took a lot of pride in knowing that his direction affected the team and their ability to win or lose.

It's funny, Tom used to say that he'd been born in the wrong time; that he should have been a 1950s husband, because that was his mannerism. He always included me in decisions, and he would ask my opinion and wanted my input. But I always knew I could rely on his decision-making skills, that he would put in a lot of thought and research to whatever decision he made, and that it would always be the best decision, regardless of my input.

Tom was very accomplished in many areas of his life, even though he was only thirty-eight years old, so he rarely talked about what he'd accomplished in his past. He always looked forward to the future, to his next goal, to his next achievement, not back to his past achievements. He didn't really talk about what he accomplished on the football field. Many of those things, I found out through other people. He was a man who always was working toward another goal, instead of dwelling on the goals he'd already reached.

"HE WAS THE ONE WHO PUT THE PLAN TOGETHER."

Tom and I spoke from that airplane four times that morning, and most of my knowledge came from those calls, and his telling me what was going on, and my being able to hear what was going on in the background. I took notes during those phone calls, so later on I had a very accurate record of our conversations. I learned that no one on the plane knew about the World Trade Center until I told Tom over the telephone. He then shared that information with the people around him, and I could hear them in the background passing it on to the rest of the passengers and crew members. I know that Tom figured out far before I did that it was a suicide mission; he voiced that in our conversation. At that point, he began asking more questions and gathering information and analyzing it. I also know that he was the one who put the plan together to storm the cockpit. He told me that that's what he was doing. I knew he wasn't going to do it by himself—I knew him better than that—so my question to him was, "Who's going to help you?"

"There's a group of us," he said.

So I knew that there were many people involved. I also knew that he was in charge, that he was playing the role of the quarterback, as he did in everything in his life.

I remember one comment that his best friend, Keith Grossman made after Tom died. We were discussing the telephone calls, and Tom's actions, and the fact that he told me that he was putting a plan together on the plane. Keith said, "We may never know exactly what happened, but we do know that it could not be any other way than for Tom to have been the leader." I think about that often. That it could not have been any other way. That characterizes who Tom was: very much of a take-charge kind of guy, able to motivate people to do whatever he wanted or needed them to do. You never argued with him; if you did, it didn't matter, you came around to his way of thinking. He just had that ability.

"HE WAS CALMING ME THE WHOLE TIME."

He was very calm and collected. It was as if he was sitting at his desk at Thornhead, working on a project. He gave me the confidence that everything was going to be okay. His voice was the same as if he was just working. That's really the image I had in mind: He's busy. He kept his answers very short and precise, so I knew that he was thinking and didn't want to go into detail as to what was going on. That was fine with me. I knew him well enough to be able to trust him and know he was going to make a good decision.

More than once he said to me, "Don't worry, Deena, don't worry." I told him that I called his parents to let them know that the plane was hijacked and he scolded me, "Why did you worry them?"

When I found out that the plane had crashed, my first thought was, Someone didn't do what Tom told them to do. And I was angry. I thought, someone else caused this, because I know that this was not in Tom's plan. Tom didn't intend for that plane to crash. He was coming home. He was coming home to the kids and me.

"THERE WAS NO DOUBT ABOUT IT, HE WAS IN CHARGE OF WHAT WAS GOING ON."

I wanted the tapes to be released, because I wanted to hear what was going on. When they called me and told me they were going to let us hear them, I was front row, center. I stayed for every minute they would let me stay. I heard it twice. The majority of the family members only heard it once. They left. I didn't. I stayed and listened twice. I heard his voice. I heard him yelling directions. There was no doubt about it, he was in charge of what was going on.

It was very intense, but it was also wonderful to have my theory about what happened confirmed. He told me what he was doing, and yet I didn't know what those last few minutes led to. I was able to hear it for myself, and know that, yes, he took those people down the aisle, and yes, he played the quarterback. It's comforting to know that he was busy with the task at hand, instead of afraid.

"HE WANTED THEM TO PLAY ON A BOY'S TEAM."

Tom had a great deal of power in his upper body. He worked out on weights regularly, and bench pressed 300 pounds. He was very strong, considering he was just under 6′ 3″ and 205 pounds. He was a very tough guy. He had a high threshold for pain. He was one of those guys who was never absent for any reason. It didn't matter what was going on, he was mentally and physically always just right there. Nothing ever held him back.

I think the virtues Tom possessed that enabled him to do what he did on Flight 93 were instilled in him by his parents. They were certainly shaped by sports and the leadership roles that he took as a child and young adult. His leadership skills were developed over a number of years.

Tom felt so strongly about his participation in team sports that he was insistent that our children choose a sport very early on in life, so that they would have the same benefit that he had had. So after he died, that was one of the first things I did was go out and seek a sport that they could participate in at a very early age. They're five, seven, and seven, yet they've been playing soccer now for two years. And they just love it. It was Tom's idea that we sign up our twin girls for Tee-ball when they were four. There was a girl's team, but he wanted them to play on the boy's team. He thought that it would be more competitive and a better experience for them, and that boys at that age may take it more seriously than the four-year-old girls would. So on picture day for the Tee-ball league, we had 800 little boys running around in uniform with their baseball caps, and then our two little girls with red bows in their hair and their baseball uniforms. But that was just part of who he was. He wanted his children to experience what he had, and then insisted that they do it at a level that would be demanding for them.

HASTERT WITH OLYMPIC GOLD MEDALIST RULON GARDNER.

★DENNIS HASTERT★

Speaker of the U.S.
House of Representatives

Wrestling

My dad was a farm service dealer, and back then in rural areas you didn't have any athletics really until you were in high school. We had chores to do. We had a feed business, so I was on the back of a feed truck ever since I was able to climb up there. After school, I'd go home and unload a truckload of feed at night. You didn't need to lift weights.

I went to a small school. We had about 350 kids, and we were probably the smallest school in the state at that time—the mid-1950s—that wrestled. We were in the fringe of the suburbs, so we wrestled all the big schools in the state. We were just a bunch of farm kids. People didn't even know who we were, or where we came from. We were just tough kids, the ones with the odds against us, who beat all the big schools in the state and made a name for ourselves. It was a great experience for us and, naturally, it gave us a lot of self-confidence.

"THIS LITTLE, COUNTRY BUMPKIN TEAMED UP AGAINST THIS STATE-RATED TEAM."

In high school and college, I wrestled at about 185, 190 pounds. I was a heavyweight, but I was always on the smaller side. I remember in high school, we wrestled DeKalb. We were undefeated, and I think DeKalb was second in the state that year. They were a very powerful team and here was this little, country bumpkin teamed up against this state-rated team. The score was going back and forth. A couple of our good kids got beat, and one of them got pinned. It got to me, and I had to break the tie to win.

The coach was on the sidelines, very nervous, of course, and my opponent tried to do something illegal. The coach got up and yelled at the referee, and the referee told him to sit down. The coach had a handful of keys and he threw them on the floor. The key ring broke and went scattering across the floor, making a big spectacle. I thought, "Oh man, now we've got this referee ticked off at us. We've got to win this match." So I wrestled my opponent, and I pinned him. It was an enormous upset. Everybody poured onto the mat, and I turned around, and the coach was gone. Somebody asked, "Where's Coach?" We went down to the locker room and we found him there, passed out.

We were just a bunch of young kids, and there was the coach lying there and we were forty, fifty miles from home. It turned out, he was just in shock. I guess he hadn't been feeling well all night. Anyway, it was a great win, but it was a sobering experience.

In college, we were always wrestling the bigger schools, like Wisconsin, Minnesota, and Notre Dame. I always found myself wrestling a Big 10 tackle who was probably 240 pounds, so I had to rely on technique more than brawn. The idea was to finesse people as much as possible.

After graduation, I went to interview for a job at this little school that happened to be our high school rival. By the time I walked out, I was hired as the wrestling coach. They had just started their program. It was a great challenge. You take kids that had never been out on the mat before, and you build them up to being the best in the state. We had nine state champions, but I probably had fifty kids who were state place winners. It's kind of fun to go to wrestling tournaments today, because their kids are wrestling, and they're back helping with the coaching or in the stands watching. I feel very proud, because those kids are growing up or have grown up to be great citizens.

"YOU CAN'T POINT A FINGER AND BLAME SOMEBODY ELSE."

Wrestling is a lonely sport. When I was coaching, just to get people's interest, we used to black out the gym, and then we'd put on a big spotlight. So you're standing in that spotlight, all by yourself, on that mat, which really makes it kind of dramatic. But at the same time you know that you've got your whole team behind you. So even though you're out there by yourself, in the spotlight, so to speak, you've got eleven other guys who are there supporting you.

Wrestling is a one-on-one experience and if something goes wrong you can't point a finger and blame somebody else. What you do is up to you. And yet it's a team sport, because whether your team wins or loses is a result of the cumulative effect of the matches. Wrestling is a great confidence builder because it's not all about strength. You have to use your balance and skill and technique and if you do, you can overcome a lot of muscle and bulk guys, and even those who have natural ability. Basically, you can out-technique an opponent.

It all comes from practice. You drill, and you drill, and you drill, and you work, and you work, and you work. But you also have to focus. You set your goals, and you have to win one week at a time. You can't say, "We're going to go win the championship." There are a lot of intermediate steps you have take to get there. You set your jaw and go at it.

When people ask me, "What's the greatest moment you ever had in life?," I have to lie to my wife sometimes by saying, "Other than getting married . . ." But you know, winning that state championship, where we took a handful of kids down to the state tournament and we swept the tournament that year—that was probably the greatest thrill of my life.

"YOU DO ALL YOUR COACHING IN PRACTICE."

I've always said you do all your coaching in practice, and I feel it's the same way in politics. You don't do all your work on election night. You do it before. You work hard during the election season, you run a good campaign, you create good policy, and that's what you do in wrestling, or any other sport, for that matter. I didn't get up and scream and yell on the sidelines very much. When I said something, the kids understood what I was saying and they listened to me. I wasn't a constant banterer on the side of the mat. If I said, "Get up," they knew what I was talking about. If I said, "Hit it," that meant something. But I didn't say something very often. People always said I sat there on the side of the mat, and compared to other coaches, I wasn't very active. But the reason was, if you do your coaching in practice, you don't have to do it on the sidelines.

I never planned to be Speaker of the House; it was just something that happened. All of sudden people turned around to me and said, "You're going to be the next Speaker of the House." It was an honor, but then suddenly you've got a job to do, too. It's like somebody turning around and saying, "You're going to be head coach." Fine. But then you've got to perform.

"MARGE, I AM WHAT I AM."

Being the speaker is very much like being a head coach. I used to kid that the reason I left education was because I didn't want to be a principal. But that's just how I ended up: being a principal. As speaker, you're the head disciplinarian. You run the place. But you're also a head coach, trying to keep the team together. I'm afraid I even use sports analogies all the time. I remember one time Marge Roukema got up in the middle of a conference, and said, "I'm sick and tired of these sports analogies!"

I said, "Marge, I am what I am."

You have to do what you believe in and what you know. What we are doing is moving a team forward. Every day, you have a challenge, whether it's getting through the practice, or getting through a game, or getting through the championship. It's all about determination. I remember that I got a lot of criticism for keeping the floor open for two hours and fifty-one minutes while we were trying to get the Medicare vote done. But, you know, I think that was part of the tenaciousness of knowing that victory was there, we just had to be able to unlock some people, so the other side could unlock some people too. We had to keep working at it, because the victory was there, if you gave up, you didn't win.

I don't think you win at all costs. You do what you think is best. And if you think what you're trying to do is the best things for the country and the best thing for your kids and your grandkids, you try to move that agenda forward. But you have to know when to step back and let the other side win, or let some things go by once in a while too. You give everybody that shot, playing that fair and even game. That's part of good sportsmanship.

"THERE'S A GREAT CAMARADERIE THERE."

Being chosen for the Hall of Fame is very special to me, because those wrestling folks, they're really my roots, that's where I came from. I was a coach for sixteen years; I was president of the Coaches' Association; I'm involved in a national coaches group, and I came up through the ranks with a lot of those guys who are my age now. They were great friends of mine and soulmates. There's a great camaraderie there.

LOMBARDO IS AT CENTER.

★MICHELLE LOMBARDO★

Sports Illustrated's 2004
Fresh Faces Winner

Softball, Soccer, Basketball, Volleyball

When I was young, my mom and dad were always outside throwing or kicking the ball to us. My dad played softball and, while the grownups were playing, my brother and sister and friends and I used to have our own little softball games on the side. I was the pitcher.

In soccer, I was the goalie and I played on a team called the Lightnings. I liked playing goalie, because I could punch and kick the ball away, which was fun. We had a great team, a great run, which included three state cups. Somewhere around the age of ten, I also started playing basketball.

I played sports by choice. My parents weren't the types who pushed us in a certain direction. They said, "If you have fun doing sports, then play sports. If you have fun dancing and you want to take ballet, then do that." Actually, I did take ballet, but I quit. I wasn't the most graceful person. And sure, I had my Barbies to play with, but I didn't take gymnastics, which was the girlie thing to do. My heart and my passion was always playing sports.

As for what kind of soccer player I was, I did what I had to. When I had to turn it up, I could turn it up. When I needed to get the ball away, then I would do that. One of my teammate's dads always called me a gazelle, because I would view the whole field, see where the ball was coming, and if there was a way, I would sprint, sprint, sprint as fast as I could, which was pretty fast, and I would get the ball away, no matter what.

I'm not sure where all that aggression came from. Maybe it was the way I grew up. My sister was very into sports, as were my dad and my little brother, and I always played with the guys. I would play touch football on the sand down at our beach house and whiffle ball with my cousins. I didn't really care about how I looked with my feminine side, because I was playing good, being competitive, and winning.

I remember this one time I was playing softball, and I had slid into the base, and my foot smacked into the base, and I fractured my ankle. It hurt so, so much, but I stayed there for the rest of the game. I wanted to make sure my team won. But the minute the game was over, my mom drove the car onto the field, I hopped in, and she took me straight to the emergency room, and I got my cast put on. Back in the car with my mom, I started crying, because my foot was so swollen. But I was dedicated and I wanted to make sure that I stayed there until it was over. I wanted to be there to support the rest of my team.

"I THOUGHT, IF I DID IT ON THE FIELD, WHY COULDN'T I DO IT IN SCHOOL?"

I grew up being very shy and I didn't start coming out of my shell until I was fifteen. In sports, though, I was different. I was vocal, but in school, I was still a bit timid. At sixteen, I started coming out, because I started becoming more confident in myself. I thought, if I did it on the field, why couldn't I do it in school? Okay, I thought, If I can communicate on the field, then I can definitely communicate in school and in classes and not be as shy as I am.

I still am; I always will have my shy tendencies, and I always will probably be a little bit more reserved than most people, but that's me. That will always be me. But sports have gone a long way in allowing me to conquer my shyness.

When I got to high school, I thought to myself, I'm starting something new. Now I'm going to have to get used to new people and new players. I decided I'd trade in my soccer cleats, and I bought a pair of volleyball sneakers, and they've been with me ever since.

I ended up being captain of my volleyball team my senior year. I was able to show the new girls that I could be a leader and that they could trust and respect me. I was always the one who had to motivate everybody. I was the one who got everyone pumped up. It paid off, though, because as a result everyone would start getting psyched, and once you get psyched, then you start playing as a team, and you start winning.

In my sophomore year, I decided I really wanted to give volleyball more of a go, so I decided not to play basketball in the winter. In volleyball, I played with the Junior Olympics team, and I made varsity as a sophomore. I loved it so much, I started playing all year round.

I liked the intensity of soccer because there's a tremendous rush when you get a goal. You scream and yell and you get really excited. But with volleyball, it's always very close and that's a different kind of excitement. You have to get the bump right, you have to get the spike right, every single thing has to be perfect. But when you base with a serve, or when you spike them and they do not even touch it, it's an awesome feeling.

"WE WOULD PAY AT PRACTICE THE NEXT DAY."

Our coach treated us tough. He was strict, because he knew he had to have respect from us or else we wouldn't pay him the attention he needed in order to get everyone focused. We were a good team, but sometimes we wouldn't give it our all. That might happen when we were playing a team that wasn't as good as we were. The attitude sometimes was, "Why should we kill them; that would be horrible." Coach would get so upset at us and, if we didn't bump the ball right, or if we missed serves. We would pay at practice the next day He might have us get ten serves in a row in different positions on the court, just to make sure that we were going to do it right next time.

"THEY WERE LOOKING FOR SOMEONE WITH AN ATHLETIC BACKGROUND."

A friend of the family saw an ad in *Sports Illustrated,* saying that they were looking for a fresh face for the magazine and thought I might be the one. She got in touch with my mom, and they checked it out on the Internet and found they were looking for someone with an athletic background. My senior year in high school, I'd won Best Physique, so I guess everybody thought I had a good "bod." "Michelle," they said, "we think this is perfect for you."

Anyway, I sent *Sports Illustrated* an application and pictures that one of my photographer friends had taken of me to send to a modeling agency. I guess they looked at the photos and the bodies and the sports angle and then they combined it all. Usually, for those things, people go around saying, "Oh, vote for me for this, and vote for me for that." For me, it was, "I don't care if I win." They ended up choosing forty from about 2,700 that sent in applications. Then they took ten of us to four different locations for the ADP Volleyball tournament, which was very cool for me to go there. Each week, they narrowed it down until they had four left, then two. Then I was the last one left standing.

I'm glad that they chose me, but it could've been somebody else. I don't have to win, because I don't want to set myself up for disappointment. Don't get me wrong, I want to win, and I will try my hardest to win, but if somebody else is having a bad day, and they're not taking the game to the next level, and if I've tried everything I can do to get them into the mind-set to play to win and to forget about anything else, and if I failed, there's nothing more I can do. As long as I know I've tried my hardest, and we as a team have tried our hardest, and if we played a great, great game, and they just happened to win by one goal or two points on the volleyball court, I won't be upset. I'm not going to go home and cry. There's no crying in sports anyway.

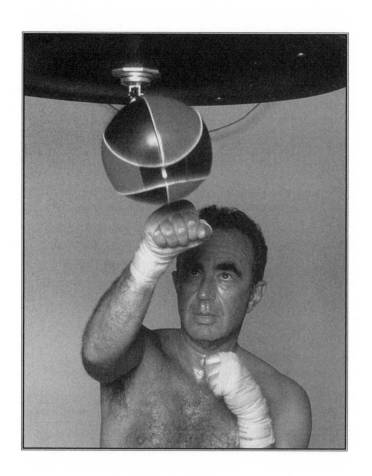

★ROBERT SHAPIRO★

Attorney

Baseball, Basketball, Boxing

I grew up in what is now referred to as West Los Angeles, which was, at the time, probably on the fringes of a middle-class neighborhood, filled with working families. I was the smallest person of 700 people that graduated in my junior high school. When I got into high school, I tried C-level sports and was fair, but I was very, very small. I was actually concerned about my growth pattern. I was so small, in fact, that I played basketball on the same team with all the "midgets." Fortunately, I had a growth spurt after I left high school and by my second year in college, I was about 5' 8" and weighed about 145 to 150 pounds, and at that point I was able to play intramural football.

I loved sports, and I was very competitive, but I just didn't have what it took, either because of size, or ability, to do anything other than play for fun. It wasn't even that I was not the best; I wasn't even close. It was disappointing, because my father was an athlete; he was an All-State basketball player and he played competitive softball well into his seventies. It was something I could never do on his level, or even come close to it. But I was very aggressive, very competitive, and despite my limited ability, I was determined to play and I played over my head.

"AT FORTY-SOME ODD YEARS OF AGE, I STARTED FOOLING AROUND WITH THE BAG."

I *love* to box.

Boxing was always something I liked to watch. My father was an avid boxing fan, so we'd go to the Olympic Auditorium, or Hollywood Legions Stadium, where they had bouts between local fighters, mostly Hispanic.

I started working out at a local health club about fifteen years ago, and they put a speed bag up on the roof. I always thought one of the most intriguing things in sports was to see a boxer do two things: skip rope, and to hit the swing bag. I thought those things took incredible ability, tremendous concentration, and speed. One day, at forty-some odd years of age, I started fooling around with the bag. I'm a very compulsive person and I was determined to teach myself how to do it right. I finally got it down to where I could hit it fairly well. They started a boxing class and I started taking that. Six people signed up, three guys and three women. They had very mediocre equipment, the kind you buy at any sports outlet—a speed bag hanging on one end, a heavy bag hanging on the other end. They also had a bicycle and a jump rope. With that, they created a little circuit. You'd jump rope for three minutes, you'd go ride the bike for three minutes, you'd go hit the heavy bag for three minutes, you'd hit the speed bag for three minutes, then you'd stand next to one of the other students and work on very basic moves, with no contact. Eventually, the class ended, because everyone else dropped out. I was the only one left and they weren't going to have three people train me, so I hired the head trainer to come to my house. This guy had boxed in the Marines, and he was a tough, young kid—a real vigorous trainer. I went out to a sporting goods store and bought the make-shift stuff—a heavy bag and a commercial speed bag that wasn't stable at all—and I started working out.

I would literally crawl back into the house after working out in the garage. I just wouldn't give up. I'd complete every round, no matter how lousy I was doing, I just wouldn't stop and say, "You know what, I can't finish this."

After a while, I was introduced to Michael Moorer, who was training for a fight in Los Angeles at the Wild Card Boxing Club, a down-and-dirty makeshift gym above a Laundromat on Hollywood and Vine. This is not a dancing gym. It's got a ring, three or four speed bags, three or four heavy bags, a jump rope platform, and a shower that is worse than any shower you'd find in a flop house. But world-class boxers were working out there, and I met Freddy Roach, who was working with Mike Tyson, and I told him I'd been boxing for a while. I said, "I'd like to work out here."

He said, "Sure. C'mon in."

I started going there four times a week and wound up training side by side with some really good boxers, trying to do what they were doing in training, though obviously I wasn't anywhere close to their ability. If they did 500 sit-ups, I'd do 500 sit-ups. I just worked, worked, worked myself to the point where I was doing a ten-round workout. I'd do shadow boxing for a couple rounds, hit the bag for a couple of rounds, then hit the focus mitts, but no sparring.

But I really wanted to work on technique, and they don't teach you technique at the gym. They expect that you know how to box when you walk in there. They ring the bell, and it's three minutes on, thirty seconds off. Everything stops, and everything starts. It's boom, boom, boom, boom, boom.

"IS THAT PIECE-OF-CRAP LAWYER HERE YET?"

After I had been working out there for maybe six months, I ran into Jackie Kallen, who introduced herself to me outside a restaurant. She said, "I understand you're a boxing fan and that you like to work out."

I said, "Yeah."

She said, "How would you like to come work out with James Toney, World Champion?"

I said, "I would love to."

She said, "Well, here's my card. During the week it's a little hectic, but Saturdays we have a closed session, it's very quiet, and if you'd like to come out . . ."

I called her on a Friday night and said, "I want to come down Saturday." I went with my wife and youngest son to a gym that Mickey Rourke owned at the time in Hollywood. It was a closed session and Toney was in the ring, training for a Super Middleweight Championship fight in three or four weeks. We walk into the gym, and he's there sparring, just beating the crap out of this guy that he's in the ring with. He was very intimidating in his language—he talks trash to everyone. Jackie must have told him I was coming, and when he spotted me he starts yelling at me in some very inappropriate language. Stuff like, "Is that piece-of-crap lawyer here yet? I'm going to kick the shit out of him; I can't stand lawyers."

I came with my bag and I had my head gear and belt and gloves and I asked, "Where do I go change?" Jackie pointed me to the dressing room.

I came back and she said, "Okay, I'll wrap you up." So she wrapped my hands with gauze, which was the first time I ever had my hands professionally wrapped. "You know," she said, "James is really high strung, and it's just before a championship fight, so I don't think it's a good idea to get in the ring with him, but I've got a couple of really good fighters here who will give you a real nice workout."

Like an idiot, I said, "I came to spar with the champ, so I'm going to spar with the champ."

She said, "Okay, go over there and work with Tom Patti," who had been Mike Tyson's trainer. He saw that I had basic skills, but when I say "basic," I mean, really basic skills.

He said, "So long as you keep your hands in front of your face . . . keep your hands up . . . you should be fine."

My wife was sitting next to James's mother—who is younger than my wife—and she said, "You know, I love my son, but he is very, very erratic, and it really is not a good idea for your husband to go in the ring with him."

My wife said, "You know what, I'm sure you're right, but he's going to do what he's going to do. I just know him too well."

And so, boom, I jump in the ring with James Toney. Tom Patti is in my corner, and Toney had another guy in his corner. The bell rang and we came out. For some reason, I think it was because I believed he really wouldn't hurt me, I wasn't scared. And remember, this was the first time I'd really sparred with a serious fighter, and he was hitting me with taps that are killing me. I mean, *killing* me. And I'm fighting back, and I'm throwing a few combinations in. He'd say, "Yeah, good combination." But he had got his game face on, and he looked mean as hell. He was staring me down, and I was trying to throw some jabs and some combinations.

The first round ended and I was ready to die. I was exhausted. I couldn't hold my hands up, I'd been hit in the stomach, and I was out of breath. He said, "One more round! You did much better than I thought. One more round." So I went back to my corner, and Patti threw water on me, and he said, "You know, you're doing pretty good. Take in some deep breaths and just keep relaxing, and keep your hands up. You're doing fine." The bell rang and just as I turned around, Toney, who had tiptoed across the ring, hit me with a right hand, right on the jaw. It stunned me. I'm sure it was a tap from him, but to me, it was like getting hit by a crane. Spontaneously, I turned around and I caught him with an uppercut, probably the luckiest punch anybody would ever throw, because if he doesn't want to be hit, you can't hit him. But he was standing flat-footed, because he sneaked around the ring, and was what he would call playing. I could see I stunned him, though not to any degree where he would be hurt. He was more surprised that I actually would land right on his chin.

Anyway, we got into a clinch, and he spit out his mouthpiece, and he bit me on the shoulder, to the point where I had blood and teeth marks. Ordinarily, he would have just thrown two or three punches, and I would not be seen on the face of the earth again, but rather than do that, he let me know who was the boss.

We finished the round, and then, just like fighters do, we embraced, and he said, "I have to tell you something. I only hope I'm in the shape you're in when I'm your age. And number two, I've been in the ring with a lot of guys, but I have never seen anybody walk in and not have fear the way you did."

I didn't move for about two weeks after that. I packed myself in ice. I was bruised, I was sore, and this is just from taps. But I learned something important from that that experience. I learned that if you don't show any fear, you're going to get a lot of respect.

"YOU HAVE TO FOCUS TOTALLY."

I used to have a terrible temper, but when I have the gloves on, I am much calmer, as are most fighters. Outside of the ring, there is no chance I'd ever get into a fight with anybody. Zero.

When you're in the ring, there are two things you have to remember. Number one, you have to focus totally. You stop focusing, and you're in big trouble. Number two, you have to stay relaxed. You cannot box if you're not relaxed. The minute you tighten up and have tension, you get out of breath, you don't breath properly, and you run out of energy easily.

The other thing about boxing is that it's very personal. It's an individual, not a team sport. It's pretty similar to what I do in the courtroom, but just in an athletic way. You have to be focused, you have to be determined, you have to be prepared.

And you can't be scared. All those things go into being a trial lawyer, and they're the same things that go into being a boxer.

I think the main thing for me is desire: desire to do better than I did the day before. I always set goals for myself and try to achieve them. I'm going to spar tomorrow, and I'm saying to myself, "You know what, I sparred last week four rounds, but I'm going to go five rounds tomorrow."

STEINFELD IS NUMBER 52.

★JAKE STEINFELD★

Personal Trainer and
Fitness Entrepreneur

Bodybuilding, Basketball

I was as the oldest of four sons, in a Jewish family, so I felt I could do no wrong. I tried out for my eighth-grade basketball team with no basketball experience, but my mother thought I was Willis Reed. Far from it. I was a fat kid with a bad stutter. After the tryouts, I just assumed that I'd made the team. The next day, we all went to the gym wall to see the posted team of the Baldwin Bruins, and my name wasn't on the list. I thought it was a joke. I literally turned this white piece of paper upside down to look to see if my name was on the back side. It wasn't. And I was devastated.

A girl I knew named Maureen Gillespie gave me a poem called "Don't Quit," and to this day it's a poem I live by, because basically it taught me that success is failure turned inside out. It was at that moment, when Maureen gave me that poem, that I said to myself that I was never going fail again.

That whole summer, I practiced, and I practiced, and I practiced. My father put up a basketball court in our backyard. I loved my train set, but we took the trains off this cardboard surface, and my father made a basketball backboard, attached a rim to it, and hung it up in the backyard. It was only eight feet tall. There was no right side, because the overhang of the house came over. That's always been my excuse as to why I have no right hand, because I could never take a shot from the right side. But my shot from the corner was always cool. I had my little brothers rebound for me all summer. I ended up making the team in ninth grade.

"WHATEVER YOU DO, DON'T TOUCH THE BALL."

The first game against Freeport I was tenth man on a ten-man team, and there was about a minute left to go in the fourth quarter. The two big guys—Mitchell Burns and Barry Field, who we called "Bone"—collided with each other. I was at the end of the bench. I had an afro, man, I mean a really great-looking afro for a Jew, and I had braces, and I had this yes-no mustache, and these yes-no sideburns, hair here, no hair there . . . it was a great look. So here I was with a minute to go, our two main guys collide, two other guys were in foul trouble, and my coach looks down the bench and says, "All right, Steinfeld, come over here. Whatever you do, don't touch the ball."

Freeport, which was an all African American school, was our arch rivals. We were down by one point and they were pressing us. The coach threw me all the way down to the other side of the court. "Don't go anywhere near the ball," he reminded me. So they're pressing us, and this guy named Mike Mailer takes the ball out, and he heaves it past half court to me. I get the ball and all I'm thinking about is the coach saying, "Don't touch the ball." But I've got the ball, and everyone is screaming "Shoot!" I turned to shoot, and this guy from Freeport fouls me. So I get two shots. They call a timeout and we get into a huddle and the coach is slapping me in the face, saying, "Take your time, take your time." (Afterward, he told me, "Jake, you were so white. You had no color in your face—that's why I was slapping you.") I got to the foul line. I took the underhand shot, like Rick Barry used to. First shot, I swish it. Tie game. They call a timeout again, and I'm back in the huddle, and the coach sat me down and said, "Take your time." I got back up to the free-throw line, and these two big, black kids from Freeport were looking at me, going, "We're going to kick your ass." The ref gives me the ball, I hit the foul shot with one second on the clock, and we won the game, 36–35.

In school the next morning, my name was announced over the loudspeaker, and from then on I started every game in ninth grade. I played high school basketball and was made captain of the team as a senior. But it was at that moment that changed my life from failure to success. It was what inspired me to start to lift weights, because that eighth-grade summer my father bought me a set of weights that I'd never touched.

"COME ON, LET'S DO SOME BENCH PRESSING."

Basketball was important, but it was the weights that truly changed my life. I was shooting around one summer and my father called me outside to the backyard. He had a bench press set up with this barbell and he said, "Come on, let's do some bench pressing."

I said, "Nah, this is not for me, Dad." He was the kind of guy who would ask you to do something once, and that was it, he'd never ask again. He kept the weights out there all summer. I never touched them once. Come fall, we had to put the weights back into the house, in the laundry room. I was living downstairs in the basement and I had my black light posters and my Jimi Hendrix and Pink Floyd posters hanging up all over.

I was looking out from my bedroom one night and I saw the weights sticking out of the laundry room. I walked into the laundry room, grabbed this easy curl bar, brought it into my bedroom, put it on top of the ottoman, took this little skinny mirror that I had in the bathroom, and put it on top of the ottoman. I put on a tank top with my stomach hanging over my underpants, and I cued up a Frank Sinatra album I loved, put on the headsets, and I stood in the mirror doing my bicep curls in front of 50,000 screaming fans at Madison Square Garden—at least that's what I visualized. And that's how it began.

I was always the fat kid in school, with a bad stutter, who was the funny guy. Suddenly people, especially the girls, recognized that something was different about me. "Steinfeld, you got biceps." When you're in eighth, ninth grade and that starts happening, that's a big deal. What's interesting was that not only did the weights build my body, but they started to build my self-esteem and my confidence.

The interesting thing about weight training is that it's you versus this inanimate object, a dumbbell, or a 45-pound plate, or 415 pounds on a bench press. You make yourself pick up that weight or do ten extra repetitions. I would visualize accomplishing things way past the ten repetitions, or the twenty reps or the hundred reps. From the beginning, I would say something like, "Okay, if I do twenty-five curls, I'm going to be able to go out with Barbara."

I don't think I'd be exaggerating to say that the essence of who I am today is a result of the weight training. It's made me and given me the life that I have.

"I'M PUTTING MY HEAD IN THE OVEN."

I'll never forget the day I made up my mind that I was going to pursue bodybuilding as a career. It was 1977. Now remember, I was the oldest son in a Jewish family. And Jews and bodybuilders don't mix, kind of like milk and meat or socks with sandals. I'll never forget picking up the phone that day and calling my mom, and her immediate reaction to my call was, "It's so great to hear from you. How's poli-sci? How's your English class?"

I said, "Ma, look, I gotta talk to you for a second."

She said, "What's going on?"

I said, "Listen, I'm going to go to California to pursue bodybuilding."

There was silence on the phone. All of a sudden she says, "Herbie, pick up the phone and talk to your kid. I'm putting my head in the oven."

After all, from her point of view, this is what it might be like. My mom might be sitting around the Mah-Jongg table and she would hear conversation like, "Oh, what is your son doing?"

"Oh, my son's at Harvard, and my son's at Yale, and Joy, what's your son do?"

And she'd say, "Oh, he's a bodybuilder. He wears these small posing trunks."

"Oh, my, sorry to hear that, Joy."

Ultimately, my parents said, "Look, you have a dream, you want to pursue it. Obviously, we'd love for you to make the right move, and we would have hoped that you had stayed in college, but we see this is not your path, so go pursue your dream." And of course, my mother had to add: "But don't worry, your bed is made, and when you get this off your chest, if you get this out of your system, you'll come home."

I'll never forget entering the Mr. Southern California contest. I read the magazines, and everybody said eat eighteen eggs and twenty-four chickens a day, and you too could become Mr. America. I came in second place; the guy that beat me was probably on steroids. I got a plaque the size of a stamp.

During that time, I was bouncing in bars at night and then I'd go to the gym early in the morning, then go home to sleep, then roll out of bed and sit in the sun. Ah, the life of a bodybuilder—it's the life of a muscle head.

"I THINK I CAN HELP YOU OUT."

One day this gal, who was getting ready to do a Club Med commercial, said to me, "You know, Jake, I see you out here every day, I like you, but I don't want to look like you. Could you help me out?" This was late 1979, at the time when women were intimidated by using weights, because they thought they were going to get big muscles. She said, "I have to wear a bikini. I have four weeks, I'm shooting this commercial."

This gal looked pretty damn good to begin with, but she needed some self-esteem and confidence building, so she could put this bikini on in front of a hundred people. I said, "I think I can help you out."

She said, "Terrific. How much is it going to cost.?"

I said, "Just give me gas money." She asked me to come over to her boyfriend's house and do the workout there.

I drive to this house, and this guy answers the door. Turns out to be this very big film director, and I look at this guy thinking, "Mmmm, this guy's a pretty heavyset guy, too. This guy could use a workout also."

She got in shape. They started going to parties, people started saying, "My goodness, you look great, what are you doing?"

She would say, "This guy Jake comes to our house. He has a broomstick, a towel, and a chair"—it's what I improvised with, during a twenty-minute workout—"and it's a lot of fun." Suddenly, people were after me to train them. It became this mystique of, "Who is this guy? Get him!" I was getting phone calls from Steven Spielberg, Harrison Ford, Bette Midler, Warren Beatty, Barbra Streisand, Madonna, the late Steve Ross, George Lucas. I mean, it was insane.

What I learned from all this, and what made me the person I am today, is that these people were no different from you or me. The only difference was, they had a dream, and they never quit on their dream. I said to myself, "I might never direct *Raiders of the Lost Ark*," but I'm going to have my own successes, and it goes way back to the eighth grade getting cut, your friends telling you that you can't do it, and you telling yourself that you can.

EMME IS THIRD FROM RIGHT.

★EMME★

Model, Author, Television Host

Rowing

I grew up in Saudi Arabia until I was seven, and as you can imagine, there isn't a lot to do there for kids. I was more athletic than my parents. My stepfather was more like a couch coach: "Do what I say, not what I do." My mom would say to me things like, "Can you give me lessons on how to dance?" Or, "Can you show me how to run?"

In 1978, we moved to Connecticut and I got into softball and volleyball in junior high.

One of my early adult mentors was my PE teacher, Mrs. Lillian Papp. She'd say, "Melissa"—that's my birth name—"why don't you go run this, try that, do this." I was very athletic, so whatever it was, it would usually come very easily to me and it was always a lot of fun.

Later, when I attended private school in ninth grade, I thought, "I want to be with a kickin' basketball team." But I was a little disillusioned that the team wasn't as serious about the game as my Bears team in Saudi Arabia was. I remember doing warm-ups, and some of the girls were complaining about it, too.

"IN THAT MOMENT, EVERYTHING CHANGED FOR ME."

One day, when I was really down because of the lack of basketball competition, I was sitting by the pond watching people rowing single shells. They were rowing around like idiots, with someone yelling at them. I said to myself, "What is this sport?"

Reverend Owen came up to me and said, "I want you to get into one of these shells."

I said, "I've never even been in a boat before."

He said, "You're tall, you look like you're athletic, and I would really love for you to get in and give it a try."

I got into that boat, and it tipped over. I got so angry about it that in that moment everything changed for me. I had never been challenged like that before, and I said, "I'm going to get in this boat, and I'm going to try and make a couple of strokes across the water."

It took all afternoon, but after a while, I was able to go back and forth across the water several times and, probably just because they needed bodies, they put me on the varsity. Of course, it didn't go so smoothly, since I'd never rowed before. I caught what they call "crabs," which is when you're rowing with one oar and you just ever so slightly over-rotate it, which can cause you to be lifted completely out of the holding and you can be thrown from the boat. I was known to be the one that would catch a crab, and almost break a boat in half.

After I while, I told myself, "Okay, I've really got to get my technique down." So I started getting some extra help in technique from our coach, Hart Perry, who was known for introducing new talent into the college system and making them elite rowers. He said to me early on, "If you continue working on your technique, you could get a full athletic scholarship to college."

That stuck in the back of my head, and I put more energy into the rowing. And I was admitted on scholarship to Syracuse University, where I wanted to go because they had a wonderful communications program.

"I DIDN'T KNOW IF I COULD ROW ANOTHER STROKE."

Rowing is pretty gruesome. It sometimes seems slave-like, especially when you're doing winter workouts when the ice is frozen. You're sweating and you're rowing, and you're rowing, and you're getting blisters, and your butt gets blisters, and your feet get blisters.

I was bench-pressing 165 pounds, my actual weight at the time, and I was leg pressing something like 450 pounds. I was so ripped. I was in the best shape I'll ever be. But I don't want to ever be in that kind of shape again, because it took so much dedication. Getting up at 5:30 in the morning, even on the weekends, then rowing six days a week. But it paid off, because I was asked to be part of the Olympic trial team in 1984.

I had been rowing for more than three years at that point, and I was tired. I didn't know if I could row another stroke. I was dying to just take the summer and work on an internship. So I sat there, and I asked myself, What is my future? Is my future this internship, so that I can get the next job after that, or is my future in rowing? And who pays you for rowing?

It was very, very hard decision, but I took the internship. I worked for the summer as an intern for free and learned about the newsroom, where I got the bug of doing the sports thing.

What I took from my rowing experience is that there is nothing that competes with winning a race, getting that gold or that trophy. It's the most incredible experience. We would work ourselves into a tizzy, running up the Carrier Dome stairs, for instance. Recently, I went back to Syracuse to give the commencement speech for the School of Visual Performance, and I was standing there in the Dome doing the school's commencement chat, and I told them, "Do you know that I have run every single step in this place for workouts! Not just once! I know each one of these stairs personally." I don't know if they believed me, but it doesn't really matter. I know that I did it. It's all part of building character when you're trying to become the highest-performing athlete. The amount of working out we did was not only to build us up physically, but to get our heads ready. If there was choppy water, if there was clear water, if it was raining like hell, whatever was going on, we had to put ourselves into that element and train ourselves to get through it. Rowing is a 90 percent mental game and a 10 percent physical game.

There's nothing better than winning, but you can't expect to win every single race, and that was a very important lesson for me, because it laid the foundation to what business is about. Whether it's an entrepreneurial business or entertainment, you're not going to win every audition; you're not going to win in every situation. In my career, I was considered beautiful, but I was curvy. When I got into the modeling industry, it was dog-eat-dog, and I learned that if I didn't look at it as a business, I'd be eaten alive.

I got into modeling by chance, because my girlfriend's brother was dating a woman who was considered a full-figured model. I looked at her and I said to myself, "She's the most average-looking person I have ever seen." She was a size twelve, and I was a size twelve at the time. When I walked into Ford Models, they looked at me and said, "You're perfect. You're 5' 11", you're size twelve to fourteen. If you were a fourteen, though, it would be better."

"I NEED TO BE NICE AND FIT FOR MY BODY TYPE AND TREAT MY CURVES WITH RESPECT."

Self-esteem was built on knowing what I was capable of as being an athlete. I have a gym in my house, and I do very light weights. I no longer try to build muscle, because I'm not a competing athlete. I need to be nice and fit for my body type and treat my curves with respect because they've been very good to me. I don't need to shrink it to anything that's not me.

I had such joy and success in athletics that it overshadowed some of the other stuff that was going on in my life. I was successful at it and that helped me get over the humps, like dieting and body judgment. When I was on the playing field, when I was on the track, when I was in the basketball arena, it was my game; it was my time to succeed and be able to figure out a way to win. It was very, very, very important for me and my self-esteem to have something in my life that was very positive. When I talk to kids for the pro bono work that I do, I always encourage them, I say, "I don't care what it is, you've got to find something that you're good at now."

You need to have something to hang your hat on and feel good about.

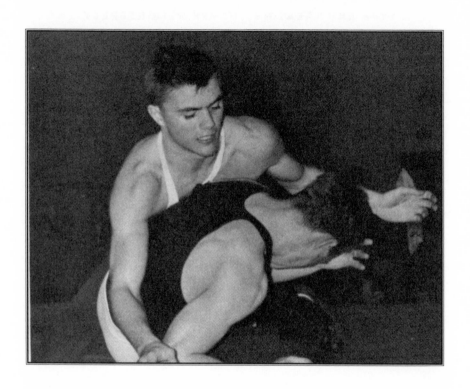

★JOHN IRVING★

Author

Wrestling

I first walked into the wrestling room when I was fourteen years old, and I first started keeping a journal at the same time, so the coincidence of wanting to be a writer and wanting to wrestle was almost simultaneous.

From the moment I set foot in that wrestling room, I thought, "Oh, this means it doesn't matter how big I am. If I'm a heavyweight, I wrestle heavyweight; if I'm 135 pounds, I'll wrestle at 135 pounds. There are no disadvantages here; it's all you."

When I entered the freshman class at Exeter in 1955, I was as big as most kids: 5′ 8″ and 140 pounds. When I graduated, I was still 5′ 8″ and I weighed 131 pounds. I was a small kid who liked contact, but it was absurd to think that you could play at football at 131 pounds. I was fortunate that I grew up in a community where there was a wrestling program.

"I THINK I WAS A KID IN NEED OF DISCIPLINE."

Wrestling was my first success, the first thing that confirmed that I could be good at anything. In wrestling, I found my niche, my calling—and my calling was to stay small. The thing about wrestling, like boxing, is that you're not only devoting yourself to the sport or to the workout, you're also devoting yourself to the diet. You learn how to eat or how not to eat.

I think I was a kid in need of discipline. I think I was looking for a mentor, someone to say, "Do this, do that." And in that regard, devoting yourself to wrestling, or tennis, or skiing, or dance, or to a musical instrument is a longing to be disciplined for a purpose. It's not simply about being told, "Pick up your plate and take it to the sink." There's a reason for what you're doing. If you put in the time, you're going to get something out of it. The idea was, "Yeah, this is tough, and there doesn't look like there's any reward, but if I apply myself there will be rewards later on." I think every kid who accepts the discipline to participate in a sport gains confidence in other things he or she does. In other words, if you work your ass off—if you do these boring, repetitive things—usually something gratifying comes from it.

"THE CONFIDENCE I GAINED FROM WRESTLING GAVE ME AN ADVANTAGE AS A WRITER."

Wrestling isn't a quick study. There are some illogical things about it that you have to learn. It's not a straightforward game, like a shot in basketball or a pass in football. I was a couple of years into it, probably sixteen or seventeen, before I really had a feel for it. But when you get it, it's a wonderful feeling. You not only understand how your body works, but you understand how everybody else's body works in juxtaposition to you.

Individual sports are those that interest me the most. I love tennis. I'm just a hack tennis player, though—probably because I wrestled most of my life, which is why I'm not good at any other sport. I love watching tennis, and I play pretty regularly, because mentally and psychologically, it's a one-on-one sport. It's life in a microcosm. A tennis match takes place over a long period of time, you can see people defeating themselves psychologically. In a wrestling match, it happens much quicker. You've got seven minutes to either defeat yourself or not defeat yourself.

What's interesting about individual sports is that your mind often gives out before your body does. I'm fascinated by that, because I think the discipline I learned from wrestling, the experience I had from wrestling, the confidence I gained from wrestling, gave me an advantage as a writer. It's a feeling that I can go back to a manuscript, not once, not twice, not five times, but ten or twenty or thirty times. I have a no-quit attitude about how many times you can do something, because you can always make it better. I didn't get that from English class. I didn't get that from creative writing. I got that from how many times I had to practice the outside single leg takedown; how many times I had to practice the duck-under. I drilled those maneuvers until they became second nature. And what possible use do I have for that experience now at my age of sixty-two? Well, I'll tell you, it is that I can read the same sentence forty times. I can read a 1,600-page manuscript ten times. I can do that, and I don't know how many of my fellow writers can.

"YOU'LL ALWAYS MEET SOMEONE WHO'S BETTER."

Wrestling gives you the recognition that you're not as good as you think you are. Every sport confronts you with that because—I don't care what you're doing—you'll always meet someone who's better, someone who will show you that you're not as good as you think you are. That's a healthy thing to know, especially if you're in a discipline where you don't have any monitors—where maybe your editor is being too kind, your wife is being too kind, or your best friend is doing you a favor, which is not really a favor at all. You have to be able to say to yourself, "This is only the first, the second, the tenth time I've done this and I'm only very good at it, if I've done it sixteen, seventeen, eighteen times."

In wrestling, you may have practiced a move a hundred times and then, after you've done it a hundred times, you might find out that you couldn't do it at all. It was not your move. Or, after practicing the move a hundred times, you gain a growing confidence that, Well, maybe in a competition, I could try this. Maybe I could add it to my repertoire. I like that kind of scrutiny. It's been extremely beneficial to me to say that at the moment of inspiration, the moment when you've thought of this metaphor, this idea, this simile, this sentence, to say, "Forget it. It's bull." It's not good until you've read it a hundred times, and you still think it's good.

"I ALWAYS FELT MORE AT
HOME IN A HOSTILE PLACE."

My mother sometimes came to watch my matches. You like the support, but the truth is, after a while, the audience, the crowd, just kind of disappears. You lose that sense of who's there very quickly, because it's a distraction. I always felt more at home in a hostile place. I always loved the sound of silence when you were in somebody else's house, when you scored the takedown, or you were racking up points on somebody, and *nobody* was clapping. I found that very gratifying. Sure it was great to have the crowd yelling for you, it was exciting, but it was nowhere as thrilling to me as being out on the road, having a crowd cheering for the other guy, and then just hear them go cold. I loved that.

"I WAS ALWAYS A CONTENDER BUT NOT ENOUGH OF A WINNER."

By my definition, I never won a major tournament. I won tournaments, but the ones I wanted to win, I never won. I was always in the semi-finals or the finals. I think I wrestled for as long as I did because I was always a contender but not enough of a winner. I was competing until the age of thirty-four. My two grown children, now in their thirties, both won New England championships. I think they were able to let wrestling go—just to let it go—earlier than I was able to let it go. That's because they had a success they could look to. They could say, "I won that tournament! I won it!" I think I hung around so long because I didn't have those successes.

The key word is "process." The gratification at the end of the day of winning a wrestling match or publishing a good book is the result of months and years of minuscule repetition. If you don't love that process, you won't have a good result, either on the tennis court, the ski slope, the wrestling mat, or with your finished book. If you don't love the process of working at something—if the process itself doesn't somehow enchant you—well, realistically, what we can expect of the finished product is a half-ass job. I mean, you have to love everything about the process, and when I say process now, I mean, whether it's training for a sport or writing a novel or a screenplay in first draft and being willing to recognize that the first draft is *crap,* and you have to dress it down and start again and start again and again and again. It's like doing sit-ups. You don't do sit-ups one day, and then you don't do them again; you're always doing sit-ups. How dare you complain about how many times you re-read or re-wrote the same sentence, the same paragraph, the same chapter? Guess what, when the book is published, you don't get to do it again. Whatever *horrible* mistake—whatever embarrassing excrescence you committed in that book—is there for all time. Why wouldn't you want to go over it as many times as possible?

"I'M GOING TO BE A WRESTLING COACH AND AN ENGLISH TEACHER."

The hunger thing is an interesting aspect. I wonder though if you don't necessarily lose that just because you've achieved. One of the guys I've known in my sport is Dan Gable, who won the gold medal in Munich in 1972 without anybody scoring a point. That's never happened before. That's like winning Wimbledon 6-Love, 6-Love, 6-Love. But he's never been someone for whom the early success has signaled a letting up. He's been a kind of hero to me. I think that the work ethic, the idea that, well, in my case, for four books, including the writing of *The World According to Garp,* I was not self-supporting as a writer. I needed to have a job teaching English and coaching wrestling. And I thought, For the rest of my life, this is what I'm going to be doing. I'll be writing these novels on the side, so to speak, which nobody reads. I get great reviews, but nobody buys them. And I'm going to be a wrestling coach and an English teacher. That was my life. I was not resigned to it; I was accepting of it. I thought, Okay, I can live like this. My kids are happy, everything's going along just fine.

When *Garp* was published, all that changed. Suddenly, I could be a full-time writer. The first time the opportunity was given to me, I realized that, like a sport, I had to learn how to do it. I began writing for the three- or four-hour time period that I was used to, and my mind wandered. I couldn't keep focus. I was *so* disappointed in myself, so down on myself. I thought, I've been given an opportunity; I can't take advantage of it! It took me the course of writing *The Hotel New Hampshire* before I could develop the capacity to stretch my concentration longer. Now I can write eight, nine hours at a time. But it took four years to build up to it. And what is that like? Just like a sport. You can't go out and wrestle for nine minutes if you haven't worked out for eighteen months. You can't do nine minutes if you haven't put eighteen months in. You have to train yourself.

If you *qualify* for the U.S. Open, I don't care whether you're 325th on the docket, you *are* a tennis player; you can play. If you wrestled in high school and college and after college, you are a wrestler; you can wrestle. But if you write, it doesn't mean that you can think. Or write.

HUNT IS NUMBER 8, AT BACK LEFT.

★DAVID HUNT★

U.S. Army Colonel
and Green Beret

Hockey, Baseball

I had two brothers, Joey and Bobby, both of whom were great athletes. Joey was a Marine and died in Vietnam in 1968 in the Tet offensive. I looked up to him and hoped I'd develop into the kind of athlete he was. He had a smoothness about him, and he was a babe magnet. Bobby was probably the best athlete of all of us. He had agility and strength, but he was a criminal. He had a learning disability, and he spent two terms in prison.

I wasn't very good at sports. I was too skinny. But it was fun, so I stuck with it. I was jealous of the talent of some of the other kids. After a while, though, I started getting competitive and I wanted to try to get better. It wasn't about gaining self-esteem, it was just about having fun.

"COME HERE. YOU'RE GOING TO BE MY CATCHER."

My high school coach's name was Bob Johnson, and he was a grizzly old lobsterman. He was a great athlete, and so were his sons. I remember when I was a sophomore he came to me one day when I was in the outfield and said, "You. Come here. You're going to be my catcher."

I said, "I don't want to be a catcher."

He said, "I'm not asking you. I'm telling you, you're going to be the catcher."

I said, "I don't know how to catch."

He said, "I know, but you're going to be my catcher." He made me warm up all the pitchers, and then he'd have somebody throw balls in the dirt to me for an hour. Eventually, I got to like catching.

"YOU KNOW, YOU'RE NOT TOO BAD."

My father, who was a great, Olympic-level athlete—he was a swimmer—wanted me to play football. We were a low- to middle-income family, and he was very upset with my choice to play hockey, because he thought it was too expensive. It wasn't until my junior or senior year that he said to me, "You know, you're not too bad."

By the time I got to prep school, I had improved enough to be named All-New England in hockey and on the second team All-New England in baseball. I wasn't getting enough ice time in high school, so I joined a semi-pro league so I could get enough practice. But although I was okay, I knew I wasn't good enough to go pro, despite the fact that I was getting hockey scholarship offers from Brown, Harvard, Boston College, and Boston University.

In college, I got clobbered. I was six feet, about 150, 160 pounds, playing against big guys like Butch Saunden, who became quarterback for the Boston Patriots. The Saunden brothers were great hockey players.

My most memorable game was for Norwich University, which is the oldest private military school in the country, in the Division II Hockey Championship. We were never supposed to get that far. Although we had the best goalie in the country, the rest of us were kind of pick-up players, but good pick-up players. We were unseated, but we beat two teams we shouldn't have beaten and we got to the finals against American International College who recruited Canadians big time. We were just a bunch of American kids and they had a great team, but for some reason, we always beat them. Of course, our goalie decided to get drunk the night of the game and it was the worst game he ever played in his life. I had a pretty good game—I think I had two goals, but we lost 5–3. Funny thing is, they actually kept the winners' trophies in our locker room and when we lost they had to take them out to give them to the AIC players. I kept my trophy; I didn't give it back. I've still got it.

"THERE'S A BIG DIFFERENCE BETWEEN BEING HIT IN HOCKEY AND BEING HIT BY A BULLET."

People sometimes think that experience in sports translates to combat, but they're wrong. Only people who have not been in combat use that analogy. I know Vince Lombardi did it, as well as some other great coaches, but they were wrong. Great soldiers aren't necessarily great athletes. It's true that having good coordination and good conditioning might help; and I guess it's also possible that if you were a team captain you learned something about leadership and cooperating with others, but there's a big difference between being hit in hockey and being hit by a bullet.

Of course, we do encourage our soldiers to participate in athletics, but in large part that's to keep them busy and to keep them in condition. You also want them as close to the base as possible, as much as you can. You don't want them downtown getting into trouble.

DOOCY IS IN THE SECOND ROW FROM THE BACK, SECOND FROM RIGHT.

★STEVE DOOCY★

Television News and Weather Anchor

Wrestling

I grew up in Kansas, where there are a lot of cows. We played 4-H basketball because when the boys park their tractors, they need something to do at night. My dad was the coach. Everyone on the team was in high school, except me—I was in fifth grade. I was just boy-size and everybody else was man-size. So the men got to play, and I didn't play much at all. But I did get to watch how team sports worked.

The reason I was so much younger than the other players was that I went to a one-room schoolhouse, where it was me and ten other kids in all the grades. There were two sixth graders—me and Jeanine—no fifth graders, three fourth graders, and two first graders, one of whom was my sister. There were three Doocys in that school. I was the oldest one in the class, and you could never play rough with the little kids, because you'd knock the soup out of them and next thing you know, you'd be in big trouble. So in those grade school days, I didn't have much team sport experience, because I was always the big boy in the school.

The 4-H basketball team would go from town to town to play other teams and our team was very good. Of course, I wasn't playing very much, because the other kids on the team were much better—and bigger—than I was. But the thrill for me was just being on the floor when I actually made it to the floor. There was always that feeling of, "Put me in, coach, put me in, coach. . . . I want to play!" But the ultimate reality is that when you get to play, you have to play, and if you're not good at it, you hate it. I was not good at it. When I did get in there, I'd say to myself, "Look, I finally made it to the floor!" But you have to be careful what you wish for, because once I was out there, somebody was going to throw me the ball and I was going to throw it to the wrong person and the other team would win and nobody would talk to me. Because of that, I kind of dreaded getting the ball.

"I WAS AFRAID OF THE WATER."

My mom put me on the YMCA swimming team when I was in second grade. But there was a problem. I was afraid of the water, especially the deep water. So mom would drop me off, and I would spend an hour talking to the locker room attendant. It never dawned on my mom, "He's just been on the swim team for an hour, why is his hair dry? Why isn't he a little wet?!"

For me, sports were just a time filler. It was just something you ought to do. I hated playing basketball because everyone was so much better than me. And I hated swimming because I was going to drown!

"I STARTED RUNNING FOR THE WRONG GOAL."

Fast forward to high school. Freshman year, I went out for football. Because I was tall and skinny—I weighed 115 pounds and I was six feet tall—and fast, they made me a halfback. I was terrified that they would give me the ball. The other kids were huge. They'd spend all summer throwing hay bales, and you didn't need no stinkin' andro, because you had a hay bale. Everybody was talented, and they'd always played football, and I had never done that. It was just another one of those things where it was a team sport that I hated.

I wish I were making this up, but I vividly remember one practice when I was halfback. They gave me the ball, and it was like one of those things in a movie, where I actually got disoriented and I started running for the wrong goal. One of my own teammates took me out—otherwise I was going to score for the other team!

"THE BASKETBALL COACH SELECTED WRESTLING FOR ME."

I said to myself, Well, you know, I've got to be better at basketball, because I played that in 4H. The football coach was also the basketball coach. I was looking for a little bit of advice, and he took me aside at the end of the football season and said, "Doocy, what are you doing in the winter?"

I said, "I'm going out for basketball. I'll be on your team."

He said, "You know what, Doocy, that's great. You're not going to be on my team. You're going out for wrestling."

So the basketball coach selected wrestling for me. At first I was thinking, well, that's kind of insulting. He's saying I'll be as bad at basketball as I was at football. But my best friend back then, Alan, who rode the bus with me every day, was on the wrestling team and he said, "Do it. You'll like it." So I went out for wrestling.

Suddenly, everything turned around. Why? Because all the other sports I was involved in were team sports but wrestling is just you and one other guy. You don't have to depend on somebody else to do it right, to make the perfect shot. It's just you.

I wound up being in the best shape I've ever been in. I also learned discipline. Some people think wrestling is just two guys rolling around on a rubber mat. But it's so much more than that. It's so scientific. It's about body physics. Where is somebody's center of gravity? How do I throw him down? There's a lot of strategy involved. It's not just brute strength. And this was when I started to like sports again. It was, "Wait a minute, I don't stink at this! I'm the only kid in my school wrestling at 112 pounds and six feet tall."

As it happened, there was a small problem. In Kansas, out there in the gravy belt, all the kids were bigger than I was, so I wound up wrestling a total of four times. That's because there were never any opponents my size. They either had somebody who was *too small*—92, 98 pounds—or too big. But I remember every one of those matches, as if they were on TV.

★CONDOLEEZZA RICE★

National Security Advisor to the U.S.
President and Former Provost at Stanford

Ice Skating

My father was a football coach and I was supposed to be his All-American linebacker, but since I was an only child, he decided to teach his girl about sports instead. I watched the NFL with my dad from the time I was four or five years old.

My father says I took to sports right away. He tells a story that when I was three or so he said to my grandmother, "I'm going to take her to an Almond High football game. I'll pick her up at three o'clock."

My grandmother said that I asked every hour on the hour, "Is it three o'clock yet? Is it three o'clock yet?" Finally, she showed me that when the hand is on twelve and the hand is on three, that's three o'clock. So I think you could say, football probably taught me how to tell time.

"I LOVED THE FEELING OF BEING ON THE ICE."

I took up figure skating during the summers in Denver, Colorado. My parents were going to graduate school in Denver, even though we were living in Alabama. Skating was sort of high-priced child care. They would drop me off at the rink for skating school, then they would go to school all day and pick me up in the evening. When we moved to Denver when I was twelve, I started skating competitively.

I loved being in the arena, I loved the feeling of being on the ice. But I was exactly the wrong body type for figure skating: size 8 feet, with, as my trainer said, "5' 10" legs," and I wasn't built very close to the ground. I probably would have been a better tennis player. In fact, I've always thought I was a little more naturally talented at tennis than at skating. But I loved skating and I worked very hard at it.

Getting on the ice at 5:00 or 5:15 A.M. in Denver, Colorado, where it's colder in the rink than it is outside, was not an easy thing to do. I always thought it was hardest on my father, who had to drive me to the rink at five o'clock in the morning and then sit there with the other parents while I skated. But it's come to be a benefit now, because I get up now at 4:45 A.M. so I can exercise before I come to work. So all those years of early skating have paid off.

I didn't want my parents in the stands, because I didn't want them there if anything went wrong. My father was always in the stands. My mother, who didn't particularly like to play sports herself, didn't like watching me skate, because she was afraid I was going to hurt my hands and ruin my piano career. So it was mostly my father in the stands, or my mother sitting there but with her eyes covered.

Contrary to what some people think, skating is not a lonely sport because the people you skate with become your best friends. You spend a lot of time with them, and the skating clubs become kind of a second home. Of course, performing itself is lonely, because it's just you and that really big patch of slippery ice.

I was not naturally talented at skating, unlike tennis or golf, where picking up a tennis racket or a golf club felt totally natural. I had to work much harder at skating than I did at either piano or academics. But I really believe that this was important in shaping me, because it taught me to work hard at something I was not particularly good at and that although sometimes you might have disastrous performances, you still have to get up the next day and the world still goes on.

"COMPETITION WAS A LITTLE SCARY FOR ME."

I got into competition at the regional level, and I was never very successful, I'm sad to say. But I always really looked forward to it. We had eight levels of tests we took, which allowed us to advance toward different levels of competition. I particularly enjoyed the testing. I found working toward the tests far more enjoyable than working toward competition. Competition was a little scary for me.

I really wanted to win. The one time that I actually came in second in a summer competition, I was so excited. It was great. If I lost, I felt bad. It took a little while, but I was able to get over it, and the good thing is it never discouraged me from trying again the next day.

During competitions, I was pretty nervous as I stood there waiting for the music to start. The problem was, I didn't bend my knees all that well, because I'm pretty tall. When I was nervous, my knees were even straighter, so you can imagine what it looked like when I actually started to skate. I sometimes had pretty successful performances, but I remember one time in particular, I fell three times in the first minute and a half of my program. The bad thing about figure skating is that you have to get up and smile and pretend that nothing ever happened. I used to envy football players or basketball players who had a chance to express their displeasure at a bad play. In skating, you're all dressed up out there, in sequins and pretty clothes, and you're supposed to get up when you fall and pretend that nothing happened. I always found that kind of hard.

"AT LEAST YOU CAN'T SLIP AND FALL."

When I gave my first speech to the Republican National Convention in 1992, I was told that there were going to be 30,000 people in the Astrodome. My first thought was, Don't they play football in the Astrodome? Why am I speaking in the Astrodome? Then, the night before, I started to get nervous. But at that moment the skating came back to me and I thought to myself, You know, at least you can't slip and fall. So, I was really glad I'd had that experience, because I was never nervous before performances.

★E.D. HILL★

Television Talk Show Host and
Emmy Award–Winning Reporter

Tennis

When I was young, growing up in Dripping Springs, Texas, a little, bitty town with one traffic light, I was known as "The Fastest Racket in the West."

If you live in Texas, you know that the only thing that matters is sports. And if you're a girl you can't play football, so that leaves you with a couple of other options, but not many. In Texas, all women are athletic or outdoorsy, so it was assumed at my school that you did something athletic, or at the very least you tried out for teams, even if you didn't make one.

I didn't have a lot of role models for sports. My dad didn't play sports. My mother was an archer and they didn't have that in high school. The only thing my family did do together was play tennis.

I started playing tennis because I got kicked off the basketball team. I always assumed that because I was tall I'd be a good basketball player. When I went out and practiced shooting by myself, everything was just fine. But once I had to play on the team, I just didn't quite get the game. In Texas, for girls' basketball, they played a three-man offense, three-man defense. It was different from boys' basketball, because they assumed that girls couldn't play a full game, so they split the court in half and you either played offense and stayed on one side of the court, or defense and stayed on the other side of the court. I never really got that. I kept thinking we should be playing the full court. But half court or not, my shooting didn't turn out to be as good as I expected, and the basketball coach had a chat with me and suggested I might be interested in looking into other activities.

This happened when I was a sophomore in high school, and it just about killed me because everybody played sports and to be told that you weren't good enough at the sport you thought you were good at was pretty awful. I remember going home that day thinking my life was over. That's when I started thinking about going out for the tennis team, primarily because in our town nobody really went out for tennis, so the competition was so limited that I was guaranteed a spot on the team.

I decided that playing tennis was something I could control. I could work out as hard as I wanted to. I could practice as much as I needed to. I didn't have to have somebody to practice with. I found a suitable back-board—the garage door—and started hitting a ball against it.

It turned out I did very well. I made the team, which was a no-brainer, be-cause there weren't enough people to fill it out otherwise, and as a sophomore I went on to win my district and went to the regionals in Texas, which was a first for someone in my school.

The whole situation—being cut from the basketball team and then suc-ceeding as a tennis player—made me realize that what you start out pursuing may not work out, but that sometimes you have to change and work with what you're given. Having a setback doesn't mean you're done. A setback just means you have to reassess and figure out what your next step is. Up until that point, I thought there was only one thing for me to do and that was to play basketball. That didn't turn out to be the case.

"THE PLAYERS WHO OFTEN WON WERE THE ONES WHO WERE ABLE TO PSYCH OUT THE BETTER PLAYERS."

I realized from watching a lot of people play matches, that it wasn't nec-essarily the best player who won. The players who often won were the ones who were able to psych out the better players and make them make mistakes, because they weren't confident enough in themselves. I realized that percep-tion often became reality, so that if a superior athlete perceived you as being better, even if you weren't, that frequently worked against them. I think that later on, this concept probably helped me with my confidence level and al-lowed me to be successful in broadcasting.

SORBO IS IN THE SECOND ROW, FOURTH FROM LEFT.

★KEVIN SORBO★

Actor

Basketball

I never wanted to be a fireman or a doctor, I wanted to be a pro athlete. I grew up watching the Minnesota Vikings with Fran Tarkenton, and I started to say that I wanted to be a pro in the second or third grade.

I was a small-town kid from the suburbs of Minneapolis—there was only one black athlete in our entire high school. We'd play the inner city schools and I found that their game was much different from ours. Ours was a pass and run and shoot from the outside game, while theirs was played close to the hoop with a lot of elbowing us around, a very physical game. I think they were surprised at how good we were, but in the end, I learned a lot from their game.

There were five kids in our family, and my mother and father would always come to our games and it was always nice to know they were up there in the stands. They were quiet supporters—my dad could get frustrated, but he wasn't a yeller. When I'd get home after a game, they weren't critical, but instead were very positive about the way I played. The fact is, I was my own worst enemy. I was very hard on myself. I could have had a sixteen point, fourteen rebound game and I'd come home and think about the three shots I missed.

"THERE WERE ONLY FOUR OF US LEFT."

I think I always had high self-esteem—my parents instilled it in me—but there's no doubt sports also helped me in that department. There was one game in particular I remember where practically our entire team had fouled out and there were only four of us left. I was one of the four and so we were playing four on five for a quarter and a half. I played unbelievably—I was always a good outside shooter—and we actually beat this other team. How embarrassing it was for them! But obviously, I felt pretty good about that and to this day it's something that's always brought up with my old high school buddies when we get together.

I was a pretty good athlete. In fact, I was probably one of the best jocks in my high school. But when I got to Morehead State College I found that everybody was as good or better an athlete than I was, which was an eye-opening experience.

In college, I chose basketball—it was my game. But I learned pretty quickly that in college sports is a business, and so that dream of becoming a pro athlete just wasn't going to happen. I was a good athlete, but the reality of college was that it was the next level up and we were only a Division III school! So I knew that sports was always going to be a passion for me, but not something I was going to make a living at.

"I DIDN'T HAVE A CAMERA WITH ME."

I'm a very competitive. Today, I play a lot of golf. I've even played with Tiger Woods. Not long ago, I found myself out on the golf course with Joe Theismann, Bob Griese, and Troy Aikman, all quarterbacks who'd won the Super Bowl. And you know what, I didn't have a camera with me, so I couldn't take my picture with them.

★SEAN HANNITY★

Television and Radio Talk Show Host
and Author

Hockey, Baseball, Basketball

All I cared about as a kid was sports. Period.

I grew up in Franklin Square, Long Island, and I participated in sports from the time I was playing stickball with my Uncle Ed. I was always a good athlete; I had very good eye-hand coordination. I played organized ball from the time I was old enough to get into Little League. Between organized basketball, street hockey, ice hockey, and baseball, I was pretty much always on the athletic field.

"IT WAS A DIFFERENT TIME THEN."

Sports for me were a matter of course. We'd play roller hockey all day—or we'd go to the duck pond during the winter and play ice hockey all day. Or we'd shoot hoops in the backyard all day. That was our whole life.

The first baseball team I played for was sponsored by Chemical Bank. I could hit the ball and, as a pitcher, I had a great sinking curve ball that I used to throw right at the batter's head. It would sink right into the strike zone and they would duck away.

I just loved being a part of it—putting on the uniform, going out there with your hat and your glove. It was a different time then. We used to get off the bus at three o'clock in the afternoon and we'd either be out playing roller hockey or baseball until seven o'clock or when the sun went down.

My parents loved it, probably because they thought it would keep me out of trouble. My father would come watch me pitch, but he and my mother didn't really take an active part in it. My father wasn't as competitive as me about it, he just wanted me to have a good time and learn some lessons from it. I had post–World War II parents, who were killing themselves working, and the idea that they could drive you all over the world every single day was amazing, because I also had three older sisters that they had to take care of. To take us to baseball games every single day wouldn't have been realistic.

"I SPENT THE NEXT SIXTEEN HOURS IN MY BACKYARD SHOOTING SLAP SHOTS."

In basketball, I was a good guard with a pretty good jump shot. I had the ability to drive, but only to the right—true story—not to the left. There was a point where hockey dominated my life. In fact, I wanted to be a pro ice hockey player. I had a mean slap shot. I used to hang around in my backyard where I had a net, and I would shoot slap shots for hours and hours. Even then, I worked at getting good. I remember the first time I tried playing hockey with the big kids and I couldn't shoot a slap shot, so I spent the next sixteen hours in my backyard shooting slap shots, so I could get it up in the air and make it fly toward the goal.

I remember a time when I got my name in the papers. That was big. That was important. It was in the Franklin Square newspaper. They'd put me in the goal, because our goalie was out, and I actually shut out an important team in a playoff game. They wrote about how a guy had a breakaway against me and I came out of the goal and stopped him. I remember a neighbor saying to me, "Hey, you're in the paper today."

I said, "Really, what paper?" Since then, I've only been in the paper for being a "horrible right-winger."

"I JUST PLAYED MY HEART OUT."

Whenever I took the field, no matter what sport it was, I felt like I was one of the better players. From the very first day I put on a uniform to play a sport, I wanted to win. Period. I played my heart out. I don't know where that came from. I think it was innate. I'm still that way today, but I'm not a bad loser.

I went to a small school, Sacred Heart Seminary, in Hempstead, and the most important day of the whole year was Sports Day, where everything we'd do that day had something to do with sports. I used to dominate because it was a small school and the kids weren't really athletes.

I once struck out thirteen batters in a row when I was pitching for St. Pius in Uniondale, against a team that was supposed to be clobbering us. It was one of those days when I either threw it over the backstop or I threw it in the strike zone.

★ROBIN WILLIAMS★

Actor, Comedian

Wrestling, Track, Soccer

In grade school, I was in good shape. I was riding bikes and I did judo, which I loved. And then, all of a sudden we moved, and I didn't have access to riding a bike anymore, so in seventh and eighth grade I was really out of shape. Then I got to ninth grade and there was wrestling, and I went, "Wait a minute, this is fun." Basically, it was a chance for a small kid like me to get a chance to wail on another small kid. I went, "I love this." The discipline of it was great. Plus, I really started to be good at it.

"ONCE I STARTED WRESTLING, I GOT TO PUSH AROUND ANOTHER LITTLE GUY."

In ninth grade, I tried out for football at the all-boys private school I was attending, and I made the team as a safety. The first game, the other team started throwing everything at me. They scored three or four touchdowns over me, and then the coach took me out. After the game, he took me aside and recommended that maybe soccer might be good for me.

I actually went and played soccer and I said to myself, Oh wow, this *is* great. Once again, it was a sport that wasn't size-reliant, so I could run up and down the field and play as well as anybody else. We had a great coach, who was my friend's father, and the game really started to kick into gear. It was this thing where, as a kid, you could find a place where you could excel. The team spirit was wonderful, because people actually came to check out the game, because we were doing pretty well.

"DURING THE SEASON, YOU'RE LIKE GANDHI ON A BUDGET."

Suddenly, everything turned around, because now I was getting into shape again and I was starting to feel pretty good about myself. For wrestling, you had to drop weight, which sometimes got to the point where people started to get very worried. The first year I wrestled, I weighed 103 pounds. The next year, I wrestled at 112. But during the season, you're like Gandhi on a budget. Everyone else is having donuts and stuff, and you're like looking at them like, "Aw man, come over here, just let me look at it." Basically, you're going, "Yes, I'll have the bone and the bread crumb, please." But the weird thing is you start to get kind of proud of the discipline. It's kind of like the monk mentality. You become like the Chinese monk where you're very proud and yet still able to kick ass.

Wrestling came at the right time for me because seventh and eighth grade were really rough. Recently, I saw pictures of myself, and I was this little dumpy kid. Then all of a sudden wrestling comes along, and you're like, *Yeah!* I remember that in seventh and eighth grade it was that thing of getting pushed around, and then once I started wrestling, I got to push around another little guy.

I was undefeated until I got to the first or second round of the state finals. The first year I was undefeated and came up against this guy who was bald and not because he shaved his head. He was this nineteen-year old freshman from Northern Michigan, who just wailed on me, and I went, "Okay, big lesson." The next year, as a sophomore, I was doing great—I think I was undefeated—then I dislocated my shoulder. I tried to come back the next year but it popped again, and I went, "Well, I can't do this anymore."

"I WAS DOING RIFFS WHEN WE WERE RUNNING."

After wrestling, I found cross country and track—and that was another great discovery, because both those sports are individual and you're pushing yourself most of the time, in cross country especially. We moved to California, where I ran cross country in these beautiful places with mountains and lakes. Suddenly, it was, "Wait a minute, this is more than just sports; it's actually a good kind of discipline where you're pushing yourself and also experiencing this kind of almost Buddhist moment out among nature on these long runs where you see no one."

I was doing riffs when we were running, because you've got long periods of time on these fire roads up in Northern California. When I ran cross country, I remember I used to do this thing where we'd be on these pace runs, where one guy takes the front and I'd specifically look for these little trails where there were bushes and go "Bushes!!" That was kind of like the fetal phases of my comedy. You're trying stuff out because you've got road trips.

I was a good runner, not a great runner. If you had the first three, I'd alternate between fourth and fifth. But you get points, so you're always helping out the group. As a track runner, I was on a two-mile relay team, and we had a record that stayed with the school for about thirty years. Maybe it even still exists; I'm not sure. But you look at this record and go, "Gosh, we're still there! That's cool."

I remember the track meets—those times, they stay with you—where you're running in a big meet and you're in a stadium. You've been doing these little track meets, and you're lucky if you get maybe fifty, sixty people. The next thing you know, you're in a stadium, and there's a couple of thousand people! It's like, wow . . . miniature Olympics . . . wow! This is cool.

Once you get into that stuff, you become endorphin-addicted, and if you don't get it, you're going, "Aw, man, I feel bad." Now, with biking, I get the same thing. When people say, "What do you do for exercise?" I say, "I ride my bike." I get the exercise and I get the solitude. A lot of people, including celebrities, play golf, because they can be away and get that kind of quiet, but for me on a bike, it's the same thing. I ride along and occasionally I get to meet someone like Lance Armstrong or Greg LeMond, or any number of people in New York, when you're riding along and all of a sudden someone just picks up and says, "Follow me." It's an unspoken thing. Yeah, bring it on, bad ass!

You talk to anybody who does these long training rides and it's all about the rush of the endorphins. It also allows you to get out of your head for a while. Especially in a career like the one I'm in, where things can be up and down—your movie's hot, your movie's not—you need to be able to be able to get away from the pressure. I do these celebrity rides where you'll be part of a relay team, and it'll kind of humble you again, because you realize you're good, but you're not that good. You get your ass kicked all of a sudden. When you're in a race or something else, you're just another guy.

"CROTCH GRAB!"

My parents loved the fact that I enjoyed sports. When I was wrestling, my mother was always going, "You're not eating." And I'd go, "I can't." But you know, my mother was always athletic; she was heavily into tennis, and I

also played tennis as a kid, I even played competitively for a while That's a really wonderful combination of mind and matter. My mother was at the
wrestling matches, and the coach kept yelling "Crotch grab," and I'm going,
"Great, that's nice. Can you lay off that, because I don't know how well mom
deals with that." The sport looks Greek enough already, so you don't have to
be yelling, "Crotch grab!"

"IF I'D HAD MY ASS KICKED, I WOULDN'T HAVE BEEN SO HAPPY ABOUT IT."

I think I enjoyed sports because I had some success. If I'd had my ass
kicked, I wouldn't have been so happy about it. I think success really motivates
you. I do remember vividly being undefeated and I was proud of that. Victory
tends to reinforce that. With cross country, it was the victory combined with
this sense of, "This is something that I'm going to do for a long time."

Being part of a team also prepares you for later life. For instance, when it
comes to making movies, you realize that you're all in this together, and your
goal is to make the best movie possible. You're doing it there in front of the
camera, but there's all these people behind the camera doing all this other
stuff. And you're all motivated toward success. When you do get an award or
when your movie does kick ass, you feel kind of a mutual pride that, "Yeah,
we made something good."

"FOR ME IT'S A LONG RACE, NOT A SPRINT."

The stamina you develop from sports also is a huge factor in later life.
When I'm on stage, some people ask, "How do you go two hours?" I say, "It's
easy." Sports give you the endurance; for me it's a long race, not a sprint.
Chris Rock said that performing is like boxing; you've got to get back into
condition, mentally and physically, especially with stand-up. Stand-up is the
long program. A lot of people can do five minutes; doing the hour and a half
is the distance.

It's the same with movies. I'm up here in the Yukon doing this stuff, and
you've got to have this physicality to keep going, because you're outside, and
it's freezing cold, and you're running and doing all these things, and you just
have to keep going. And the people are going, "Do you want to go again?"
And I'm like, "Yeah." It's like when you were doing wind sprints, except this

time they're filming it. The prep is kind of like athletics, because it's training and discipline and getting ready. It's this weird thing that goes back to my history teacher, who was my wrestling coach. He gave me a double bill of wrestling and this love of history that helped me in preparing for anything that I do that's a period piece. All of that stuff just helped you just kick your ass, move you forward rather than sit back and go, "I can't do this." Instead, you go, "You've got no choice."

When I'm watching someone like Lance Armstrong or Greg LeMond, I'm watching the discipline and the focus. It makes me go to myself, "Wow, I can add a little bit more of that to the mix." It is a combination of intense concentration and relaxation, the ability to keep going when the going gets tough.

KERRY IS IN THE BACK ROW, FOURTH FROM RIGHT.

★JOHN KERRY★

U.S. Senator from Massachusetts and the
Democratic Nominee for President in 2004

Football, Baseball, Hockey

I loved to play baseball and I remember taking my glove and rubbing it with linseed oil and then wrapping it around a ball. I played with friends on our front or back lawns, or in the street, or in an alley somewhere, just hacking around. I loved to play catch or just bang the ball against the wall. Nobody pushed me to play, and it wasn't about competing, it was just about having fun.

As a kid, I also played football. I loved the smell of a football helmet. I started off playing on the 90-pound team and then eventually moved up to the 110-pound squad. I was a linebacker, believe it or not, in fourth and fifth grade.

It wasn't until seventh grade that I began to learn how to skate, and that's when I got interested in hockey, which was about the same time I began to play soccer and lacrosse. I loved every one of those sports and didn't concentrate on one of them exclusively, although I was probably better at hockey.

"IT WASN'T LIKE ANYTHING YOU'D NORMALLY HEAR AT A SPORTING EVENT."

One of the indelible memories I have was being on the soccer field when JFK was killed. We were in the biggest game of the year, Yale versus Harvard, and suddenly there was a ripple through the stands. It wasn't like anything you'd normally hear at a sporting event, and we could tell that people were not involved in the game itself. It wasn't until I went to the bench that I learned that Kennedy had been shot. The game went on, but I was in kind of a fog. I honestly do not even recall who won the game, and

I've never bothered to look it up. The game ended and then we learned that the president had died. The game itself became meaningless, and we were in total shock.

"YOU LEARN A LOT ABOUT LEADERSHIP."

I think there are several good reasons why you want to play sports. First of all, you learn about discipline. You also learn how to play as a team and how to dig deep inside yourself to get that something extra, if you need it. You also learn about adversity. You can't play sports without losing sometimes and, in losing, you learn something about grace and how to act under pressure. These are all things that can help you later in life. I think it made me a better naval officer and a better warrior. In fact, it taught me a lot about politics.

There's an old saying that goes something like, "You play the way you practice," and I think you apply some of those lessons of athletics in the rest of your life. If you like sports and working out and trying hard like I did, it was quite a thrill if a coach walked up and said something encouraging to you. As an athlete, you live for times like that. You learn a lot about leadership and about being a great motivator, because you learn what people respond to.

As a teammate, I always tried to be supportive. I was fortunate enough to be part of a couple of great teams. My senior year, we had a great lacrosse team that beat Maryland, University of Virginia, Johns Hopkins, Army, and Navy. I mostly played attack and midfield, though I preferred attack. There are a couple of games we played that still burn me up today if I think about them. I remember playing against Cornell and getting a fantastic feed and putting it right into the dirt. Amazingly, I can still feel it crunch and miss.

"I LOOK UP AND IT'S GORDIE HOWE."

I've had some great moments in sports, but the best of them came later in life when I was able to play with some of the legends of hockey. It was like dying and going to heaven. I remember sitting on the bench and a guy reaches over and says "great shift," to me and I look up and it's Gordie Howe. I look to my left and there's Ray Boruque, and next to him is Phil Esposito, and next to him is Wayne Cashman. These are the heroes that you grow up with as a kid and to get on the ice with them as an adult is just a kid's dream come true. It really is like going to heaven.

I had have some great moments as a player. I remember in the last soccer game getting a hat trick against Harvard, and we won 6–3. That was fun, and it was also really the last organized game of any seriousness that I played in any sport.

★JOAN LUNDEN★

Television Host

Gymnastics, Dance, Horseback Riding

When I was young, I was never involved in organized sports like soccer or baseball. Consequently, I always say I was not athletic as a child. But when I really stop and think about it, I realize I was dancing every day, which certainly was a kind of organized sport. After school, I'd take the bus to the dance studio and I'd be there until my mom picked me up at six o'clock in the evening.

Because I didn't choose the path of organized sports when I was young, I allowed myself to think of myself as nonathletic. But now, when I say that to my mom, she says, "You danced until 6 P.M. every day. You rode horses. You jumped off a bridge when you were eleven." Looking back, I think I did have an adventurous spirit by nature, but I didn't think that then. I was in more individual types of sports, like gymnastics and ballet. I didn't go to any particular sporting events on the weekends, but I did march in every parade and did acrobatics, like headstands in moving cars.

My father was a dedicated cancer surgeon and my mom was one of those vivacious, effervescent women who would light up a room. They were never physically active in a sport type way, but they both knew they had to involve their kids in something, and I chose dance.

"YOU CAN'T KEEP A HORSE IN THE DORM."

I used to dance and perform all over the place and all the time, but when I got to high school it wasn't cool anymore, so I stopped. That's why I wanted to get my girls involved in the type of sports that would carry them through life, because you can always grab a basketball or a tennis racket and play, and this carries through to adulthood.

The other athletic thing I did as a child was to ride horses, but not competitively the way my daughters have. I grew up in California and we used to take horse rides through the countryside and watch the sun go down. I did that until I reached college, because you can't keep a horse in the dorm, so I stopped.

When I had children, I got my oldest daughter, Jamie, riding. It only took a month of watching her do the jumps and seeing the joy in her face, smiling from ear to ear, for me to say to myself, Wait a minute, why did I give that up? Who says I can't still do that again as an adult? So I got back involved in riding competitively. But again, this was an individual sport as opposed to a competitive sport. I'm out on my own, instead of with a group, saying, "Hey, let's cream the other guy!"

About the time I got back into riding, I asked myself, Where did I lose the physical activity that I used to do? When did I lose the personal challenge and the physical feeling that I used to get from being athletic? I knew I had to get the physicality back that I had when I was thirty-nine, so I drastically redesigned my life. I took lessons and started playing tennis. I started mountain climbing and managed to climb the Grand Tetons. It extended my life, I think. It added challenge and excitement and vigor and joy to my life.

"I THOUGHT THAT GEORGE PLIMPTON HAD THE BEST JOB IN THE WORLD."

The past ten to fifteen years of my life have been so much more fun than the previous ten years, and it's all because they've been active and challenging. About the time I began redesigning my life, I created a show called *Behind Closed Doors*. The idea was to take viewers on a journey of life's challenges with the aim of getting them to participate eventually. Keep in mind, I thought that George Plimpton, who tried all those different professions and wrote about them, had the best job in the world.

The show was really an attempt to test myself with situations like being with the Marine special forces and, as my husband said, it would have just been called stupid human tricks if I wasn't in shape to keep up with them.

For ten years I was sleep deprived, exhausted, with three kids, watching everybody else race the race. And all the time I was wishing that I was in it. So I just made a choice to get back in the race. By getting back in the game, you actually have more energy to do things. For example, people can't believe that at fifty I'm having more kids. "At your age," they say, "aren't you going to be exhausted chasing them around?" But it's the opposite of what people think. I've got so much more energy now.

I didn't push my kids into sports, but I did insist that they do something. Now, seeing my daughters having so much success in equestrian events and climbing mountains, I say to myself, "Wait a minute. Now I get it. If I'd pushed myself harder, I might have gotten that unbridled confidence that they have." I might have realized that there are no boundaries. We create those boundaries for ourselves. We say, "I can't do that."

When you are walking onto the court to shoot a basket or walking on stage to do a three-and-a-half minute dance routine, you're still doing something that requires you to concentrate and perform and live up to your level of performance. Boys in sports have an edge because they learn to expect to win, to play as a team, and they're instilled with a desire to win, along with the concentration and dedication required to achieve a goal. Often, girls don't have that experience growing up.

I know women who interview people for jobs and they will look for a candidate who played in competitive sports because they know that person understands strategy and teamwork in order to achieve a goal. We need to provide girls with opportunities to play as a team. It doesn't have to be a sport like baseball, for instance, but it should be something that requires them to dedicate themselves to a group.

These are the kinds of things that made my daughter what she is today: outgoing, bright, hardworking, gregarious. She will go a hundred times further than the next girl because of what she learned playing sports as a kid. She also knows that when she gets into the ring and blows the first jump, she won't fall apart. She knows you have to shake it off and keep going, with the idea that you can and will win.

My husband always says that my motto is, "No matter what anyone asks me to do, just say yes and figure out how later on. Someone just asked me if I want to climb Mt. Kilimanjaro and I said yes. Does it scare me? Would it have been easier when I was younger? Yes! Do I pass on it? No way!

Once you say yes, you figure it out.

★DAVID POTTRUCK★

Co-CEO of Charles Schwab

Football, Wrestling

I'm a baby boomer, and you can imagine all these GIs from World War II returning to the suburbs, places like Levittown, and they all had kids about the same time. Every street had a billion kids, and they were all my age. Every day there were stickball games, touch football games, all kinds of team sports like that.

In the beginning, I was big fish in a small pond. And when I moved up to a bigger pond, I wasn't such a big fish anymore. Somehow, even though I was often extremely intimidated at first, I learned how to step up to the level of competition and then, eventually, I did become a bigger fish.

I was the best football player on my block, but then I went out for junior high football and I was lousy, so I sat on the bench. In fact, as an eighth grader, I sat on the bench the entire year. The next year I started on the freshman team, and then I moved up to varsity. But that didn't last long, because I got cut from that team and wound up on the JV squad, where I sat on the bench again most of the year. But senior year, I made it to the varsity as a starter and became the MVP, as a fullback and linebacker.

To be the MVP of your high school team was hot, but when I got to college I was with a whole team full of all-league captains and MVPs, and this was in the Ivy League.

Overall, I was late bloomer. When I graduated high school and went out for football I was 185 pounds. By the time I left Penn, I was 235 pounds, and I wrestled at 190 pounds the whole time I was there. I became bigger and better in both sports.

My sad reflection is that I never had a coach that said, "Oh, my God, you could be unbelievable, and here's the program you have to follow to get yourself into the NFL or into the Olympics as a wrestler." My coaches took me to a higher level, but they never saw in me that kind of potential. I don't think they understood my level of determination. Even today, I am continually redefining my success. My athletic gifts were limited, but my determination was enormous.

So my college career is pretty darn mediocre, and it was painful! I don't like to think of myself as a failure, but I was, which was pretty humbling.

I don't think I got the most out of my abilities. I thought so at the time, but I have now come to realize that I limited my ambition by what I thought was possible and so I set my goals much too low. I thought if I outworked everybody else I could rise to the top. Only when I became a coach did I realize that you have to do more than outwork everyone else in the room. You have to work harder than anyone *outside* of the room. You have to realize that you are competing with everyone on the planet. You have to go home every night and say to yourself, No one worked harder than I did today.

"SUDDENLY, A LIGHT WENT ON IN MY HEAD."

The turning point for me came in my second year of college. I was at a tournament and had already lost. I was watching this awesome wrestler from Cornell and I started talking to the guy next to me and I said how good this guy was. He said, "I'm from Cornell and I know that guy and last year he had a losing record. Man, did he turn things around!"

As silly as it seems, in my head I thought I had a pretty good pecking order of athletic prowess. Either you were good or you were not good or you were somewhere in the middle. This notion that you could have a losing record one year and become a regional intercollegiate wrestling champion the next never occurred to me. Suddenly, a light went on in my head. It made me realize that you could control your destiny. That it wasn't all about talent. It was about your level of commitment and the work that you put into it. You could perform or you could underperform, based on your commitment level. It seems obvious now, but it was not obvious to me at twenty.

This epiphany stuck with me, and the next year my work ethic doubled. My goal was to outwork everyone on the field. I knew I could not control my talent, but I could control my work ethic. I went on to go undefeated, and I was runner-up in the Eastern Intercollegiate Championships, making me ninth or tenth in the country. It was also my breakthrough year in football, and I was named MVP of the team.

The second breakthrough for me came when I was the wrestling coach at Penn while I was going for my MBA. I could not believe that I hadn't been drafted by the NFL. I thought that if the scouts didn't draft me it was because I was not good enough. I had some contact from the Oilers and the Dolphins, but I since I didn't think I was good enough to make the team and since I didn't want to fail, I said to myself, "Why work out and then show up and get cut and be embarrassed? Why not retire while I still have some dignity?" I didn't know that the greatest failure is not trying.

So instead, I coached wrestling and I saw these men doing what I was doing: limiting their ambition because of what they thought was possible as opposed to putting no limits on what they could achieve. If they lost, they said the other guy was better than they were. I was trying to convince them otherwise, but I had failed to convince myself of the same thing. I realized how much our mind controls what we accomplish, as opposed to simply our athletic gifts. It's all about what's in your head.

I became determined to make the adjustments to not limit myself. I wanted to not only outwork my colleagues, but outwork anyone everywhere that I could imagine. I set huge goals for myself that involved a work ethic, moving to unexciting parts of the country, taking on roles that were not so glamorous. I made huge sacrifices in the name of my career, including, sadly, two failed marriages. At the time, I thought I'd picked the wrong people to marry, but to be honest, they failed largely because I did not put the time or energy into my marriages that I needed to. My priorities were elsewhere.

"NOTHING IS EASY. EVERYTHING WORTHWHILE IS DIFFICULT."

I have never ever felt my athletic training so profoundly as when the dot-com bubble burst. It had been utterly defeating and certainly disappointing. I had to face my company's failures and my failures. There are always times when you think you want to give up, where you ask yourself, "Where's the joy?" It's terrible when you are pushing layoffs in the midst of downturns. When you have to face something like that, it's extremely challenging. That's when I feel my preparation from playing on losing teams that eventually became champions was important. That's when I realized that hard work does not turn things around immediately. Nothing is easy. Everything worthwhile is difficult.

You don't achieve a high level of success without drive and determination. Between my athletic career and my business career, I have to say that I am prouder of my professional career and grateful for what my athletic career taught me: the value of hard work and tenacity and the resiliency to get back out there and try again. Everyone of us has had disappointment in life, but we've just got to get back out there and do it a little better next time. That's the way to win.

★CAROL ALT★

Model and Actress

Gymnastics, Basketball, Track, Lacrosse

I went to a Catholic school that did not have a gym. Nevertheless, we did have sports, but nothing was really organized. In sixth grade, I moved to Long Island and switched to a public school, where all the girls had grown up playing sports. These girls knew how to do cartwheels and handstands and I remember the first time I took gymnastics I was shocked because these girls were like pros, and I had never even seen this kind of equipment before. I had to play catch up, but for me rather than being intimidated it became a challenge. I never felt like I was a natural athlete, but I just loved the challenge of sports, and I said to myself, I have to catch up to these girls.

I didn't go out for the gymnastics team, but I did try out for everything else. My mind-set was always to find out what the hardest maneuver was and then try to master it.

I played left attack wing on our lacrosse team, left attack wing in field hockey, and center in basketball. Playing on these teams was a blessing, because as a fireman with a big family my father could not afford to keep us in the coolest clothes and the nicest outfits, but he could afford the uniforms.

Among all the team sports, I liked cross-country best. I never had great speed, but I could just run and run. It helped me clear my head, and I loved to use the time to think about things that were on my mind. I would run through the woods and fields all alone, and I loved it. I just wish I had the time to do it today.

Out of all the sports I played, basketball is what I was best at, and my team always seemed to win. My coach was great with me. He knew and understood that I had to work in a bakery after school, and he knew I had to leave practice early and on Wednesdays I couldn't practice at all. On the days I could go to practice, I would go straight to work afterward, where I'd stay through seven o'clock at night. I also worked all day Saturday and did some babysitting at night. So, throughout school, I was very busy between sports, keeping up with classes, and work.

What's made it great for me was when my parents came to watch me play. They couldn't come much, especially my dad, because he worked two jobs. But when they came, I always played better. Every time I saw my dad in the stands he always had this grin on his face. He was just so proud and happy being around his kids, watching all of us take part.

"I DID NOT MAKE ONE TEAM THAT I TRIED OUT FOR, AND THAT WAS CHEERLEADING."

As a player in every sport, I prided myself on my anticipation. I tried to be where the ball was going to go. I was able to get to a spot on the floor before the ball got there and go around a player rather than through the player. I also brought a sense of humor to my teams. If I was better at something than someone else, or not as good, I would try and make light of it to break the tension of competition. This worked, I think, because so many times the better players would make you feel so bad when you couldn't do something. I wasn't like that. I always tried to be a good teammate in that regard.

I did not make one team that I tried out for, and that was cheerleading. I practiced hard for it, but I just didn't do well. Maybe I struggled because my arms were the length of everyone else's body. This kind of underlined how I felt in high school, because those were my awkward years. I found that most of my model friends were the tallest and goofiest girls in high school.

It's the same approach I have today on any modeling shoot: Don't try to intimidate the makeup artist. Things like that. They hear they are going to be working on a big-name model and they get nervous. I always try to defuse that by just being nice. If I have a problem with their work, I never make demands. Instead, I use self-deprecation to defuse any tension and get my point across. I want to make sure they stay on my team.

After high school, I was not done with sports. I went to Hofstra University for one year where I played lacrosse and joined the Army ROTC. I also held a job at a clothing store and then a restaurant, where I was more or less discovered.

"ONE PROBLEM I OFTEN SEE WITH WOMEN IS THAT WE DO NOT HELP EACH OTHER."

Something important that sports did for me was to help me with my femininity. I was very tall, and athletics helped me with my coordination and balance. One problem I often see with women is that we do not help each other, and sports also teaches you the idea of teamwork. We are on a team, and we are in this together. Men do it all the time, but historically I don't think women were ever taught this.

"THOSE THREE PLAYERS HAVE
TO BE ON THE SAME PAGE."

I have had $40 million movies with my name attached to them. It's a lot of pressure on my shoulders, and I think that my athletic background has absolutely helped me handle the responsibility. The feeling on the set comes from the top down. If any of the top three players are having any problems, it permeates throughout the set. The lead actors and director have to get along and work well together, and I know how to make that happen. Those three players have to be on the same page, and I have often sacrificed to make that work.

The one time it was most obvious was in a movie called *Vendetta 2*, with Eli Wallach, Burt Young, and just an all-around great cast. The director walked up to me the first day of shooting and said, "You are my weakest link, but I had to take you," and then he proceeded to blast me for forty minutes in front of the entire cast and crew. *Vendetta 1* had been a huge success, and it was the story of a woman, and that woman was me, so it made no sense to blast me like that. After day one was over, I went to Burt Young's door. I was upset and he gave me the best advice: "Just do what you do. You'll always run into people who will not like you and all you can do is the best you can." That's just what I needed to hear. So I called my acting coach and she came to the set and we went to work. By the end of the film, the director was coming to me asking my take on different scenes. I'd completely won him over. It was very similar to trying to win over a coach who doesn't think you can play. In movies, the news business, modeling, and sports there are always going to be people who want you to do well and ones who want you to fail. The only way to handle that is to block it all out, do your best, and whatever happens, happens. What you can't do is let these people get into your head and affect your performance.

This is why today I really have no regrets about what I did in sports or in my career. I didn't always win or get the job, but I feel that my effort was there and I did the best I could. And without sports, I just don't think I would have known what I was made of and what I could actually do.

WOLFE IS AT RIGHT.

★KEN WOLFE★

Former Chairman and CEO of Hershey's

Football

A t this stage of my life, there are two periods in my past that come to mind. Number one was when I started playing football and number two was when I was about to conclude playing football.

I started playing football in seventh grade in Lebanon, Pennsylvania. Some ninth grader came through and smacked me in the mouth and knocked me down. I was bleeding and my lip was cracked, and the coach had to come over and help stop the bleeding. As my face was puffing up, the coach said to me, "Look, Ken, you should tell Harry to stop, or else he'll do it again when I turn my back. So you'll have to deal with him somehow." I'm not sure what possessed me, but I was on defense and I made a seven-yard run and smacked into that son of a bitch as hard as I could. I was able to knock him down and there was dust kicked up all over the field. I braced myself for the retaliation, but much to my surprise, there never was any. I think the reason was that he knew there would be a response on my part.

I was twelve at the time, and what I learned from that incident was never to walk around acting like a tough guy because there's always someone tougher than you. If, in fact, someone comes your way and slams you, you have to slam them back twice as hard. And I don't mean physically.

I've carried this lesson into my adult life. I've learned to respond forcefully. If anyone ever puts me under attack, I always confront that person immediately and, figuratively speaking, of course, deliver a blow that puts an end to the intimidation.

What football does for a young man is make him feel confident which is, I think, unique to any contact sport, like hockey and football. There's an element of physicality to those sports and you can't just let anyone run over you and that's something I've never forgotten.

"FOOTBALL GAVE ME THE CONFIDENCE
TO DO MOST ANY JOB."

When I was in my senior year at Yale, we were undefeated and untied. We were ranked twenty-third or twenty-fifth in the country, which might not have been fair, considering our competition, but we were. That season I learned that everyone has a role to play, and if someone falls down on a play, the team does not go anywhere. This taught me about individual responsibility, about doing your job while at the same time not letting your head get out in front of you. We knew we had talent and yet we were humble and worked hard, despite the fact that we thought we could win every game we played.

As we went through the year, we began winning by larger and larger margins. The last two games we played, against Princeton and Harvard, we won handily. What you learn from all this is that if you have an organization, you must make sure that everyone knows that they have an individual role and if anyone breaks down and doesn't do their job, you let the entire team down.

I used this philosophy in business, where I tried to make everyone feel like an integral part of the team. They had to do well because that would be the only way the team could do well. Football gave me the confidence to do most any job and the notion of teamwork, learning to delegate and the sense we are in this together which ultimately yields better results.

At Lebanon High School, I was, by all accounts, a tremendous player—I was first team All-State (the other half-back on the team that year, by the way, was Herb Adderly). We had a great team, and since I was the only running back I scored a lot of touchdowns. My senior year, I think I had twenty of them. If you remember Lenny Moore, from the Baltimore Colts, we both shared the state record for touchdowns.

Football helped me get into Yale, because they could have had plenty of people with perfect SATs, but schools need bands, skating, swimmers, and football players, so it made me a better package. At Yale, I caught passes and had touchdowns, but I certainly wasn't the best back in the Ivy League.

I was fortunate that I never let myself get too carried away with my accomplishments. I always had a good team and a very good line in front of me. I actually got invited to the LA Rams training camp, but I was too small and too slow and generally not good enough to make the NFL. But I didn't have NFL dreams, because I knew I just wasn't up to that level of play.

"MY MOM HAD ASKED ME TO WEAR A MOUTHPIECE."

Over the years, I can't tell you how many times I've gone places and someone has said, "I remember you when you played for this school or that school." I have to tell you, I almost never remember the particular game they're talking about. But my football team from high school is still very close, and the fellows I played with at Yale get together every two or three years for mini-reunions. And yet, I don't remember too much from those days.

But I do remember when I was playing junior high football and my teeth were knocked out. My mom had asked me to wear a mouthpiece, but I told her I couldn't breathe with it on, so I didn't wear one. It was a Thursday afternoon and I ran through the line and got held and a guy came up and just kicked me in the mouth. My teeth came right out. I came off the field and I sat on the bench bleeding all over the place. Coach came over and asked how I felt and I said, "Not great. I can't feel my mouth."

He said, "Okay, want to go back in?"

I went back in and scored two touchdowns. It hurt later that night, but I got some new teeth—and I always took them out before I played.

★BERNIE MAC★

Comedian and Actor

Basketball, Baseball, Football, Boxing

I got cut from the basketball team five times as a freshman in high school and five more times from the varsity team. But I kept sneaking back and finally, because I just wouldn't go away, I made the team.

I also played baseball, but I didn't get cut from that team. And in football, I was pretty good, too, as a quarterback. But it was cold in Chicago, where I grew up, so I said, "I ain't playin' no football because it's too damn cold out there."

My brother, who was a chiseled six-footer, was a fifth-degree black belt who busted bricks with his bare hands. He used to win a few dollars betting folks who thought he couldn't bust them, and that was a lot of money back then.

My brother was the one who forced me into boxing when I was about fourteen or fifteen, because he could see that I was into physical sports. I started boxing, which was an indoor sport, so I didn't have to contend with the Chicago winters, but I didn't like it much because I didn't have the mentality for hurting people for no good reason. Defending yourself is one thing, but the mind-set you have to have in boxing is having the killer attitude, which I had in basketball and football and which I have in comedy, but I didn't have it in boxing. I was afraid to be hit in the face. I was scared to get it in the jaw. The first time I got hit it scared me, but you know what, it didn't really hurt that much. I took his best. Sure, that night I couldn't open my mouth, but I still got confidence. I got hit and I was okay. You learn about yourself. It's a process.

Boxing is something you have to sleep, eat, and drink, and I didn't like that. I like entertaining, love, and peace. But the thing is, I was very good at boxing.

"I'M COMING RIGHT BACK
YOUR WAY, SO GET READY."

I was also good at baseball, which I liked. For example, if you threw in-side and hit me, that was a treat. I wasn't going to charge the mound. I was a real devil. I'd get on and, taking a page from Joe Morgan, Curt Flood, and Lou Brock, I'd steal second. I learned how to turn on it, get the hit, then take the base. I prided myself on being able to keep my head.

Same thing in football. I'd get hit when I was out of bounds, I'd go flying 15 yards in the air, and I'd just get back up and let the other guy know that he didn't do anything to me. Sure, he was bigger than me and yeah, I was hurting. But I got up as if nothing was wrong, with him yelling at me, "I'll get ya again."

I'd say, "I'm coming right back your way, so get ready." That's how it was.

In basketball, it was the same thing. You fouled me hard, I would not miss the free throws. I learned that from my high school coach who would have us run laps. After thirty laps, he'd toss us the ball, yelling, "Mac, go to the line." If you hit the shot, you and the whole team could stop running, but you had to hit the free throws. It got to the point, where he'd never call me because I didn't miss. That's how focused I was. I just loved the pressure and even now, I love it in the shows that I do. I wish I could tell you where it came from, but I can't. Maybe it's because I don't look at it as pressure, but as an opportunity.

I guess it kind of started with me as a kid in fifth grade. I got to talking in class and my teacher said, "Bernie, you are talking and I'm talking, so why don't you come up here and share your story with the rest of the class."

I said, "Okay," and I told a story off the top of my head.

The next Friday, the kids were acting up so Mrs. Cochran said, "If you don't settle down, I will not let Bernie tell any stories."

I had no idea she wanted me to tell stories. I asked, "What kinda story do you want to hear?" The kids hollered something out, and I told a twenty-minute story off the top of my head.

Mrs. Cochran told the principal, "I've got this kid who can tell a story. I'm not sure where he gets them from, but you've got to see this." The next week, the principal and two other classes, totaling about sixty people, were there waiting to listen to me. Again, I asked them what they wanted to hear. They told me, and I did thirty minutes this time.

They ended up putting me in this district competition. I was in the finals and this girl from another school was ahead of me and she had everyone howling with laughter. My friends kept telling me, "Don't freeze up. Don't choke."

My mom heard this and said, "Just be yourself. Don't hear the voices."

"What voices?" I asked.

She said, "Talk from your heart, play from your heart, and you will never lose. And even if you do lose, you win."

They gave this girl a standing ovation. She walked off and I got introduced and I looked at my mom and she winked at me. I didn't think about it. I went with what got me there. I told my story and I won.

"I WAS NEVER PICKED FIRST TO DO ANYTHING."

Sports taught me a lot about sacrifice, obedience, love, and dedication. New day, new practice, new game. I thought you always had to prove yourself every day. I was never a thrill seeker. I saw guys in high school who would finish the game and run to the scorer's table and say, "Look, I scored 7," or "I scored 12." I went right to the locker room. It's the same with comedy. When I'm done, I stick the mike in the holder and I'm gone. Applaud if you want, but I'm thinking about tomorrow, because I get a kick out of topping what I've done. I took my sports experience to my life on stage. That's why I'm so disciplined.

In my career, it took me eighteen years to get to a point where I understood what comedy was all about. It was the same thing in baseball. I studied Rod Carew and Pete Rose, so I would not strike out. I noticed how they moved their feet, how they changed their stance, how Pete ran to first base. You can be good at something, but still not know what it's all about. You have to have physical skills. You have to want to look good.

Playing sports, I was always underestimated. I was never picked first to do anything. I never walked into a party and had women say, "Who the hell is that? Damn, he's something." But at the end of the party they would always say, "Are you coming back tomorrow?" This always helped me. It taught me how to push myself. Boxing was good for me because it taught me how to fight tired. Sometimes I let people think they are winning.

I went through a stage when I was an All-Star in practice, but I didn't have the confidence to do it in games. You get benched, you wallow in pity.

But you get better, then you get lucky, make a few hot shots, you smile all night. It's all part of the growing process.

A lot of cats have one or two good years and then they believe the hype that they read in the papers. "He is the best running back in the league," or "He's the best quarterback since such and such." And then they believe all that. They listen to that bull, which only puts the pressure on.

My brother was an example of what not to do. He should have played pro. He was brought up to the Cardinal's farm system. In one game, he was 2 for 3, but he went to a bar and bragged about it and never developed any further. I'd hear these old stories over and over again, 203 times a night, games from years ago. That's not me.

★JIM CAVIEZEL★

Actor

Basketball

I grew up just north of Seattle, where everybody loved the Sonics. Lonnie Shelton and Lenny Wilkens were my heroes, and that's why I went to their basketball camps. I played every day after school and I'd wear my wristbands like they did and even had a signed shirt from both of them.

I was good athlete, but I really worked at it. My dad, who earned a full ride to UCLA to play basketball under John Wooden, and my brother were better players than I was, but they always marveled at how hard and how often I worked. I got everything I possibly could out of my physical ability, out of my body. I made starting lineup in high school for a team that was third in the state, and I had opportunities to go to a NAIA Division 2 school.

Coming out of junior high school I was a very good player, so good that my freshman year in high school I started talking about playing on the varsity and so I got the nickname, Varsity.

I wasn't the greatest student, but I wanted to be good at something, so I trained heavily every day for basketball. I had a regular shooting workout. My sophomore year, I broke down my shot because a coach had told me that I was a streak shooter and I wanted to be a pure shooter. To do that, you have to make believe you are shooting in a telephone booth—straight up with back spin—so you hit the rim and it goes in. I would work on my weaknesses, learn to change direction, to change speeds, to go left.

"I WAS MOTIVATED BY FEAR."

I knew my friends, my teammates, were not working nearly as hard as me, and yet they were still better than I was. I just didn't get it, and eventually I burnt out. That's because I was motivated by fear, which burns you out. I would be very nervous, saying, "I should be training instead of doing this or that," instead of saying, "I love to train." I always feared that someone was getting better than me. It was also hard for me because my younger brother was an All-American, recruited by three or four hundred universities. He was a 6′ 8″ point guard who could pass like Pistol Pete Maravich and had an uncanny ability to see the whole court like Jason Kidd does.

Soon my body helped me out by getting bigger and stronger, and I was able to go further because I got bigger than the others.

"I HAVE TO GET BACK IN THE GAME."

Basketball taught me to train for every possible situation but always stay in the moment. One time, in high school, I received a severe head injury, which turned out to be a concussion. It was the district finals and I was going for a loose ball at the same time as another guy. We hit each other when we were going at full speed. I got caught the wrong way and stepped on the ball, and it twisted me around. My leg shot out from under me and I landed head first, and he landed on my head. The trainer came over and all he could say was, "Oh, my God. Oh, my God." I thought that was it. My eyes hit a tunnel and I went out thinking, I have not lived my life yet. I was so sad and I was asking for another chance. I thought I was dying. I had to be airlifted to the hospital but all I could think about is, I have to get back in the game.

"I KNEW I HAD THE TALENT, I JUST HAD TO GET OUT OF MY OWN WAY."

Here's how participating in sports played into my life in Hollywood. At first I would go to an audition and blow it. I realized I was not getting any opportunities, and my agent got rid of me. It took a lot of pain, but I said, Okay, I didn't do this right in basketball. I could have been better, but physically and mentally I would sabotage myself. And now I'm doing it again. I knew I had the talent, I just had to get out of my own way.

Mondays were always my worst auditions, because I would go out all weekend. I gave that up. I changed my whole approach, and the night before an audition I would not go out. I really started to improve quickly. One Monday I had an audition for *The Thin Red Line*. I walked in and through the wall I could hear some of the others auditioning and I could tell they hadn't prepared. Their timing was off. Or they didn't sound natural. It gave me confidence, and as a result I was comfortable when I walked in. The casting director told me to stand here and I said, "I need to be there." She was not happy, but I needed to take control as if I were on the court. I was right. I didn't push it or force anything, and so it flowed. And I got the part.

Acting is all about focus, something you learn in sports. In basketball, you shoot 100 shots a day, just trying to get better, always moving, always looking for the open shot, then running to get your own rebound. Practice does make perfect. And that's also what I love about acting.

In the movie in which I played Bobby Jones, I had to hit this putt with 400 people watching. I nailed it and the place went nuts. It was all about preparation. It's about having the work ethic, the discipline. In basketball, I would arrive at practice an hour earlier just to drill my shot.

I learned to play with pain, and now I've learned how to use that in acting. I've done some roles that were very physically taxing. I came back from filming *The Passion of the Christ* with gray hair and a separated shoulder, and I was struck by lightning. On the cross, I used the pain of being in a defensive stance. I'd squat and put all my weight on one leg on the cross. I was freezing. I wanted to hold my hands in tight. There I was, with the wind howling, shivering, my shoulder was separated so there was a shooting pain with every move. I had hypothermia, so I couldn't keep any food down. So, I played in pain for that entire movie. And it was my years in sports that got me through the biggest movie in my career.

McCAIN IS IN THE FRONT ROW, THIRD FROM RIGHT.

★JOHN McCAIN★

U.S. Senator from Arizona

Wrestling, Boxing, Football

I f I were to describe myself as an athlete it would be, "mediocrity at its finest." And yet, if I took sports out of my life there would be a huge vacancy.

I wrestled and played football in high school and, in my last year, I started as a wrestler and actually had a fairly good record. But I hated to lose. I always gave it everything I had which, unfortunately, was not as much as I'd hoped for. But keep in mind, I feel like I got the most out of my ability.

There is one match that I will never forget. I was wrestling and my opponent had been interscholastic champion the year before. Our bout was in this tiny gymnasium, and right away he put me on my back. I spent the whole period trying not to get pinned. Well, right before the match was going to end, I escaped, and suddenly I heard this tremendous scream from somewhere in the audience. We both stopped, I looked up, and I saw that it was my mother. She was just so happy that I hadn't gotten pinned.

I started boxing in high school and boxed at the Naval Academy as well as in the summer when the midshipmen would cruise around to different places. In the Naval Academy, every Saturday night they would have boxing matches—smokers, actually—and I boxed for my battalion in front of 1,000 shipmen, the faculty, and their wives. It was a thrilling experience, and I just loved it. I didn't have any fear of losing or getting hit. Instead, I just felt anticipation and excitement.

One moment that was special above all the rest was winning my last bout at the Naval Academy to finish the entire summer undefeated. That was thrilling, but what's more, it helped me in prison because the first time I got knocked around by the Vietnamese, it did not come as a total shock.

When I was in prison for five-and-a-half years in Vietnam, I got beat up a lot. It wasn't easy, but I'm sure glad I had the experience of contact sports, because I learned perseverance and how to recover. To this day, I have never learned how to lose.

I was lucky at both the high school I attended and at the Naval Academy that participation in sports was required. I have this theory that people who are fairly decent high school athletes have the greatest appreciation for high school and college. I really believe the committed sports fans are people like me, because I had a level of participation in high school and college that allowed me to appreciate the enormous talent that's needed in order to excel in these sports.

"HE SAID HE'D RATHER BE DEAD."

My biggest thrill was meeting Ted Williams, because growing up he was everything I ever wanted to be, and I idolized him. He was a great player, but he was also a fighter pilot. I was like any fan. I had questions ranging from asking him about Joe DiMaggio, to why the hell he didn't eject when his jet was on fire in Korea. His answer, by the way, was that he was too big for the cockpit and he was afraid that if he tried to eject his knees would get caught. They'd be wrecked and then he wouldn't be able to play baseball again, and he said he'd rather be dead.

All this plays into why I am fighting to clean up sports, especially boxing, the Olympics, and baseball steroid abuse. These sports are very important to America. They provide us with entertainment, but also knowledge, and they create a sense of unity. When the Diamondbacks won the World Series, the citizens of Arizona were together like no other day since we attained statehood. Only sports can do that. When Charles Barkley brought the Suns to the NBA finals, that was another galvanizing moment. Boxing today pains me, because these fine athletes are being abused by unscrupulous people who use the system to exploit these often unsuspecting men. We have improved it some, but until we get a national boxing body, it will not have legitimacy, in large part because states like Nevada don't want to give up their power.

Over the years, I've met some of the most powerful people in the world, but when I see a great Hall of Fame player I have to marvel. Why? Because it takes such great skill, concentration, dedication, and focus to reach that level. Like Randy Johnson. Anytime I'm around him, I'm just in awe. After all, here's a guy who just pitched a perfect game at over age forty. Not many people can say that.

★HANK PAULSON★

CEO and Chairman of Goldman Sachs

Football, Wrestling

had a fifth-grade teacher who did two things that changed my life: He took me to a Cubs baseball game, and as a result I became a lifelong Cubs fan; and he taught me how to play flag football. I also played Little League and played baseball and basketball in grade school through junior high. But my eye-hand coordination wasn't good, so I knew I was never going to be a terrific baseball or basketball player. It was only when I got to high school that I played football and wrestled.

As a child, I could beat most kids in sprints, but overall, wrestling was the most natural sport for me. In fact, I was a pretty good high school wrestler. I was unusually quick and strong. That translated over to football, where I was quick off the ball, stayed low, and was able to overpower bigger guys. It never occurred to me that I would be hurt, and I never missed a play because of injury.

When I was at Dartmouth, you couldn't play varsity as a freshman, so I started on the freshman team. I was small and got buried on the depth chart. Fortunately for me, we had a challenge system. It was a nutcracker drill, where two linemen squared off with each other and if you won, you started and played, and I kept winning.

When it came to my sophomore year, I was devastated because the freshman line coach moved up to coach varsity. I didn't think the coach liked me and, once again, I was buried in the depth chart, actually behind some of the teammates I beat out my freshman year. I was going to quit and I told my parents about it. They simply asked, "Would you be happier if you quit?"

I thought about it and said no, and so I decided to go back and give it my all. Once again I was saved by the challenge system, which allowed me to move up.

Nonetheless, as the first game of my sophomore year approached there was still some question about whether I would be a starter, so I asked head coach, Bob Blackman, what my status was. He wasn't keen to start sophomores the first game because, he said, they made lots of mistakes. I managed to convince him to give me the chance to start from the first play of the first game. We ended up winning the Lambert Trophy, and I led the team in minutes played.

I learned early on that there was a direct correlation between how hard I worked and how I did. I also learned to talk through important issues with the boss.

"IT'S TOUGH TO TELL HOW AN OFFENSIVE TACKLE IS PLAYING."

My parents were not particularly interested in team sports, but once I got involved they were at all my games and gave me great encouragement. Being the parents of an offensive tackle, well, I'm not quite sure they knew what they were looking for. It's tough to tell how an offensive tackle is playing. But they would say, "Hey, that's my son, number 76, out there." They liked the fact I was on a team, enjoyed it, and was doing well.

Anyone who plays the offensive line understands the meaning of being a team player and, for the most part, does not need the spotlight or media attention. I was just one cog in the wheel, but I knew the way I did my job could make a big difference between success and failure for the team. And my whole team was made up of high school football stars. We didn't do it for the perks or the glory we played because we loved the game.

There's something special about being a lineman. If someone cares about being a star or getting attention, then they don't want to be a lineman. If you're out there in the dirt and the mud, play after play, loving it and doing well for the team, then you more than likely will do well at a firm like Goldman Sachs. It's all about teamwork, and if you're a real team player it's hard to be arrogant about your position, whether it be at work or on the field.

My seminal moment was when I got the award for best lineman in New England and Greg Landry, former Detroit Lions quarterback, won it as the best back. I was about 200 pounds, and it was a running joke that he was bigger than I was—and he was a quarterback.

"THE BIGGEST SINGLE FACTOR HOLDING
PEOPLE BACK IS FEAR."

As a businessman, I like people who are participators. It could be in sports, on the debate team or in the school play—whatever. I just want to see if you work well with others and put yourself on the line. The single biggest factor holding people back is fear. Fear of getting hurt, fear of failing. The self-confidence that comes from working hard, getting better, and growing as a person is part of being happy. I feel true happiness comes from challenging yourself, working hard, and achieving success.

Football added to my confidence, and it taught me how to fit in with others. I achieved success in sports and in business because I worked very hard. I can't say that if hadn't wrestled and hadn't played football, I wouldn't be where I am today, but I would say that I would not be the person I am if I hadn't played football. I was fortunate that my coaches were intelligent people, and they dealt with us in a mature way. We learned to play by the rules, and if you didn't, you got penalized. I have never forgotten that lesson. Never.

★KURT RUSSELL★

Actor

Baseball

When people know you from acting, that's what they know you from, but the friends I had growing up knew me from playing baseball, and they were mystified as to how my television and movie career developed. They used to say, "Hey, get me into that. You get to meet girls and stuff, so help me get out there."

My world growing up much more revolved around baseball than acting. I played baseball about 350 days a year, and when I went on to pro ball it continued. The world was gauged around baseball, and my day revolved around practice and games. Acting was just a way to get myself money to live on, but baseball is how I intended to spend my life.

I didn't join a baseball team until I was nine years old, when I joined a Little League team. I started playing and found I was good at. I began to stand out when I was eleven years old, and by fourteen or fifteen, I said that I wanted to make baseball my career. My dad, Bing Russell, had a big role in this goal. He played minor league ball in the Yankee and White Sox organization. His godfather was Lefty Gomez. Eventually he had to leave the game with a head injury. He was the best, most knowledgeable coach around, and he kept increasing his knowledge of baseball. He was a terrific teacher of the game, and I was lucky to be his son. You always knew what he was thinking, and you always knew where you stood. He was tough, but very fair.

Baseball shaded my entire outlook on life, because that's how I first saw the world. I looked at everything, even today, through what I learned about the game. Like pacing yourself, focusing yourself, preparing yourself for what you want to do, keeping yourself healthy for the game. I do all that through the eyes of a ballplayer.

"THE PRETENDERS SPEND A GREAT
DEAL TIME MASKING THEIR REALITY."

When I was playing Herb Brooks in *Miracle*, I was struck by how much Herb and my dad, Bing, were alike. My dad was always trying to get the best out of every player through manipulation and hard work. Physical errors didn't mean anything to him, while mental errors meant everything. Once you understood that, you began to see the value in paying attention and focusing on the task at hand. I grew to learn and apply in every aspect of my life the need to pay attention to all areas, especially as you rise up the ladder. When the competition gets better, even the smallest error can make or break you. You realize that he who has the supreme confidence got it because he paid attention to every aspect of his task. Working hard with the correct coaching gives you a confidence that's invaluable at the highest level at every task. Even if you hit a slump in any sport or your career, if you have that supreme confidence, you know you will recover. The pretenders spend a great deal time masking their reality.

Sadly, my dad died while I was filming that movie, and so did Herb.

"DO YOU THINK YOU COULD HAVE
PLAYED IN THE MAJOR LEAGUES?"

I know I was born to be good at the game. I could hit in my sleep. I started off fast as a kid with a strong arm. I could turn the double play. I was a switch hitter. The questions always asked me is, "Do you think you could have played in the Major Leagues?" That's a really lame question. The better question would be, "Do you think you could help a team win consistently?" Could I have been an impact player? That's a question you can't answer until you go out there and do it.

Did I ever coast on my talent and get a wake-up call? Only in that I began to work on my weaknesses after going through a period where I was thinking I was working hard and wasn't working on the right things. I started to work on the right things, and when people talk about an athlete maturing, that's what they're talking about: Working on things you need to work on, and working hard.

"I HAVE NO REGRETS."

I have no regrets. I was injured and never got my Major League shot, but I feel fortunate because for me, my injury came at the right time. If I had not gotten hurt, I would have played forever and not had the full life and career I am enjoying today. I would not have met all these great people from around the world. I would have taken great pains not to ski or do anything else in the off-season. As a ballplayer, I would not have been able to spend the quality time I spend with my family. But don't get me wrong. When I got hurt, I cried for three days and felt sorry for myself, and it wasn't because of the torn rotator cuff. It was because I knew it was over. And yet I picked myself up and started acting again.

What truly hurt is that six months into my final season I was hitting .562, coming out of being named to two minor league All-Star teams in two years. I am just so lucky that my life turned out to be so wonderful that I don't have sit there and think, "If only I didn't get hurt . . ."

I have so much appreciation for these players who do what they do every day in baseball. That's why you see these guys cry when they win a championship. It is such a long haul and you are overwhelmed when you reach the top. Sure, I wanted to experience that. And I regretted that an injury took away my career, but I had to move on.

"IF YOU GET HURT, YOU GET UP, MAKE THE ADJUSTMENT, AND GO FOR IT AGAIN."

From playing the game, I learned that if you have a setback, if you get hurt, you get up, make the adjustment, and go for it again. Make as few mistakes as possible, and that's what takes you higher.

I took that lesson into my life. Yes, the games do count—if you get the right coach. Because bad coaches can be extremely destructive, not just to talent but to the psyche of the individual. It can be devastating, and I see it al the time. These coaches want to be good, but they are in it for the wrong reason. They only want to win. A coach should just get the best out of all their players, and the wins will follow.

I have a son who is paying minor league hockey. I am happy because he has talent and a bright future. I just want him to have a well-rounded life and not be myopic about the sport. I just want to make sure that he keeps his eyes open to the rest of the world.

★RON SHELTON★

━━━ Director and Screenwriter ━━━

Baseball

I first started playing sports when I was three years old, and to prove it, there are photos of me holding a ball. We lived out on the West Coast, and Jackie Robinson was a family hero. I knew my mom and dad thought he was a great player, but only later did I realize all the other great things he stood for. I was also a huge fan of the Milwaukee Braves because Eddie Matthews was on the team, and every little boy from Santa Barbara wanted to be Eddie Matthews.

We never had Little League in Santa Barbara, and they still don't. They do have recreational leagues, but the parents aren't allowed to have anything to do with it, and there are no uniforms until kids turn thirteen, which I think is visionary. I am not a big fan of Little League, because I think there is just too much pressure. I don't think an eleven-year-old should be dealing with regional finals.

I started to realize when I was young that I was a pretty good player because when I got to high school I was able to beat out upperclassman. I started playing second base and then, when I grew a little, I moved over to shortstop. I hung up a carpet in my backyard and kept hitting at it until the carpet fell apart. The practice paid off, because I won some hitting championships in high school, then I hit .500 my senior year.

I was a tough, hard-nosed competitor who played hurt. I was kind of old school in that way. I got that approach to baseball from my dad who was a baseball player in college. Those were the rules he laid down for me growing up: You play hard and don't complain.

My dad came to all my games, to the point where I wish he would have let me alone a little more. I got to like high school road games because he wasn't in the stands. Not that he put pressure on me, it was just that I reached a point where I wanted to make it on my own. I needed a little room. Which is why I think parents should show an interest in their kid's game but not be oppressive about it. The kid is out there playing for himself, not to please you. Let the kid be a kid.

Almost all the good memories I have from when I was young were in sports and they usually include my teammates and the games we won and lost. For instance, I remember the college championship game I played in for a small college on the West Coast that sent us to the nationals. We scored four runs in the bottom of the ninth to win 4–3.

The only way to get me to quit baseball was knowing I could move on to another "show," to borrow a term I used in *Bull Durham*. I felt like I was going to be another Crash Davis, a career Triple-A player. I didn't know which direction I was going in. I always knew it was going to be a lot of hard work, but it was also fun. There's a lot of pressure on baseball players. They live and die by their statistics. A player goes 0 for 5, and he starts to go crazy. A pitcher goes winless in five starts, and he begins to look over his shoulder.

Almost everything I know that's worthwhile I learned playing sports. All the critical lessons, from the time I was a boy through college and my years in the pros, came from athletics. It was all part of my education, and in fact it helped me get a formal education by way of getting a scholarship to college. Sports teaches you so much: how to lose—not to be happy with it, mind you—but how to deal with it. For instance, in marriage you have ups and downs, and in your work life you have ups and downs, and sports teaches you how to deal with those ups and downs without lessening your commitment.

As a director, I love dealing with ex-athletes. They are the easiest guys to direct. They respect authority. They listen and they give input, but they know where the buck stops. And, they are used to doing the same thing over and over again, because rehearsal is just like practice. Instead of, "Give me 100 ground balls," it's, "Redo that scene again." They are on time and they don't complain. Athletes also know how to turn it up a notch and perform in the clutch. Tommy Lee Jones, who was All-Ivy League in football, was great when I directed him in *Cobb*.

"I DON'T LIKE LOOKING BACK IN THE REARVIEW MIRROR."

I am proud of what I accomplished, but I don't like looking back in the rearview mirror. I did what I did at the time and then I moved on. It's not that I don't think about it, because I do. It's just difficult because you tend to remember failures, not successes: that hanging curve you didn't hit that would have gotten the team to the next level in the playoffs; the ball I misplayed at short that I wish I could have charged harder to make a better play on. Some guys dwell on successes and say, "Hey, Ron, you won the league championship and you led the team in hitting."

"Yeah, but I should have handled that groundball."

I played pick-up basketball into my forties, right up until the time I made *White Men Can't Jump*. I knew the game because I was a college All-American basketball player. I just loved that world. But the thing about baseball is that it's played every day, sometimes at night. In the minors there was hardly a day off.

What makes sports so compelling is that we don't know the ending. We never know how the third act is going to wind up. We live out the soap opera with real guys who are really good at what they do. We are fascinated by their successes and their failures. That's why we watch.

I've never been in awe of the tremendous athlete. I think some get a gift from the gods and work at it and become great. I tend to be more impressed by a guy who has achieved greatness outside of the spotlight, against bigger odds, with less going for him.

As for me, I didn't max out my talent. Looking back, I see I could have approached it differently. I worked hard but I never worked out in the off-season, like guys do now. But I guess, at the time, I did all that I could.

★DONNA LOPIANO★

Executive Director of the
Women's Sports Foundation

Softball, Basketball, Volleyball, Badminton

I grew up in Stamford, Connecticut, on a street with fifteen boys and one other girl, so I don't remember sports not being a part of my life.

Our house was on a dead-end street, and as soon as we got home from school, all the kids were outside playing some kind of sport. We painted bases on the curb in the middle of the street and played baseball, for instance. I realized right away that I was pretty good at all these sports the same way all kids know how good they are. You win all the races and you're always picked first for a team. Or, you got to be captain.

If we weren't playing baseball with a taped up ball, we were playing PG ball, which was a game played with bat or broomstick and this small whiffle ball. We played it in a driveway between two houses. Your hit was determined by where the ball went. For instance, if you hit it above the second story window it was a double; on the roof, it was a home run. It was great fun.

"I WASN'T ALLOWED TO PLAY BECAUSE I WAS A GIRL."

One season, I played both basketball and football, but when it came to Little League and I was drafted first, I wasn't allowed to play because I was a girl, and those were the rules at the time. It bothered me when they banned me—I was the best player—and I cried for three months. It was a hard thing to deal with. It wasn't until I was sixteen that I was old enough to play in industrial women's league softball. I never forgot what it felt like to be prevented from playing Little League. Although I didn't vow to change things at the time, it does result in your developing a social justice mind-set.

In high school, we played all sports, but the seasons were so short. Our basketball season for women only last six games. The same with softball. So I played volleyball, badminton, and field hockey.

I knew I wanted to stay in sports after college, so I started to go for my master's, specializing in the social aspect of sports. This was well before any women's movement and before most women felt they could question the way things were. I was done with my master's before the 1970s began, so when change started to happen, I was well prepared to take part fighting for women and trying to level the playing field.

The first activist thing I ever did was testify before Congress at twenty-nine against the Tower amendment to Title 9. My work in helping to get Title 9 on the books and keeping it there is a source of great pride for me, and it didn't come easily, since it's taken thirty years of hard work. Now, the Women's Sports Foundation has become the equivalent of a trade organization for women's professional sports. You could call it the national advocacy organization for those who have been wronged because of their gender.

As far as my athletic career is concerned, it doesn't bother me that I never had a WNBA or WUSA to try out for, because I really believe athletes know how good they are. I knew how good I was and sure, I didn't get an opportunity to play in those leagues because it was a different time and a different place, but I did get a chance to play internationally in softball.

"I APPROACH EVERYTHING THE SAME WAY I DID SPORTS WHEN I WAS YOUNGER."

When I was growing up, there was no weight training and certainly no weight room. I can't envision how much better I would have been with advanced training and better coaching. I have to wonder sometimes how good I could have been.

Even though I don't play today, I approach everything the same way I did sports when I was younger. You can't separate me from sports, because sports is the most multicultural learning environment you can find anywhere. I used it as a training ground. It's an ongoing reality play. Will you choose to polish your skills or won't you? Will you take responsibility for your own performance? Instead of a ball and glove, today it's all about research and facts. Instead of pitching, it's my communication skills. I am what sports made me, and I am better for it. I learned simple things, like how to behave when speaking in public. I just follow the first rule of sports, which is to learn not to show that you're nervous. If you create a persona of confidence, then you become confident. You also learn how to deal with pressure. Playing in a World

Championship for your country, going into the seventh inning trailing by one run, that's pressure. Speaking to a couple hundred people, that's not pressure.

My memories in sports are not about the winning home run or the great pitch, they're about the throw I didn't make, or the pitch I didn't hit, or the catch I didn't make. However, the moments I like best are the plays I made that didn't get noticed. Like getting to a ball I didn't think I could get to, or beating out the slow ground ball for a single. But the best moment ever had to be playing for my country in the first World Softball Championship in Australia. It wasn't what I did, it was just being good enough to represent this country. That's something I will never forget and something I think about often.

★LAURIE DHUE★

Television Anchor
and Reporter

Track, Swimming

Sports began for me at a very young age because of my father, who played football at Virginia Military Institute. I'm not sure if he was hoping for a boy and got a girl, but I actually looked like a boy. I had a Dorothy Hamill haircut and braces, and I wore sports jerseys.

My dad started taking me to the park on the weekends, and he says it was evident at an early age that I was coordinated. I had no fear. I would run and hang onto the jungle gym from the time I was three years old. I learned how to swim when I was three or four, and my dad says I would play handball on the beach where we lived in Florida.

Playing sports was a way for me and my dad to bond without even knowing it. I just loved hanging out with Dad. Before I played sports myself I was going to ball games with Dad and running around with him. I went on to become one of the top female athletes in my prep school in Atlanta.

"THAT WAS ONE WAY I EARNED RESPECT, BY BEING ONE OF THE GUYS."

To be honest, I was not too attractive growing up. I was tall, skinny, gangly, and unattractive to the point where I used to get made fun of because I was so ugly. I was a huge pair of lips on this little face. As painful as it is to discuss even today it just made me try harder in everything I did, because that was one way I earned respect, by being one of the guys. I was the only girl to play on the guys' football team and I would take them down. It used to be, "Oh, my God, Laurie Dhue is coming." I think this was a way for me to overcome being a dork. Sports was also a way to be better than the boys.

The key to my being good at sports may be that my dad never pushed me. He just said, "Do your best," and told me that there wasn't anything I couldn't do in sports or otherwise. Today, there are so many absentee parents or pushy parents in sports—they are the new version of backstage moms, but my parents were just supportive. They let me do it on my own, and that's the way I liked it.

My sophomore year in high school is when I began to take sports very seriously. I participated in cross country, track, and swimming. My junior year I quit track to concentrate on swimming, because it was the sport in which I showed the most promise. I was MVP my junior year, and my senior year I was captain and ranked fifth in the state in swimming.

"REPRESENTING THE UNIVERSITY OF NORTH CAROLINA, FRESHMAN FROM ATLANTA, GEORGIA, LAURIE DHUE."

When it came to college I chose North Carolina and walked onto the swim team without a scholarship. The coach liked me, and I worked hard and earned a place on the team.

Nothing could prepare me for the thrill of standing on the starting block for my first meet. It was against another ACC team, and I will never forget standing there, staring down on the pool and hearing on the PA system, "Representing the University of North Carolina, freshman from Atlanta, Georgia, Laurie Dhue." People applauded and that was the thrill of my life.

Now, everything has reversed. Today, I am this person who is known more for her looks than as an athlete. And although that may be the perception, I still think of myself as this unattractive girl who had to work extra hard.

Sports instilled in me a confidence and discipline I still carry with me to this day. It also taught me time management and the concept of team, as well as a sense of competition that I have never lost. I just hate the idea of letting anyone down, whether it's for an interview or an adventure for Fox that entails jumping out of a plane. I just want to be the best. I want my dad to be proud of me, and that's probably why I am so driven in my career, having become one of if not the youngest national cable anchors ever. CNN put me on the air when I was only twenty-six years old. And I think that I've benefited tremendously from my sports career, because I learned how to perform under pressure. And I just love that.

★DARIUS RUCKER★

Lead Singer of
Hootie and the Blowfish

Football

When I was six years old, playing Pop Warner football was my life. All the guys in my neighborhood in Charleston, South Carolina, played Pop Warner, and the practices were awesome, but the games were even more awesome. I remember watching Dallas beat Miami in the Super Bowl when I was five years old, and that's probably when it all began for me. My whole family was football crazy, but I was the only Dolphin fan, which wasn't easy. I knew football was the greatest game going. I loved anything having to do with football, but let's be honest, all we had in South Carolina were the Gamecocks and Clemson, so if we weren't playing the game we were reading about it or watching it. We took it so seriously that if you played soccer, you got beaten up.

I had dreams of playing in the NFL, and here's some news for you, I still have dreams of playing in the NFL. I always said I would give up all my years of success in the music business to play center on one drive in the NFL. Rock and roll was something to fall back on. If I had my choice, I'd be Jerry Rice and I'd be playing until I was forty-five.

The indelible moment for me came in ninth grade, when I looked at myself and then at some of the guys I'd be playing with and said, "I'm five-nine, kind of light, this is not going to happen. I am not going to be a football star." So, I started looking at Plan B, which was music. But I never left the team. I still went to all the games and truly enjoyed it.

I was quarterback most of the time, from the age of six to fourteen. I always thought of myself as the coach's dream. I wanted to be there on the field. I arrived early and stayed late and went all out. Unfortunately, football was the only area of my life where I had this kind of discipline. I could have been a good student, but I didn't focus enough.

Two years stand out for me as a player. At ten years old, I played on a team that went 0 and 10, but the next year, with the same guys, we went 10 and 0. We had a different coach and we were just so embarrassed by the previous year's record that we would do anything not to repeat it, and we ended up reversing it. The amazing thing is, I still see those guys today.

What I took from those two years was learning how to deal with failure. We really thought we were good, but it took a year before we really got good, and as a result of that losing season, we were able to keep our success in perspective.

"YOU'RE NOT HURT. GET UP!"

My mom was at every game, and when she was there you knew she was there. She was loud. My favorite story was about these twins who were huge and played defensive end. As quarterback, I'd go back to pass, and these two guys just crushed me. There I am, lying on my back. My ribs and back are killing me and I have the wind knocked out of me and all I hear is "You're not hurt. Get up. Get up!" Other moms might yell, "Stay down!" or run out on the field to see their kid was. But my mom just demanded that I get up. So, I got up. I loved that.

Another thing I learned from playing football was teamwork. I don't play football today, but our band is a team. The dressing room is our locker room. When we get on stage or we're in a meeting with the record label, we're a team. Now, as the quarterback of Hootie and the Blowfish, I know, for instance, that true discipline is not going out before a big gig, so I make sure we stay in if we have somewhere to be in the morning.

We started to break into the sports world with the hit, "Only Want to Be with You." We called up ESPN and the Dolphins and invited them into the video. We wanted to meet those guys, so that's why we cast them. Today, Dan Marino and I are best friends, but even though we're friends today, I still can't help being a fan.

What's great about music is that I can play through age forty, which is past the average athletic career. And I've still been able to maintain my sports connection. I have been asked to sing the national anthem dozens of times, including days after 9/11, which, with F-16s flying overhead, had to be the most emotional thing I've ever done.

It was also amazing and mind-blowing for me to be asked to sing "America the Beautiful" and "Amazing Grace" at Pat Tillman's funeral. Just to be a part of it at the memorial service was one of the greatest experiences of my life. It's very moving for me to think that I am included in the sports world, and that I'm called on in good times and in bad.

I sang the anthem on national TV in Atlanta before a World Series game, and guess who they sat me next to during the game? Cal Ripken. It was the best time I ever had at a baseball game. I met Jimmy Carter, too, but Cal's the one I remember. A World Series with Cal Ripken. It doesn't get much better than that.

TRUMP IS IN THE FRONT ROW, FOURTH FROM THE RIGHT.

★DONALD TRUMP★

Real Estate Developer, Author,
and Television Personality

Baseball, Football, Soccer

Sports, for me, is a microcosm of life. There is something about being an athlete that helps you become a successful businessperson.

I always had good eye-hand coordination. When it came to anything involving a ball, I was just very good at it. But if you took the ball out of the equation, it wasn't a pretty sight. For example, something like gymnastics wasn't for me. But it was something else if it came to hitting a baseball or a golf ball or throwing a football. I was supposed to be a pro baseball player. At the New York Military Academy, I was captain of the baseball team. I worked hard like everyone else, but I had good talent.

I am not sure if I was a competitive person who played sports or became more competitive because of sports, and I guess I'll never know the answer because I started playing when I was three and I always wanted to win.

I remember a number of moments in my sports career that really stood out. In baseball, I was a catcher and a first baseman and a pretty good hitter. There was an upperclassman who was an established player, and he was the first baseman. He was good, but I thought I was better. I was trying to beat him out at the position and he just forgot how to throw, the same way Chuck Knoblach, Steve Sax, and Mackey Sasser did. He may have felt the pressure of being challenged for the job, but there was this one ball he not only threw over the catcher's head, but over the entire backstop. I saw that and said, "Man, that better not happen to me." And it didn't. I ended up starting, but it was at that moment I realized what the mind can do.

Another moment I will never forget is the first time I saw my name in the newspaper. It was when I got the winning homerun in a game between our Academy and Cornwall High School. It was in 1964 and it was in a little local paper. It simply said, TRUMP HOMERS TO WIN THE GAME. I just loved it and I will never forget it. It was better than actually hitting the home run.

People asked me if I worked hard in sports. I didn't. I loved it too much to call it work. When people ask me, and they do all the time, "How do you become successful?" I say, "Love what you're doing." The second thing I tell them is that you can't stop. If there's a wall in front of you, you just have to get through it or over it. Just get to the other side. I see the most successful people love what they do, and they don't stop. I know people who are much smarter than other successful people I know, and they're still total failures. They don't have the drive. That drive comes automatically if you love doing what you're doing.

"WHAT I LOVED WAS THE PRESSURE AND THE CHANCE TO WIN A GAME WHEN IT WAS ON THE LINE."

I tried playing football and soccer the same year, which is pretty tough because they're both fall sports. Ultimately, I loved soccer more, but soccer in the sixties was just not as big a sport. I was a kicker on the football team because I had a very strong leg. What I loved about kicking was the pressure and the chance to win a game when it was on the line. It was the focus on execution in crunch time that was the attraction.

I loved sports, but I always had an eye on business and I was always prepared to move on. The problem with some of these great pros who I've had a chance to meet over the years is that they are true jocks who can't think about anything but sports. Ultimately, they will have hard time making the transition to business because they can't get their mind off the game. They struggle with retirement because they can't turn the page. I like to think I cared just as much, but I knew when to move on.

When I played high school ball, being a pro was in the equation, but it wasn't such a big deal for me in that those guys did not make a lot of money. Mickey Mantle, one of baseball's biggest stars, was only making $100,000. Still, I was still thinking in high school that I had a shot at the Major Leagues until I attended a tryout with another young kid named Willie McCovey. I watched him hit the ball, and I said I really believe I will enjoy the real estate business for my entire life. I had always felt like the best player until I saw that man hit. I said, after seeing him, "He will be great," and he turned out to be great. Sometimes you have to step aside. I knew I wouldn't be better then Willie McCovey, and even though I could play, I knew I would never be better than Mickey Mantle. But I also knew that I would be better at real estate than both of them. I never played baseball after that because there was no future in it for me. I would have had to have done it just for the love of the game, and that wasn't for me.

I hate to lose, and if anybody gets used to losing they are going to be a loser. I'd like to tell you losing is part of the game, and it is, but I hated it. I still hate to lose. And that will never change.

I learned a lot from my USFL experience. I learned that you are truly only as strong as your weakest link. We had a number of owners who did not have the money to play the game. But we did have a lot of stars—Jim Kelly, Hershel Walker, Doug Flutie—and almost all of them are great guys. They're all mentally tough.

If you think about it, I am the Michael Jordan of real estate. The only difference is that my window is not closed, and even the best athletes are rarely productive in their forties. So many of them have their career end and they just fold up. The superstars seem to have a harder time making the transition, while the borderline pro can usually hit the ground running when they put down the bat and take off the cleats. They are used to outworking everyone on the roster, and maybe the success came too easy and too early for the star.

By the way, just because I turned the page and poured all my energies into business does not mean that I don't miss organized sports. I do.

BRUCKHEIMER IS AT LEFT.

★ JERRY BRUCKHEIMER ★

Film and Television Producer

Baseball, Hockey

I first got involved in organized sports when I was eight years old. In fact, I was the one who did the organizing. I put together a baseball team and found a sponsor, and then the neighborhood kids and I went out there and played ball.

As a player, I was not every good—I was fair, at best. I tried hard and I competed, but I'm not a naturally great athlete. But, of course, that didn't stop me from playing or wanting to play. Most of the time, I made myself the catcher.

When I was eleven years old, I did for hockey what I did for baseball—I formed a neighborhood team and got sponsors for it. We didn't have any coaches. We just showed up for games. When we moved from Detroit, when I was twelve or so, I left hockey behind and I didn't pick it up again until I was out in California about fifteen years ago. It was then that I met Wayne Gretzky, who was with the Kings at the time. He told me to come to a game and after I did I was so enthused that I went out and bought some skates and started taking skating lessons. That led to starting to play hockey again.

As I did when I was a kid, I put together a team and today we play a couple of games a week. We make time to play at 6:15 P.M. on Sundays and 8 on Monday evenings. Those are the times that work for me when I'm in town.

"ANYONE WHO'S INTERESTED IN HOCKEY KNOWS TO CALL US WHEN THEY'RE IN TOWN."

At any given game, you might find businessmen as well as actors like Keanu Reeves, Kiefer Sutherland, Cuba Gooding Jr., and Mike Myers out there on the ice with us. Anyone who's interested in hockey knows to call us when they're in town.

Today, when I'm putting together a movie, I try to hire people who have what I didn't have in sport: major league talent. With my company, you either have it or you don't. We have to get the Barry Bondses and Wayne Gretzkys of film to join us for a project if we want it to be successful. Today, my job as executive producer is to be the ultimate manager. I put the great team together and then I let them play. That's what I concentrate on.

"THE SAME SENSATION I GOT AT ELEVEN PLAYING HOCKEY WITH MY FRIENDS AND WINNING IS THE SAME FEELING I GET TODAY WHEN I MAKE A MOVIE THAT WORKS."

Growing up in Detroit, I looked up to Gordie Howe. His skill, toughness, and ability were traits that I very much admire. And what I learned about competing and winning and losing undoubtedly helped me survive and excel in Hollywood. The same sensation I got at eleven playing hockey with my friends and winning is the same feeling I get today when I make a movie that works.

Today, I still have a hockey tournament that I started. We play once a year in the summer and we call it the Bad Boys Tournament. We put together six teams and we play in Las Vegas. We have professional players like Wayne Gretzky and Rick Tocchet playing alongside with civilians, celebrities, and businessmen. It can be a hard-fought game, but it's also fun and it's given me some great thrills. My greatest moment had to be scoring a goal off a pass from Wayne Gretzky. It's something that I'll never forget.

Making a hit movie is great, but winning and scoring at an event like that is something that far exceeds that.

★ MELISSA PAYNER-GREGOR ★

President of BlueFly and
Former CEO of the Spiegel Catalog

Gymnastics

I was always a motivated, independently driven athlete.

It all started when I was eight when I got a pair of roller skates and then hooked up with a partner and started doing routines. But my coach at the time demanded that my mom take me to practice four or five times a week, and that was more than she thought I should be doing, so I was cut off from skating.

It wasn't until I was eleven years old that a friend of mine told me to go and try gymnastics at the Y, which was so close that I could walk there myself. I liked it right away and started going there on my own every day after school. It wasn't long before I had a private coach along with my high school coach.

I was in the gym all week and during the weekends. When I wasn't doing gymnastics, I was doing ballet, jazz, and tap dancing. I did manage to fit in some kind of social life, but not much, because gymnastics is such a mind sport and you have to be so focused. But I enjoyed it so much, I never thought about what parties or other events I was missing.

When it was time for college, I went to Ohio State, and I was one out of only seven freshman girls to make the varsity gymnastics squad. It was a tough life. We packed all our classes into the morning, so we could train in the afternoon and evenings. We were constantly having our body fat measured in water tanks, and if you had any fat they put you on a very strict diet. It was quite stressful.

"EVEN TODAY I CAN'T HELP THINKING THAT I COULD WALK ACROSS THOSE BEAMS."

No one particular performance or event stands out for me—probably because now, looking back, it's all just a blur since I worked at it every day for my whole life. Yet, I think about those days on the balance beam all the time. Even today, if I walk through our office building and I see the unfinished floors above us, I can't help thinking that I could walk across those beams. But other than that, I've put those days behind me.

Looking back, I see that I was robotic, totally focused on training until I experienced an injury while performing a floor exercise. I was told that my arm would be paralyzed, but I said, no way will my arm be paralyzed because I knew my body. After ten days, I demanded the doctor cut my cast off so I could start working at rehabilitating my arm. It took me two years to straighten my arm out.

"I FOUND MYSELF UPSIDE DOWN IN THE AIR AND I DIDN'T KNOW WHICH WAY WAS UP."

What I got from gymnastics is the incredible focus that you have to have. You have to be able to compartmentalize. When you're on the beam, you can't think about screwing up on the next floor exercise or else you'll fail on the beam. In fact, my injury was the result of not being able to completely focus. I was in the midst of my floor exercise and as I got to the tumbling part I said to myself, You'll never make it, which meant that I broke concentration. I should have stopped, but I didn't. I found myself upside down in the air and I didn't know which way was up and I blacked out.

Now, when there are eight thousand things that need to be done, I've learned how to compartmentalize. I don't think of everything that needs to be accomplished, but rather I just take one thing at a time, focusing on what needs to be done. In that way, I'm able to make great progress. Repetition is the key to getting things right. If you fall, you just get up again. It's not the time to have fear and not take risks.

Another thing I learned from gymnastics is how to be disciplined and how to accept it when things don't go as planned. Every day involves problem solving and if things don't break the way you want them to you can't give up.

My goals in gymnastics were the same as they are now in business. It's not about being president or winning every time. It's about doing my best, and if I come in first, that's okay. Gymnastics is all about individual performance, but it only works within the context of a team. It's the same with business. I have to do my job well in order to help my company.

People have told me that I am very calm under pressure, especially when I'm involved in the business world of turnarounds and start-up companies. These are the most pressure-packed situations, but I actually enjoy the pressure and the challenge. Just love what you're doing and everything else falls into place. As long as you see improvements from yesterday, you are moving in the right direction. Not all progress goes in a straight line and knowing this helps me solve the problem at hand.

★GEORGE W. BUSH★

President of the United States
and Former Governor of Texas

Baseball, Basketball, Rugby

It all started for me when I began playing catch with my dad, who, along with my mother, instilled a great love of baseball in me. There are photographs of me attending games when my dad was a player at Yale, so obviously I was exposed to the game at a very young age.

Some of my first memories are of Little League baseball in Midland, Texas, at age six. We lived to play the game, and I remember hanging out on the dusty fields, playing in the park behind my house for hours and hours. Mother, who was sometimes the scorekeeper, would have to come and get me.

As a player, I was good, although I like to tell people that I peaked in Little League. I was a catcher and a pretty good hitter. Did I have to win? Well, I guess you could say that. I'm from a very competitive family, and I guess you don't get to be president unless you have a competitive streak in you.

Most people in Texas in the 1950s never heard of Yale, and if they did they thought it was a strange place in a foreign land. My dad was captain of the baseball team there, but he never set false standards. He never said, "I want you to be like me," or "You have to hit a certain way because I hit a certain way," or, "I was better than you." He just said, "Son, if you love baseball, play baseball."

I took the game seriously, but I never felt the pressure to be a better player than he was, even though I went to Andover, where my dad went. I played second base and pitched. But I was at a disadvantage because when you go from Little League to high school you have to play summer ball to help with the transition, and I never did. The kids who ended up being good high school players found a Pony League or American Legion team, and I didn't, because we moved to Houston from Midland the summer all my buddies joined a Pony League, so I missed out. But I don't regret it because I went to camp and worked at Sears in the Sporting Goods department and I became the ping pong ball sales champion. I learned a little about business that summer when I started off selling the big-ticket items and then had my manager tell me that I had to handle the ping pong balls. So I backed off, made a few bucks, and he was able to put dinner on the table for his family.

Some of my fondest memories were playing pick-up basketball games on Sunday afternoons with friends in Houston. I just liked to compete and I still do, although now I do it playing golf. I didn't have what it took to be a big-time varsity player, but I have no regrets about it. I always tried to make up for lack of talent by working as hard as I possibly could and by out-hustling the next guy. That's the way I was brought up. It's in our genetic makeup to be competitive so when you combine the hustle with the drive, you turn out to be a certain type of player.

"I LOVED THE GAME, BUT FRANKLY MY TALENT DIDN'T MATCH MY ENTHUSIASM."

Not playing summer ball didn't stop me from going out for the freshman team at Yale, where I was fairly decent as a relief pitcher. I had a pretty good curve ball and I pitched in the Harvard game. I just didn't take it as seriously as a lot of my buddies who played varsity. They were pretty good baseball players and I was getting by just on talent. I loved the game, but frankly my talent didn't match my enthusiasm. When it was clear that I wasn't going to be a varsity player, I switched sports to rugby, which is a good team sport where you can get your licks in.

Dr. Britt Kolar
Yale classmate, rugby teammate, and lifelong friend

George started on the rugby team his junior year and made it right up to the first fifteen, which is a big deal. We had four sides back then. He not only made the team but ended up breaking through as a fullback, the last line of defense, which is a skilled position usually played by soccer players, because you had to be fast, tough, and know how to kick and kick under fire. The year 1968 was a watershed for us. The wheels were coming off the war train and most of us were facing military service.

Rugby was an outlet from that stress, and a sport we could play to bond and have fun. George was the ultimate team player, loyal and committed. He would also provide encouragement in his own unique way, mostly through some self-deprecating humor.

As a player he had excellent balance and was a shifty runner and surprisingly good kicker, especially on the run. I think the best moment we had was beating Harvard. The fact we were able to best them was really something I know we will never forget.

As an owner of a sports team, the Texas Rangers, my philosophy was always less about the stats and more about the man. Lance Armstrong is a good example. Look at who pedals harder. In terms of energy given out, size, and weight, all those stats look the same. But he has something in his heart that gives him that little extra. What do you learn from this? That there is something beside physical talent that drives these elite athletes. I think it's courage and the desire to win.

The one athlete who made a greater impact on me than any other is Nolan Ryan, who at over the age of forty was incredibly competitive. He wanted to be fit and go at it with twenty-year-old kids who were getting by on raw talent. And there he was throwing 100 mph fastballs because he was in shape. I'll never forget the look on Nolan Ryan's face when he was standing on the mound as Robin Ventura charged him. I had this perfect view of Ventura heading up the line and then just taking off for the mound. Let's just say he showed Ventura he was someone you don't want to tangle with at that moment. He was a very tough guy.

"JUST ABOUT ALL THESE LEADERS TAKE CARE OF THEMSELVES."

I like to find out what sports different world leaders played before I meet them, as well as how they stay fit, if they do. The prime minister from Slovakia is an avid runner, a marathoner, who's always after me to run with him. The prime minister of Denmark is a very fit guy. At our last NATO meeting, the prime minister of Norway was talking about how he still plays soccer. Tony Blair and I went for a jog on my ranch; prime minister Berlusconi of Italy and I made it a point to walk at the ranch. Vladimir Putin made sure to show me when I went to visit him the gym he works out in, and it's pretty nice. We're in an era when just about all these leaders take care of themselves.

"WHEN WE GET TOGETHER, THE TALK IS USUALLY ABOUT SPORTS."

Sports are an important part of the American way of life. The best health care plan for Americans is to watch what they eat, stop smoking, and exercise. Teaching kids team sports is so important. They learn how to play and sacrifice for something greater than themselves: the team. The idea of people watching sports and cheering for a team is also part of the social fabric.

As a family, we may be involved in politics, but when we get together, the talk is usually about sports. The fish we caught; the golf we played, things like that. Today, I still play sports because it's part of my makeup. I work out on an elliptical machine and swim for 20 minutes or so, and I feel better for it. There could be a lot of stress with this job if you didn't have an outlet. And for me, sports are that outlet.

I think people involved in sports have a responsibility to send the right messages. They must take their role seriously as sportsmen. That's why I put the steroid issue in the State of the Union address. I don't want some pro athlete feeling like he can increase his worth in the marketplace by taking steroids. He or she is hurting his or her body and at the same time sending messages to eighth-grade kids that if you want to succeed all you have to do is take steroids. It's an irresponsible message sent by professional athletes who should know better.

"I LOVED SEEING THE PICTURES OF THE PLAYERS."

I still remember getting on my bike and riding over to John Ashman's, a friend of my dad's, and getting a copy of my first *Sports Illustrated,* with a photo of Eddie Matthews on the cover. I just loved seeing the pictures of the players. So I got the idea of sending baseball cards to the players with a note asking them for autographs, and they usually sent them back signed. I think I still have a few left.

When I became owner of the Rangers, I made myself a baseball card. I did it for the fans, really. It's hard to get a player to sign something at the park, and as owner of the Rangers, I wanted the fans to leave with something because kids always want to take something home with them from the ball-park. I thought at least I could make myself available to them to sign my card.

"HIS GREATEST GIFT WAS UNCONDITIONAL LOVE."

I never felt pressure to live up to my dad, like saying that I wanted to be president just because he was. And I don't remember a time when I said to my-self, Oh, God, I let him down because I'm not a great baseball player. The rea-son is, he never put that on me. His greatest gift was unconditional love, saying, "Son, I love you no matter who or what you are." He was never the type of dad who said, "Let's go outside and hit the tackling dummy because I want you to be a great football player." His attitude was, "If you want me to hold the tackling dummy I will; if not, don't worry about it."

And I didn't worry about it.

ALEXIS IS IN THE FRONT ROW, SIXTH FROM LEFT.

★KIM ALEXIS★

Model, Television Feature
Reporter, and Talk Show Host

Swimming

When I was six years old, I had a girlfriend my age and she started swimming, so I joined the YMCA program with her. From that day on, I didn't stop swimming for twelve years, until I graduated from high school. It was a serious commitment and took a lot of my time, and I thought about quitting when I was fourteen, but my dad talked me out of it.

I trained five hours a day but all that training paid off when our team ended up being number one in New York State. I participated in the medley relay, and I was number nine statewide in the 100 yard fly. Being on the swim team worked out for me in other ways, too, because all my very good friends were on the team.

When I got older, I didn't go out for any AAU team or for the Olympics because I had other interests. I worked in a pharmacy—that's what I wanted to be, a pharmacist—I belonged to a youth group, and I was in the band.

Swimming taught me how to compete when the pressure's on and you're nervous. I used to step on the block and my heart would race. Even today, the smell of chlorine gets my heart going and my blood pumping. I also learned how to win and lose gracefully, and that every day is not always going to be *your* day.

I took a great deal of pride in my performance. I remember one particular state meet when I was a senior in high school. My coach picked another girl for the 50 fly in the medley relay, and I knew I was better. Normally, I would sit back and let things happen, but this time I said no. I said I deserved that spot because I was a faster swimmer, which was a very bold move for me. The coach said, "Okay, then race." So, I raced her—and, by the way, she was one of my best friends and still is to this day—and I beat her by a full body length. I went on to the meet, and the relay team won first place.

Looking at my make up, I would have to say that competing comes naturally. My husband, Ron Greschner (former New York Rangers hockey player), and I even compete over who eats dinner faster. I don't like competition with strategy, I like it with strength. For example, let's take golf. I would just crumble under pressure in those celebrity golf tournaments. But in terms of physical tests, the power events, I do very well. I have run seven marathons, and if anyone is in front of me in the last 100 yards I will catch them. My best time to date is 3 hours 52 minutes.

"SPORTS GIVES YOU A SENSE OF CONTROL ABOUT YOUR BODY."

Athletics have helped me a lot in my modeling career. You are judged as a woman by how you look, and sports gives you a sense of control about your body. I also learned how to pace myself, and it helped me feel strong and confident. If I knew I had what was right for a shoot or a part, I was not going to give it away to anyone else. I would fight for it. That came from competing in sports. Swimming also gave me a sense of team, even though you are swimming for yourself and by yourself.

Participating in sports also taught me how to listen to people with more experience than I have—in other words, to be open to good coaching. When I first went on *Good Morning America,* Joan Lunden went out on maternity leave. We had not met, but when she came back after having given birth and was perhaps not feeling great about herself, the last thing I wanted to have happen was for her to look over and see this bratty supermodel who was the new fashion correspondent. I went right up to her and said, "Joan, I respect all of what you've done. Can you please take me under your wing and teach me?" It was one of the smartest things I could have done. I got to learn from one of the best in the field and she didn't view me as the enemy because I let her know I was on her team. We ended up doing live interviews together.

"AS I GET OLDER, I ALMOST FEEL LIKE I HAVE TO TRAIN LESS."

I can't imagine my life without sports, not being fit, not working out, laying in bed with my muscles not being tired. Since I am married to a professional athlete, he's coaching me all the time. Just this morning he said, "Forget about running, go lift weights." As I get older, I almost feel like I have to train less. Now that I am in my forties, I know I can't go out and run ten miles and burn up all those calories. Number one, I can't run ten miles—I have too many kids and too much going on to do that.

★BRIAN KILMEADE★

Television Host and Sports Anchor

Soccer

I couldn't believe my parents wouldn't let me join a baseball team. Here I was, a first grader, and they told me I was just too young to play a sport. To their credit, they saw how upset I was and on some level, they probably felt like they had made a mistake, but by this time it was too late to register. They tried to make amends by pledging, "The next sport you want to play, we'll sign you up for it."

Yeah, right, I thought.

The next fall, in second grade, I had my chance to test their sincerity. We got handouts for a sport I never played: soccer. I knew next to nothing about it, but registration was fast approaching and I wanted to test their pledge. I asked, they said yes, and next thing I knew I was playing with a bunch of kids I had never seen before, competing in a game I had never played before.

The first practice was a disaster. I was a charter member of the school for the chubby, and from the moment I arrived I got a bad vibe. It seemed that everyone on the field were already friends. I was from the other side of town, my parents left me alone on the field while they went shopping (they deny this, of course), and so I felt as comfortable as a runaway in a homeless shelter. Here I was, on a strange field, among strange kids, playing a strange sport, running laps with my monstrous cheeks and my baby jelly belly. So, after a few head balls too many, I did what most any hardworking, never-say-die working-class kid would do: I retired from soccer.

"I GOT BACK ON THE FIELD AND PLAYED."

While waiting by the fence for my parents to come back and pick me up, I thought twice, then three times about quitting, and then made the decision that would affect my life and my family's life more then any other I'd made: I got back on the field and played. And later, when my parents picked me up, I kept my brief retirement to myself, because even then I knew there was no place in our house for quitters.

I finished the season strong, made a team of friends, and exposed my brothers to the sport—which they both would later join, and later even my father would get involved by becoming a soccer coach. Every weekend for the next fifteen years, our entire family would go from field to field, town to town, gym to gym, playing in games and tournaments.

Before long, it became even more intense with tryouts for select teams, State cup finals, and division titles. As a family, we played one sport in fall, winter, spring, and summer, every weekend, at least three times a week. I took it all very seriously. I made lineups with my dad, I coached my younger brother, and carefully studied my older brother for any tips I might pick up. By junior high, my dad was coaching my travel team, and I was hunting talented kids for our roster, reprimanding teammates who missed practice (just making sure my dad wouldn't be embarrassed on game day), thus building a bond most of us who played on those teams still share today.

Our town of Massapequa, Long Island, was a flat-out soccer power from day one. Three times in our age group, our town's first and second select teams would meet in the state finals. In high school we would be divided into two schools, and still my senior year team was only one win shy of a state title.

Now here's the kicker: through all this I was just a good to okay player. Nothing special. Sure, I had my moments. Yes, I was good enough to be a travel player and in other towns probably would have stood out more. But with all that drive and dedication, I was just an average player. I would work on my own, train for the season, focus on the game, never miss a practice, but in the end was nothing special. Can you imagine that? Caring so much about something and not being that good? That was my reality. I played four years of Division 2 college soccer. For my first two years, I was playing and starting just about every game. In fact, I might have been on path to be captain, but then there was an unexpected twist—a coaching change. This new coach had little use for me—he wanted his guys, most of whom were not from this country. I would end my junior and senior year in extreme frustration. Talk about unfinished business! It was a disheartening conclusion to eighteen straight years of year-round soccer.

Don't get me wrong, I had great games, made great friends, and loved training, but I just didn't understand why I never reached the pinnacle, why I was never a great player. I wanted to be the guy in the sport movies who works hard, is a great teammate, a leader, a great student, who scores the winning goal in the championship game, and lives happily ever after. But no such luck.

My dad, my best coach ever and my biggest fan, died when I was in ninth grade. I did not become an All-American, and I was so burnt out after college I left the game hating the sport. I always believed I was better then most coaches thought and suspected I'd have my revenge with a furious finish to a mediocre career.

But it didn't happen, though it would have made a nice story, a nice way to reward my dad's belief in me. And my disappointment wasn't made any easier by the fantastic conclusion most of my lifelong soccer buddies enjoyed: Bruce and Rob, a six overtime conference final win; Rick, a captain, All-American, and runner-up Big East player of the decade at Syracuse, and Tom, a four-year starter and captain at U-Mass.

In truth, I now know I needed to leave the game hungry, driven, in order to prepare for my career or real-life quest to be an All-American, Hall-of-Fame TV personality. Of course, I didn't think that way back then. TV is as competitive and cut-throat as any business there is, and cutting my teeth in sports provided a great boot camp. Playing soccer gave me confidence—confidence that was transferred to my TV career. I knew I was not a great athlete and rarely felt like the most talented guy on the field, but I outworked just about everybody. When it came time to dive into broadcasting, I did the same exact thing, only without the cleats and shin pads.

When I first began, I believed in my sense of humor. I always thought I could ask the right questions, and I embraced the *live* pressure. So, along with my future wife, Dawn, and my superstar friend, Rick Fatscher, we started our own local show. Quickly, we got three sponsors—a catering company, a clothing store, and a limo company—and we were on our way. It wasn't great TV, but we thought it was, and best yet, I wound up with a tape and a rolodex of contacts. From there, I just kept striving and getting a few jobs—just enough to keep me going, but barely enough to survive. Just like in soccer, it seemed everyone was doing better then I was. Okay, everyone *was* doing better than I was, but I just knew I was on the right road.

My side job was scouring the trade papers and then cycling my tapes out looking for new opportunities, while blitzing regions around the country where I hoped to work. I also did a lot of cold-calling to program directors, telling them I was coming to town on a certain date and setting up get-to know-you interviews. I kept all the rejection letters, because after my experiences in soccer I was not fazed by a swing and a miss. In fact, on some level I think I even embraced the setbacks.

Now, I'm on the #1 morning show (*Fox & Friends*) on the #1 news network in the country (Fox News). I get to use my personality and my love of news and sports, while seeing most of the world and meeting the most important people on the planet working alongside two pros, E. D. Hill and Steve Doocy, with an unbelievable staff who are just as driven (if not more) then me.

"I'M IN THE GAME EVERY DAY FOR THREE HOURS A DAY."

I'm not the Bob Costas of sports, the David Letterman of late night talk, or the Bill O'Reilly of news, but I'm in the game every day for three hours a day. I have three great kids and a sensational wife, who knew me when I was the less than impactful midfielder on our high school soccer team, and yet she still stuck around. I know I am the least accomplished person in this book, but that won't be the case for long. And although I'm just forty, I've now been able to make sense of my entire athletic career. I believe I had to struggle and be disillusioned at a young age, or I would never have stuck out the highs and very lows on this career. Most of the criticism I got and still get it rolls off my back because after having my self-esteem in my coaches' hands for nearly twenty years, I swore that would never happen again. You can bar me from your station but not the industry, and right now, I feel so lucky, it's scary.

"IT ALL HELPED, AND NOW IT ALL MAKES SENSE."

What I didn't do in soccer is address my weaknesses in the right way. I was too slow, but did I seek out a track coach? No. I felt too embarrassed. I was too heavy on my feet, but did I pull a Lynn Swann and take up ballet? No. Why not? Because none of my friends did. And did I develop a superior game sense by playing with the older guys at the park? No. I practiced on my own, because I was concerned that those older guys would think I wasn't very good. Dumb? Yes! I was a great endurance guy who kept improving his endurance, and I was an aggressive player who focused on weights. This just was not a smart practice regimen.

TV Brian changed this line of thinking. I had a thick New York accent, so I saved my money and took speech classes. I wanted to get better at memorizing, so I bought taped courses. I wanted to refine my comedic skills and test this new memory, so I took a class and spent five years doing stand-up wherever and whenever I could. I also found a way to get to know and at least talk to everyone who was doing a job I aspired to have—Matt Lauer, Jim Caldwell, David Letterman, and Regis Philbin, to name a few. It all helped, and now it all makes sense.

And oh, yes, I always wanted to write a book, and I've just done that, and I'm honored that you read it.

AFTERWORD

I cannot tell you how much I enjoyed and benefited from this journey to collect the sports stories of the most accomplished people in America. It was a privilege to talk openly and honestly to a collection of such fascinating people as they re-connected with a life they never quite let go of, but often had filed away. Many of the interviews seemed to me to be therapy sessions. By asking the questions, I helped these former athletes dust off their memories and share a original story that they have rarely if ever told before.

Something about this book prompted the most in-demand people in America to set aside time to thoughtfully tell their personal sports saga. As much as I would like to think I was the attraction, it just wasn't the case. It was the subject! Why else would Robin Williams reach out to me from the outer reaches of Canada? Why would Kurt Russell pick up my fax and call me back at the office with his home number? Why would the president of the United States say I could stop by the Oval Office for a ten-minute chat—which turned into a twenty-five minute talk and a signed ball? Why else would Senator John Kerry use my call-waiting feature to share his memories on a Friday afternoon in between a mind-numbing number of campaign stops? It's sports, stupid! They have a story to tell and knew that people could benefit from hearing about it.

Now, we know that these accomplished winners weren't always the best at everything they tried, but they strived, overcame, and to use tennis analogy, dropped a game but won the match. As we have learned, without a few losses they wouldn't have eventually won.

Okay, maybe Condi Rice would have been successful with or without skating, but how else would she have learned to keep her cool under pressure in Washington, D.C., if she didn't first try to do it alone on the ice in competition? Why is Bernie Mac the funniest yet one of the most down-to-earth celebrities in America? Maybe it's because he got a huge dose of humility riding the bench in basketball with his friends and family in the stands.

It is my sincere hope that by reading these personal sports stories from America's best and brightest, you will see you can lose a contest, be cut from a team, be benched in a key game, and come out a better person if you can make a classroom out of the court or the field.

One important note: If there is one element of sports that's simply exploding, it's women's sports. Thirty years ago, fewer than two hundred thousand girls in the United States played varsity sports; now more than three million do. I hope that trend continues, because girls and women should have the same shot at fame, fortune, and frustration that men have. It was more of a challenge finding women to interview than it should have been because for a generation of girls, organized sports are what the boys did. Finally, that's changing.

In closing, a reminder: If you're a coach of any sport at any level, be aware of the power you have on athletes' lives. If you are a sports parent, I hope you now know that it's not about turning pro or the college scholarship—it's about the journey. And if you are a player, pour your heart out on the field, but don't let your minutes or stats define who you are. Identify your weaknesses, work hard to make them your strengths, and remember to think of the team first. Apply these lessons, and your personal glory may be delayed, but it will never be denied.

ACKNOWLEDGMENTS

There are so many people to thank for taking this project from concept to completion that it's almost impossible to remember all of you, but I will try. First, I have to thank Judith Regan for green-lighting the book while pushing for the very best subjects this country has to offer. Also, thanks to Cal Morgan for reviewing the manuscript, Cassie Jones for editing it, and Anna Bliss, Marissa Shalfi, and Liz Grotyohann for handling the photographs. I particularly want to thank and acknowledge Charles Salzberg, a terrific writer, editor, teacher, and sports fan. Trident Media's Paul Fedorko has been a tremendous asset, as has the indefatigable Shannon Firth, who had the unenviable task of tracking down these photos from the busiest people on the planet. Dana Benningfield was also a key member of the team. I'd like to single out two people who helped me assemble this team and school me on the business: Joel Mowbray and Monica Crowley. Speaking of business, for clueing me on the many athletes in the corporate community and providing unwavering support, I'd like to also pay homage to Peter Kash.

Many people have supported me from beginning to end, but I have to salute Fox News Channel Vice President Jack Abernathy. I felt this concept would work, but it wasn't until Jack was sold on it that I truly believed this book should and would happen. He's also one of the few diehard Nets fans I know.

Stepping back even further, I would like to thank the people who placed me in a position to pull off this project, and that's the first-class management at Fox News Channel. Legendary TV executive Chet Collier took the risk and brought me to the Major Leagues in 1997, and Kevin Magee kept me there, and for that immense sustained break I am forever grateful. I'm also honored to have news superstars Bill Shine and John Moody in my corner (most days). This job gives me a chance to cover every major sports story and event while cohosting the number one morning cable show, and it's an honor I relish and cherish every day. It's allowed me to meet the most important and interesting people in the world, many of whom are featured in *The Games Do Count*.

When I reached a certain age, I thought I had stopped looking up to people, but that changed when I began to work for Fox News President Roger Ailes. He has achieved more than most could dream of in his career—and seems the least impressed by it. He's a master communicator from whom I learn every day. He has allowed me to stumble and shine for the past seven years and to be who I am, while making sure we all strive for excellence. Not only did he green-light the book, he provided one of the most inspiring personal stories included in it.

Providing incredible support in every way is the morning show team at *Fox & Friends,* headed up by Matt Singerman. Matt and his A team have been an invaluable sounding board and great resource for contacts while making all three hosts look good by producing the most important people on the planet three hours every day, seven days a week. I have to recognize Stephen Herzog, Joe Kraus, Megan Abernathy, Kim Agle, Fred Cwerner, Maria Donovan, Marcelo Grate, Paul Guzman, Sebastian Hill, Karrah Kaplan, Joe Kraus, Paulina Krycinski, Jose Lesh, Ron Messer, Tara Ruotolo, Jess Todtfeld, Melissa Smith, Laurie Weiner, Jonathan Glenn, Sean O'Heir, Kate Policastro, Kyle Crise, Lauren Sivan, Alexis Valez, and Mavel Jimenez.

The studio crew did a wonderful job of pretending to be interested in the book for the past year, and I'd like to give this all-star cast, led by director John Basuino, its due. I salute Don Presutti, Chris Ciullo, James Burt, Joel Fulton, Steve Gender, Hardy Kluender, Ian Faust, Toba Potosky, Anthony Aurecchione, Frank Scudero, Brenda Salamon, Laura Finan, Mark Togno, and Jim Gorman.

Of course have to recognize Steve Doocy and E. D. Hill, the two blue-chip cohosts of *Fox & Friends,* who have to deal with me every day, who made it clear they were in my corner (at least for this anthology), and who also tell their moving personal sports story in the book. And who can forget the former Miss Minnesota-turned-anchor Lauren Green?

I'd also like to salute the other outstanding hosts on the *Friends* franchise—Kiran Chetry, Juliet Huddy, Mike Jerrick, and Julian Phillips—along with sometime hosts and contributors Judge Andrew Napolitano and Dr. Georgia Witkin.

For every superstar in business politics, television, sports, and modeling there was a stalwart member of their support staff championing this book's cause. I know how much weight most of you have with your clients, and how many calls we all had to make to get this to happen, and I am truly honored to have earned your trust. An extra-special thanks to Dan Bartlet, Pam Stevens, Krista Ritacco, Ed Gillespie, Tom Frechette, Dag Vega, Jim Wilkinson, Colby Cooper, Mara Boxbaum, Laurie Famera, Mike Simon, James Dixon, Penny Circle, Norma Foerderer, Jessica Incao, Scott Novak, Jeff Smith, Steve Greener, Eric Kritzer, Chip Unruh, Bill Bosen, Julie Polkes, Makida Wubneh, and all the many others who helped make the seventy-three-plus interviews happen.

The most enjoyable aspect of this project was actually conducting the interviews, and many of them were done over the phone. I knew that sound quality mattered, and the Fox News radio crew took time out of their busy news day to help me each and every time. I'm not sure how Condi Rice got disconnected, but apart from that they were simply A-plus. A big thank you goes out to Mitch Davis, Bernie Pigott, John Griffin, and Jim Donaldson.

And most of all, thank you for taking the time to read *The Games Do Count.*